SHAME

Other Books by Dr. David F. Allen

In Search of the Heart

Shattering the Gods Within

Contemplation: Intimacy in a Distant World

Crack: The Broken Promise and James F. Jekel

Pudgy: A Bahamian Parable

SHAME

The Human Nemesis

David F. Allen, M.D., M.P.H.

ELEUTHERA
PUBLICATIONS

Washington, DC • Nassau, Bahamas

To purchase additional copies of this book online go to:

www.shamebookstore.info

Requests for information should be addressed to:

Eleuthera Publications
#207 Lagoon Court
Olde Towne Sandy Port
Nassau
Bahamas

publisher@eleutherabooks.com
www.eleutherabooks.com

Cover photo: "Expulsion and Fall" by Michelangelo

About the Author

Dr. David Allen was trained in medicine at St. Andrews University Medical School in Scotland and in Psychiatry and Public Health at Harvard Medical School where he was a Kennedy Fellow. He did work in religion, psychiatry, and ethics under Professor Arthur Dyck at the Harvard Divinity School. He has also taught psychiatry and religion at Harvard, Yale, and Georgetown Medical School.

Dr. Allen was mentored in theology by Dr. Francis Schaeffer at L'Abri Fellowship in Switzerland. He studied contemplative psychology under Dr. Gerald May at Shalem Institute in Bethesda, M.D. and psychiatry and spirituality under Fr. Henri Nouwen at Yale Divinity School.

Dr. Allen was awarded the RB Bennett Commonwealth Prize by the Royal Society of Arts in London for his international contribution in the field of cocaine addiction and treatment. He was featured in the PBS special "The Drug Wars" which documented his identification of the crack cocaine epidemic in 1985. He was one of the authors of a groundbreaking scientific article in the *Lancet*, June 1986, which heralded the crack cocaine epidemic.

Voted one of the most outstanding psychiatrists for 2002-03, Dr. Allen was also named a Distinguished Life Fellow of the American Psychiatric Association in 2008. He was honored for his work in addiction by the Royal Society of Arts in London.

He has established drug and alcohol treatment clinics in Washington, DC and Nassau, Bahamas. He is a popular conference speaker and has an international private practice in the Bahamas. His television show, "People to People," and his radio show, "Coming Home to Face Our Heart," are on the air weekly in the Bahamas.

Dr. Allen is the author of a number of books including: *Crack the Broken Promise*, *In Search of the Heart*, *Shattering the Gods Within*, and *Contemplation: Intimacy in a Distant World*. Most recently, he published his first children's book, *Pudgy: A Bahamian Parable* and an award-winning DVD version.

A renowned psychiatrist and author, Dr. Allen is also a popular and powerful conference speaker. He has conducted conferences and seminars for many organizations including the Young Presidents Organization of Washington D.C., the Chautauqua Institute, Chautauqua, New York, and the Institute for Applied Theology and Behavioral Sciences [IATBS] at the Psychiatric Institute of Washington. His widely acclaimed marriage, grief, and shame seminars have been hosted by churches as diverse as Dallas Bible Church, Dallas, Texas and St. Teresa of Avila Catholic Church, Washington, D.C.

Dr. Allen is the director of the Renascence Institute, Nassau, Bahamas where his team of psychoanalysts and therapists serve an international clientele and specialize in marital therapy, depression, grief and loss, addictions, and crisis management.

David lives in his native Bahamas with his wife, Victoria, who is an author and assistant professor at the College of the Bahamas. Their home on the Bahamian sea is full of love and the Real Presence of Christ. Most of all, they enjoy living near their children and grandchildren.

Contact Dr. Allen at the Renascence Institute

P.O. Box SP 63124
Sandyport, Nassau
The Bahamas

renascence@coralwave.com / 242-327-8718

This book is dedicated to all of the courageous men and women who have suffered from drug and alcohol addiction who have given me the courage to honestly face my own shame.

Table of Contents

Foreword

Dr. David Allen provides an unusual, insightful treasure to readers of this book. It is based on a symphony of Dr. Allen's God-given gifts of empathy, a loving heart for people, and the ability to connect instantly to human beings of all walks of life. He integrates his skills as a psychiatrist with a deep knowledge of Scripture and rich experience from his counseling practice. Perhaps, it is his sensitivity to the Holy Spirit that distinguishes him from his peers. He draws strength from his meditation and contemplation of God's Word. He radiates God's love as he counsels complex and emotionally laden issues.

This book focuses on shame as the *Master Emotion*. Dr. Allen carefully applies the teaching of Scripture to this fundamental human problem. Chapters of the book are skillfully introduced by stories from his vast experience to illustrate psychological principles. Particularly relevant is his discussion of the Ego Addictive False Self and its resolution through the love and forgiveness of God.

As Dr. Allen points out, Jesus bore *our* shame not his own. This analysis of the psychodynamic and spiritual concepts of shame, defined as **S**elf **H**atred **A**imed at **ME**", is explained so skillfully with examples from the Bible and contemporary life that it is a misleadingly easy read. This is a book that the reader will want to return to over and over again and give to friends.

Thank you, David, for this book. I am honored to have you as a friend and colleague.

Frank E. Young, M.D., Ph.D.
Former Commissioner of FDA
Dean Emeritus, School of Medicine and Dentistry,
University of Rochester

Preface

This book has grown out of my professional and personal experience with shame. I am often struck by how many people know they are forgiven for their behavior, but still suffer from the debilitating, self-destructive power of deep shame. God, in his mercy, created human beings with a capacity to feel the remorse of shame whenever we engage in behavior and attitudes that are hurtful to others or ourselves. This *good* shame is a blessing that encourages surrender to God's healing grace and power.

Michelangelo graphically depicts the shame of Adam and Eve on the ceiling of the Sistine Chapel in "The Fall and Expulsion" reproduced on the cover of this book. In Genesis 3, God commanded his first humans to not eat from the Tree of the Knowledge of Good and Evil warning them, "In the day you eat of it, you shall surely die." Adam and Eve exercised their free will and chose to eat the forbidden fruit. Their eyes were opened to see their shame and they immediately sought to cover their nakedness. God expelled them from the garden and paradise was lost.

Shelves are filled with books rightly proclaiming the message of the forgiveness of sins through the sacrificial death of Christ. There is no more important doctrine for the world than the cleansing of guilt from the human heart. Whether guilt is caused by willful disobedience, deception, a mistake, or the false accusation of others, it is always about behavior or attitude, about what I have done. Shame, on the other hand, is about who I am as a person. Guilt says, "I made a mistake." Shame says, "I *am* a mistake."

Somewhere along the line we only received half of the Gospel message. Even when our guilt is removed, we tend to carry the shame cross. Shame voices cry out, "I am a failure!" "My ministry is finished!" "I messed up my life."

"God may forgive me, but the damage is done." "There is no hope". As one lady said, "When my marriage broke up, I asked God's forgiveness. I kept on performing – but I stopped living!"

This book addresses the shame we continue to feel even after we know that we have been forgiven by God and others. It takes a long, deep look at the shame that is destroying so many of us, i.e., the shame of failure, anger, arrogance, regret, and transgenerational wrongs to name just a few. Most importantly, it is a book about the good news that the death and resurrection of Christ will not only remove our guilt, but will also remove our shame.

It is my prayer that through this book, you will be freed from the shame that so easily besets us. You may also find help in my previously published trilogy: *In Search of the Heart, Shattering the Gods,* and *Contemplation: Intimacy in a Distant World.* Finally, I want to hear your story. Please write to me and share your heart.

Peace,

David Allen, M.D., M.P.H.
Renascence Clinic
P.O. Box SP 63124
Sandyport, Nassau
The Bahamas

renascence@coralwave.com

242-327-8718

Prologue

A Mother Confronts Shame

One of the most common 'Faults' regarded as shameful is social weakness, whether it is poverty, dependency upon others especially in the form of accepting charity or reputation as a loser. Poverty in particular has been viewed as a disgrace from antiquity.

–Leon Wurmser

On the Monday after Christmas I was in the community health center known as Knowles House when Ms. Adderly stopped by to say hello. After our initial greetings, she said, "I have a story to tell you." I invited her into my office and asked her to share her story with me.

She told me she was a poor, single parent with a nine-year-old boy named Johnny. Johnny's dad had dropped out of their life shortly after Johnny was born leaving her responsible for her son's welfare. It was not easy. She was a straw market vendor and made her living by making straw products to sell in Nassau's international straw market to visiting tourists.

Sometimes she did well and was able to get enough money to get by. But at Christmas, every parent in the Bahamas wants to do something special for the family. In an old Bahamian tradition, especially in the family islands, everyone has a Christmas meal with chicken or ham. More recently, families have sought to give their children toys.

Ms. Adderly worked hard all Christmas week to make as many straw products as she could sell – hats, bags, dolls – to the tourists. She worked throughout the night so she would be able to buy a ham and a toy or two.

Laden down with her straw goods and with high anticipation and the excitement for Christmas, she walked to the straw market early in the morning. She decorated her stall with all her new creations. Then she waited for the tourists to come. Sadly, it was a cold and rainy day.

At 10 a.m. the rain was falling strong and very few tourists came to the market. By noon the weather was still bad and the rain and wind blew through the market. She had made no sales. Now Ms. Adderly started to worry. She knew that Bay Street started to slow down around 4 p.m. as people headed home to prepare for Christmas with their families. But Christmas for her and Johnny depended on what she sold that day. By 5 p.m. she had sold nothing.

The other vendors started to pack up and head home to celebrate Christmas. Ms. Adderly was stunned, upset, angry, and disappointed. She began to pack up her wares. Her heart was downcast. What could she do? She had no money. She had no husband and no family to support her. She felt trapped in her poverty. She was broke and broken. She had nowhere to turn. How could she break the news to little Johnny?

Depressed and grieving, she took her bag of wares and headed towards home. Her mind was filled with shame thoughts, "What kind of mother are you? You are a failure." The shame voices were like people shouting and jeering at her, "Lazy woman, you should know better." "You should have planned ahead." "Your mother always said nothing good would come of you." Like a self-imposed shame whip, she felt the words beating her back, breaking her heart.

All the way home, negative thoughts pounded in her head like sea waves against the sand. Everything looked dark and hopeless through the eyeglasses of shame. The voices in her head continued to scream at her, "You bad woman! You made a mess of your life. Now you have ruined Christmas for Johnny! You should be ashamed of yourself."

Confronted by her own self-hatred and the perceived hatred of others, she nailed herself to a shame cross. The only way out of her shame appeared to be death.

As she approached the western shore, she threw the straw goods into the sea and watched them float away. Overwhelmed and unable to take it any longer, she walked into the water determined to kill herself. She waded out into the water until it reached her shoulder, then her neck. In her mind, there was no way out. The magnification of her problem created a hopeless scenario as she walked into the darkness!

She put her head under the water and waited. Then a thought struck her. If I kill myself, who would be there for little Johnny? No one! She prayed, "O God, give me the courage to face my shame. I know I am a failure." She pulled herself out of the water and went back to the beach still shaking inside.

In her wet clothes she walked over the hill and down the long winding lane leading to the two-room clapboard house to face little Johnny. When she reached her corner, she felt afraid and apprehensive. She prayed again, "Please, God, help me." She summoned up the courage to face Johnny. She walked up to the door and knocked.

When Johnny opened the door, Ms. Adderly burst out crying, "Johnny, I am sorry, I am really so sorry. I made nothing today. The weather was bad and no tourists came. Mommy made no money today. I have nothing to give you for Christmas. I am so very sorry."

To her surprise, instead of crying, Johnny hugged and kissed her and said, "That's okay, Mommy, I know if you had it, you would give me something." Then Johnny went outside and disappeared for a while. He came back with a branch broken off a tree decorated with foil paper which he found in the garbage. He said simply and with a smile, "This is our Christmas tree, Mommy!"

On Christmas day they had no food or toys, but they read the Christmas story in the Bible and prayed together. Pausing, she said, "It was as if someone else was with us. We did not feel alone."

At the end of her story we were both crying. I found myself saying, "You and Johnny did not have food or gifts, but you experienced the true meaning of Christmas in being present to each other with the *Eternal Presence*. The Love that never lets us go and the Face that never turns away was with you. In your emptiness and brokenness, you made space for the Christ child."

The purpose of this book is to provide the help and hope we all need to face our shame. You may be deep in the sea of despair and ready to give up, but, like Ms. Adderly and Johnny, you too can find the Love that never lets you go and the Face that never turns away.

Introduction

Shame (Self Hatred Aimed at ME) The Human Nemesis

Self-contempt (shame) is difficult to eradicate.
—Derek Walcott

The word *shame* is derived from a Germanic root word meaning *disgrace* and has been traced back to an Indo-European root meaning *to cover* or *to hide*. The notion of hiding is intrinsic and inseparable from the idea of shame. It is an ancient concept; shame appears in the Genesis story of Adam and Eve in the Garden of Eden. When Adam and Eve disobeyed God, they felt "naked and ashamed" and instinctively covered their nakedness with fig leaves.

In spite of its ancient history, shame has been little discussed in the psychological literature. Why is this so? One hypothesis is that shame was repressed, denied, and ignored because therapists themselves were not in contact with or had not worked through their own shame.

No longer neglected, shame is now called the *Master Emotion*. It combines the powerful affects of anger, hurt, remorse, rejection, abandonment, and humiliation. Shame is a powerful bolus of pain that strides like a colossus across the length and breadth of so many hearts, minds, and lives.

Examining the dynamics of shame has become imperative in our culture because shame is the principle impediment in all relationships whether husband-wife, parent-child, teacher-student, or therapist-client. It violates inner security and interpersonal trust. It inflicts wounds not only on the self, but also on families, groups, entire nations, and even on international relationships.

> Shame is the most disturbing emotion we ever experience directly about ourselves, for in the moment of shame we feel deeply divided from ourselves. Shame is like a wound made by an unseen hand, in response to defeat, failure or rejection. At the same moment that we feel most disconnected, we long to embrace ourselves once more, to feel reunited. Shame divides us from our selves, just as it divides us from others, and because we still yearn for reunion shame is deeply disturbing.[1] –Gershen Kaufman and Lev Raphael

Shame is the gap between the expectations we have for ourselves and the reality of what and who we are. Shame is an internal, hidden phenomenon that appears in society as the unmistakable external faces of inferiority, shyness, failure, anger, addiction, shattered dreams, and broken lives. Shame destroys the quality and the meaning of life and causes psychopathologies such as depression, anxiety, intimacy dysfunction, and violence. In modern society shame has become a predominant factor for the following five reasons.

Shame-based dysfunctions such as sexual and emotional abuse, drug and alcohol addiction, and eating disorders are now society's dominant diseases. Treatment is often sabotaged or inadequate unless the shame core in these illnesses is worked through.

The breakdown of the family creates a multitude of problems which include an increasing number of single parents, blended families, dual careers, latch key kids, post divorce families, etc. Each of these exposes children to painful experiences that result in evolving layers of shame.

The burden on the educational system due to the breakdown of the family has placed an enormous burden on schools by mandating teachers to act as parents. Teachers cannot replace parents. Children are raised with a deep sense of inferiority, anxiety, and pain which develops into shame. The absence in the home of meaningful, comforting environments leads to poor separation, individuation, and identity formation. This, too, feeds into the development of shame.

The exploding technological revolution in modern society has produced a new transparency and openness. Facebook, email, YouTube, MySpace, Twitter, and smart phones have revolutionized our way of life. Everything is open and out there for everyone to see. Shame implies hiding and there are few places to hide.

The development of Self Psychology[2] through the work of Heinz Kohut, Joseph Lichtenberg, and others has created a greater awareness of the development and importance of the self as opposed to the dynamics of intra-psychic conflict. Since shame involves the evaluation of the self, the evolution of the Self Psychology movement has projected shame into public prominence.

Shame is <u>S</u>elf <u>H</u>atred <u>A</u>imed at **<u>ME</u>**. It exposes a rupture of the self to the self and others. Shame interferes with personal experiences and communication with others. It is evidenced by looking down and is associated with a feeling of terror and withdrawal. Shame makes us feel worthless, self-conscious, and embarrassed. It is associated with disappearing, covering, or hiding.

Feeling useless and fundamentally flawed, shame-prone persons have a sense of deep loneliness and haunting self-doubt. Shame seeks a reunion with the person who shamed us which creates in us an internal conflict between simultaneously hating and needing to be loved. There is an intimate connection between the shamed person and the person doing the shaming, i.e., our Nemesis. Nemesis was the Greek goddess of retribution and indignity. She was a personification of the resentment and humiliation aroused in us when we are shamed by others. Thus, the title of this book, *SHAME: The Human Nemesis.*

Shame is a longing for what we wish for, a deep desire which is elusive and often illusory. According to Leon Wurmser, "Shame is the shadow or night side of love and love is the true transcendence of shame."[3] Friedrich Nietzsche says that in shame "everyone is farthermost away from himself."[4] One cocaine-addicted person asked me, "How can I get out of my own way?" Another man exclaimed, "I have a great life, but I can't show up for it."

Blocking our dreams and the life we desire, shame or self-contempt causes us to deny certain aspects of our lives. For example, it is not uncommon to hear people say, "I am living my second-choice life." Shame has blasted the dreams of their first-choice life. So often, wherever we are...*we* are what is missing! To experience the life we want, we have to let go of the shame, open up, and accept the life we have.

Shame may result from the deep pain of a child brutalized by a parent or sibling. Shame may come from a discrimination against a minority person by the dominant culture of the majority, the breakdown of a boring career, or an empty marriage. The shame core is associated with self-deficiency and self-blame. It is a feeling of not being good enough to belong.

Shame is also manifested by a false character where phony kindness and submissiveness disguise contempt and disregard. Charles Dickens' character Martin Chuzzlewit describes this in Mr. Pecksniff who is: "full of promise, but not performance. He was always, in a manner, going to go and never going. When I remember the hypocrisy, the knavery, the mean-nesses, the false pretenses, the lip service of that fellow and his trading in saintly semblances for the very worst realities I almost despise myself."[5]

Constructive shame implies having a conscience so that when we do wrong, we feel shame, seek to correct it, make amends, and then the shame is removed. Conversely, to be shameless is to have *no* conscience or moral development. This leads to corruption and fragmentation. The purpose of this book is to look at the untreated, unrecognized, and unattended shame core which creates self-contempt and the shame of being ashamed.

From a Contemplative Psychology perspective which integrates Judeo-Christian spirituality and psychiatry, this book discusses the psychodynamics and spiritual concepts of shame. It challenges us to seek a more contemplative life as an antidote to shame and to experience our true identity as the *beloved of God.*

The photo on the cover is of Michelangelo's "Fall and Expulsion" of Adam and Eve from the Garden of Eden. The angel's sword is pointed at Adam's back. He is distraught, hurt, and disappointed in himself. Eve cowers in remorse and the embarrassment of brokenness. Humiliated and bowed down with shame, Adam and Eve remind us of many experiences which have characterized our own lives.

The prologue of the book is a true Bahamian story of how a poor distraught single mother faced the shame of being in such poverty that she is not able to provide food or toys for her little boy at Christmas. To her surprise, her son expresses deep love for her and graciously faces and accepts the sad situation. Having no food or gifts, they experience the joy and meaning of Christmas in the simple blessing of being truly present together with the *True Presence.* They bear witness of meaning beyond poverty and possessions.

The first chapters of the book explore the different external faces of shame. The latter part of the book invites readers to make the journey to the heart, not only to confront their shame, but also to encounter the Holy Other, the Eternal Mystery, the Love that will never let you go and the Face that will never turn away.

Chapter one explores shame as a consequence of the human condition. Shame is defined as **S**elf **H**atred **A**imed at **ME**. The psychodynamics and characteristics of shame are discussed with a review of some ideas which may be helpful in the healing of shame.

Chapter two explores the shame of arrogance with particular reference to the ancient Jewish stories of Cain and Abel, the narcissistic grandiosity of Prime Minister Haman, the pride and fall of King Uzziah, and the deceit of Abraham in the betrayal of his wife Sarah.

Chapter three explores failure and how King David faced the shame of his throne being overthrown by his own son Absalom. It includes a ten-step, shame-busting process for overcoming the shame of failure.

Chapter four explores the shame of anger and betrayal as a portal into *evil* – spelled backwards is *live* –and describes evil as the destruction of the quality and meaning of life.

Chapter five explores the development of idolatry or pseudo gods as a compensation for shame. These idols include: narcissism, materialism, conformity (relevance), the sacredness of the affect (high experience), the illusion of permanence, and the bane of the extraordinary.

Chapter six covers the psychodynamics of surrender as a gateway to make the perceptual shift from fear and shame to our true identity as the *beloved of God*.

Chapter seven discusses aspects of Christ's life on earth with a development of the characteristics of authentic faith as taught at the Last Supper, in the seven last words from the cross, and of the victorious resurrection as seen through the eyes of Mary Magdalene.

Calling us to a contemplative spirituality, chapter eight explores our inner life to discover that "God has more to do in us than through us", by encouraging us to pursue the meaning of *stillness* expressed so poignantly by the psalmist's words: "Be still and know that I am God" (Ps. 46:10) and "My soul waits in stillness for you, and you alone" (Ps. 62:1).

The epilogue is a riveting personal journey of theologian and former pastor Curt Ashburn coming face to face with his own shame. Looking *beyond the veil*, he helps us to see *things unseen* and explore *things unknown*.

I am greatly indebted to Curt Ashburn who helped to clarify, design and edit this book, and to Alison Peet who faithfully prepared the manuscript. Deepest thanks to my dear friend Dr. Frank Young for his kind expressions in the foreword. Most importantly, I am grateful for my wife, Dr. Victoria Allen, whose keen intellect and theological insight kept me on the path to clarity, succinctness, and truth.

My hope in writing this book is that God, the *Hound of Heaven*, will touch our hearts, heal our shame, and open us to the love and grace of his eternal presence.

> O God, all hearts are open to you,
> You perceive my desire.
> Nothing is hidden from you
> Purify the thought of my heart
> With the gift of your spirit
> That I may love you with a perfect
> Love and give you the praise
> You deserve. [6]
>
> —Unknown author
> *The Cloud of Unknowing*

Chapter 1

Shame: The Human Condition

Liberation is no longer being ashamed in front of oneself.
–Friedrich Nietzsche

She was a lovely lady, but deeply hurt. Married and pregnant, she was terrified when her husband left her for another woman. Her shame came from feeling abandoned, rejected, and humiliated. Hate for her husband drove her to constantly contemplate revenge. As she drove past the exit on the highway leading to his house, she would scream out at the top of her voice, "I wish you'd die. I hate you. You destroyed my life. You betrayed me." The thoughts of revenge were so deep she even thought of paying someone to kill him. Crying profusely, she told me, "I know I shouldn't think like this. But it really hurts."

She thought of killing herself or running away. What about the children? Why should they suffer? They were not at fault. The shame penetrated her emotionally and then started to affect her physically. She developed muscle aches, irritable bowel syndrome, and periodic, severe heart palpitations. Thinking of her husband, she would literally shake and break down crying uncontrollably.

Life was miserable and almost intolerable. She felt like exploding. Even church became routine. The songs and the sermons had no effect on her. She tried to pray, but it seemed as if her prayers bounced back to her off the ceiling. The pain was immense. Life lost its luster. She kept on performing, but she had stopped living. She was ashamed!

What is Shame?

Shame (Self Hatred Aimed at ME) is a feeling of self-castigation, self-loathing, or hatred arising in us when we feel something about us is wrong, flawed, or weak. Shame is a hateful vision of the self through our own eyes. As a result, it may determine how we expect and believe that others see us.

> Much of human misery stems, I believe, from the gap between what we wish to be (or think we should be) and what we believe we are. This gap – influenced by the largeness of our aspirations on one hand, and lowness of our own self-image on the other – is the breeding ground for shame. The nature of this gap, between our ideals and our convictions about our selves, is both universal and individualized, often leading to feelings of embarrassment, self-loathing and humiliation.[1]
> —Andrew Morrison, *The Culture of Shame*

Accompanied by a sensitive self-consciousness and conviction of failure, we are driven to hide or conceal ourselves. Hence the common expressions when we feel embarrassed, "I could have died" or "I could have sunk into a hole." Mortification is a synonym for shame. Guilt is not equivalent to shame. Guilt is an evaluation of behavior. It generates confession and hope for forgiveness. Shame, on the other hand, is an evaluation of the self and seeks concealment and self-deprecation. We drop our head, cover our faces, and lower our eyes when we are ashamed.

One young professional describes the shame and turmoil of his life like this:

> Harsh words and violent blows
> Hidden secrets nobody knows
> Eyes are open, hands are fisted
> Deep inside I'm warped and twisted

So many tricks and so many lies
Too many whens and too many whys
Nobody's special, nobody's gifted
I'm just me, warped and twisted
Sleeping awake and choking on a dream
Listening loudly to a silent scream
Call my mind, the number's unlisted
Lost in someone so warped and twisted
On my knees, alive but dead
Look at the invisible blood I've bled
I'm not gone, my mind has drifted
Don't expect much, I'm warped and twisted
Burnt out, wasted, empty and hollow
Today's just yesterday's tomorrow
The Sun died out, the ashes sifted
I'm still here, warped and twisted.
—Anonymous, "Warped and Twisted"

Shame has emerged as the *Master Emotion*. Shame can spur major achievements or create unthinkable and devastating violence. Beginning in early childhood, shame influences the total human experience and, although rarely recognized, shame may be the cause of much conflict in interpersonal relationships. Shame is a powerful internal phenomenon which penetrates every segment of life. It produces mortification and makes us want to disappear into some deep hole.

In his classic Invisible Man, Ralph Ellison describes the shame of being a black man in America:

I am an invisible man.... I am a man of substance, of flesh and bone, fiber and liquids – and I might even be said to possess a mind, I am invisible, understand, simply because people refuse to see me.... When they approach me they see only my surroundings, themselves or figments of their imaginations – indeed, everything and anything except me.... I am only ashamed of myself for having at one time been ashamed.[2]

Shame is having a diminished vision of the self. Shame impales us under the magnifying gaze of our own eyes. Like a deer in the headlights, "We are," in the words of Jean-Paul Sartre, "frozen by our own inner gaze." He goes on:

I was a fake child...I could feel my acts changing into gestures. Play-acting robbed me of the world and of human beings. I have no scene 'of my own'.... I was giving the grown-ups their cues... my own reason for being slipped away; I would suddenly discover that I did not really count, and I felt ashamed of my unwanted presence in that well ordered world. My truth, my character, and my name were in the hands of adults.

I had learned to see myself through their eyes... when they were not present. They left their gaze behind, and it mingled with the light. I would run and jump across the gaze, which preserved my nature as a model grandson...a transparent certainty spoiled everything: I was an imposter.... The clear sunny semblances that constituted my role were exposed by a lack of being [a real self] which I could neither quite understand, nor cease to feel. I was not substantial or permanent...I was not necessary.... I had no soul.[3]

We have all experienced shame at some time or other. At times it motivates us towards positive action. At other times, however, shame becomes toxic and destructive. It overwhelms and blocks our relationships with others and our own true self. Multi-layered, multi-dimensional, and transgenerational, shame beats at its own frequency and self-replenishes, triggered anew by life's events. Shame is ever rising like the phoenix. We cannot eliminate shame from our lives, but we can learn to recognize the difference between constructive, God-given shame and self-destructive shame, the human nemesis.

The Impact of Shame

The principle affects of shame are hiding, paralysis, and transparency. Hiding is an attempt to reduce scrutiny by seeking to cover the self. In paralysis, speech is silenced, movement interrupted, and the self frozen. Feeling the total exposure of our innermost being with our insecurities and flaws produces a painful transparency, nakedness.

Shame makes us want to be found out when we feel like imposters and failures. For example, an expert witness in a trial said he was so ashamed of doing such a terrible job in court that when the police came to handcuff the defendant, the expert witness thought they were coming to handcuff him. Overwhelmed with shame about his poor performance, he felt that he deserved to be punished. This is consistent with shame being an evaluation of the self.

Self-validating shame makes us believe that we deserve the pain we feel inside. Shame is an experience of exposure *of* the self *by* the self which blurs the distinction between subject and object. The universal look of shame is the head bowed and eyes looking downward and away from the shaming persons. It is accompanied with blushing of the face because of self-visibility known as "the loss of face." A head lowered in shame or an inability to look others in the face is associated with low self-image.

Shame has many faces. Embarrassment is shame in front of an audience. Shyness is shame in the presence of strangers. Discouragement is shame about failure and defeat. Inferiority is shame permanently located in the self. Self-consciousness is shame about performing before others. Father Thomas Keating says, "Shame is felt as inner torment. A sickness of the soul...the humiliated one feels himself naked, defeated, alienated, lacking in dignity and worth."[5]

Shame causes many reactions. Fear is the warning anxiety of anticipated shame. Distress is the crying and sadness that covers the underlying shame. Rage is the protection we use for the exposed self.

> If distress is the affect of suffering, shame is the affect of indignity, transgression, and of alienation. Though terror speaks to life and death and distress makes of the world a vale of tears, yet shame strikes deepest into the heart of man....[4] —S. S. Tomkins

The Psychodynamics of Shame

After the traumatic process of birth, we are ejected from the safe cocoon of our mother's womb into the world. The umbilical cord is cut and we are pushed further away from the last vestigial connection of our home in the womb. Adding insult to injury, we are spanked and sent on our way to live — or to try to do so.

No wonder Wilhelm Reich felt that birth is our greatest trauma of life. Delivered into the caring arms of the mother and under the loving gaze of the father, family, and community, we begin our trek towards maturity. Unlike other animals that mature quickly, human beings have a long journey to maturity.

Human beings are created in the image of God. This bestows on each of us an Identity comprised of Dignity, Meaning, and Value (I-DMV). *Coming* from love, we are *born* to love, and to *return* to love. Henri Nouwen said that our true identity is in being the *beloved of God*. "Though the mountains be shaken and the hills be removed my unfailing love for you will never be shaken" (Isa. 54:10).

Keating again writes that this deep yearning for unconditional love is manifested by three instinctual needs.[6] These instinctual needs are energy centers creating in us a desire to seek fulfillment at any cost [Diagram 1].

Survival-Security (Safety)
Affection-Esteem (Connection)
Power-Control (Adequacy)

Margaret Mahler says that a child who is exposed to a meaningful environment of stability, consistency, and predictability, will undergo an individuation process, a separation from the primary care person (usually the mother) and identity development. The internalization of the caring object allows the development of object constancy or self object transference within the child.[7]

According to Heinz Kohut, and validated by Joseph Lichtenberg, all children have three major self object transferences or relationships.[8] First, *Mirror Self Object Transference* affirms the child as he or she grows up in the delighted gaze of the mother producing a sense of safety and wellbeing. Second, *Twinship Transference* relates to the development of empathic feeling with others and self. Third, *Idealized Transference* allows children to be attached to something or someone greater than themselves.

We are born in relationships and we live and die in relationships. In Kohut's perspective, the self cannot exist outside of a matrix of self objects. Self objects are relationships that maintain the cohesion, vitality, strength, and harmony of the self. They emphasize the instinctual energy zones of safety, connection, and power. They form the basis for the development of human community.

Life is wounded [Diagram 1]. We all experience hurt in one or more of our instinctual needs. This woundedness is described in psychology by Sigmund Freud as the conflict between *Eros* (life force) and *Thanatos* (death force). Philosophy calls this woundedness *alienation* and theology calls it *original sin.*

Hurt or deprivation in one area of instinctual needs resonates with hurt and deprivation in the others because they are interconnected. Deprivation or hurt in the *survival-security* area leads to feelings of abandonment, e.g., divorce, alcohol, death, natural disasters. Busyness or spending insufficient quality and quantity time with children can also lead to abandonment schemas.

Hurt or deprivation in the *affection-esteem* area leads to feelings of rejection. Sadly, this occurs in our homes where parents choose favorites among their children because of intelligence, athletic ability, spirituality, or looks. Parental favoritism wreaks havoc in our children even after we are gone. As parents we must be ever vigilant against this. Rejection may occur in school or church as it relates to such issues as obesity, academics, athletics, attractiveness, or general popularity.

Hurt or deprivation in the *power-control* area leads to feelings of humiliation. Physical or verbal abuse in our homes produces hurt and humiliation in our children. Paradoxically, we are kind to strangers. After work things fall apart at home. Tired and stressed, we scream at our kids and each other. Anger turned to rage is displaced on the minor infractions or misbehavior of our children. As a result, we discipline them in anger which is not really discipline. It is abuse.

Childhood Shame

Describing the scene when his parents arrive home, a young boy said, "Dr. Allen, I have to go next door until the hurricane dies down." As strange as it may seem, if the phone rings, the tone changes in the midst of the anger and confusion. The parent answers the phone saying something pleasant like, "How are you? We're just fine. We're blessed. Johnny's doing well in school. Thanks for calling. See you in church on Sunday. God bless."

As the chaos, anger, and frustration swirl around his head, we can only imagine what Johnny is thinking. The cognitive dissonance makes the child wonder, "If this is being blessed, what would it be like to be cursed?" He feels abandoned, rejected, and humiliated and withdraws from his true self giving way to the Ego Addictive False Self.

Fear Defenses

The false self seeks to create opportunities for fulfillment or happiness to medicate the pain of fear. Fear also causes the Ego Addictive False Self to *defend against abandonment* with self-absorption, *defend against rejection* with high experience seeking tendencies, and *defend against humiliation* with self-inflation or pride (Diagram 2).

Keating says this reflects three dynamics of original sin:

1. The false self is attached to our central passion and diminishes our determination to seek happiness in the right places.
2. Not knowing the place of true happiness we waste much time and energy in the illusion of seeking it in the wrong places.
3. We tend to exhaust happiness by making it an end in itself which only creates more unhappiness.[9]

Shame is a powerful internal phenomenon with many external faces including anger, addiction, blaming, learned helplessness, and victim behavior. Like a fire burning in our psyche, shame is so painful that the mind, through a series of neural and psychological mechanisms, defends against it by creating a false self-image. This false self is created, not in the image of God, but in our own.

This false self is an illusion. It needs attachment to such things as persons, objects, situations, behavior, and drugs for stabilization and validation. Addictive in nature, the false self seeks happiness and fulfillment as ends in themselves resulting in a vicious cycle of more shame.

Shame usually occurs in the presence of an idealized image of some thing or person. This creates intense feelings of worthlessness, inferiority, unlovableness, defectiveness, failure, etc. Guilt condemns behavior saying, "You made a mistake." Shame condemns our very existence saying, "You ARE a mistake!" God says, "You are my beloved child."

Five Components of Shame

There are five components to shame that generally progress and manifest in the following order: shame scene and scripts, shame thoughts, shame voices, shame whip, and shame behavior [Diagram 3].

1. Shame Scene and Scripts

Shame is an affective experience stored in memory as scenes which are dynamic, photographic slices of life with scripts such as being slapped in the face or laughed at. The storage of a shame scene depends on the intensity, duration, and repetition of the affect. Negative affects are more easily remembered than positive affects. Shame or fear scenes are more easily remembered than those of joy.

Interconnected with and magnified by other affect laden scenes, they combine to form the hurt trail or shame core. Continuously beating at its own frequency, the shame core seeks replenishment and may capture or dominate us.

All shame scenes have scripts, that is, voices or language which allow us to predict, interpret, and re-live them.

Shame scenes and scripts are reactivated by the affects of imagery and/or language. Images include people who were present at the shaming, facial expressions, and actions. Words, spoken or unspoken are consciously or subconsciously remembered. Some shame reactions occur unconsciously without imagery or language. One gentleman recalled a powerful shame scene from his childhood:

> The door to my room suddenly burst open. My father rushed in screaming and angrily criticized me for my poor report card. Shouting at the top of his voice, he called me stupid and said I would never amount to anything. Shocked, I became extremely anxious. My face flooded and I was lost for words. In the dreadful silence, looking down and away from my dad, I felt like a total failure. Hopelessly ashamed, I wanted to disappear.

This scene and script is permanently etched in his memory. It is reactivated at home by his wife and at work by his boss. He became emotionally upset as he described the shame scene in therapy. His father is dead and long gone, but the shame scene and script play on. In his own words he said, "My father is controlling me from the grave!"

2. Shame Thoughts

Shame thoughts come to us as a very critical inner voice that demeans our personhood. Shame thoughts are painful, soul destroying, and destructive. The nature of shame thoughts are, "I am alone," "Nobody cares about me," "I am ugly," "I am a failure," "I cannot make it," "I am stupid," "I should have known better," and "I am weak". These thoughts are incessant and bombard our minds creating depression, anger, and isolation.

3. Shame Voices

Shame voices are the words of others playing over and over again inside our minds. Note how our shame thoughts echo the shame voices of our parents, relatives, teachers, employers, peers, or partners. Shame voices are heard as painful, destructive, and hypercritical memories of the words of others. Shame never stops judging us.

Shame voices criticize and demean with statements such as, "You stupid person, why did you do that?" "Can't you do anything right?" "You're a loser." "You had it all and you blew it!" "You should be ashamed of your self." "How could you mess up so badly?" "People are laughing at you." "No one likes you."

4. Shame Whip

Shame-based persons develop a masochistic whip to beat, punish, and eventually destroy the self. This is a form of chronic penance in which shame-prone persons create their own shame cross. The shame cross has a vertical pole of self-hatred and a horizontal pole of hatred for others. The intersection is the shame violence point where there is danger to self (suicide) and to others (homicide).

A man who had attended a top boarding school in England since he was seven years old told me this shame memory. He had received years and years of severe corporal punishment from a tough and cruel senior master for bad behavior, poor class work, and refusal to do homework. Now married and successful in business, this man lives a shame-based life with a shame whip and a shame cross. Arriving home after a bad day in the office, he screams at his wife, goes into the bathroom and repeatedly slaps himself in the face for about three minutes. Relieved, he then joins the family for dinner. The shame recording of his youth keeps on playing. Like footprints on fresh cement, shame lasts for a long time!

5. Shame Behavior

Shame thoughts, shame voices, the shame whip, and the shame cross lead to shame behavior. Shame behavior validates the unworthiness, failure, and pain of internalized shame. The shame that we fear and despise often leads us to a cycle of more shame.

Factors and Associations of Shame

Shame has multiple factors and has many causes and associations. Freud, who believed that shame was caused by genital deficiency, wrote, "Shame...is considered to be a feminine characteristic par excellence."[12] Females and males each have specific shame-based areas in their lives. Females tend to feel shame about relationships and body appearance. In males, shame is usually associated with failure in achievement, jobs, competition, and finances.

Primary Causes of Shame

1. Abuse in all its forms, sexual, physical, emotional, mental, and cultural produces repeated cycles of shame.

2. Addictions and eating disorders subtly tend to be shamed based in causation and effect. They cannot be treated effectively until the shame is identified, defined, confronted, and resolved.

3. Natural disasters and illness impact people negatively producing various levels of shame.

4. Oppression and discrimination dehumanize people and create deep shame and low self-image. This type of shame is common in certain populations or minorities.

5. Failure and the shattering of cherished dreams of all types result in unending cycles of pain and shame.

6. Stress overload reduces our margin for compassion and love when it exceeds our limits resulting in a painful saga of shame.

Characteristics of Shame

Shame radiates continuous waves of deep hurt and fear as a result of the gap between our expected self (what we and others expect of us) and our actual achievement. Shame is a complex, evasive, but ever-present phenomenon occurring throughout our lives. The following is a limited discussion of some of the characteristics of shame I find in my own experience and work with others.

1. Constriction of Emotion

Shame-based persons have difficulty integrating feeling with thinking and act out of emotion rather than cognition. But the affect tends to be consumed with one form of anger or the other. Anger pervades all of life from constant complaining to fear, paranoia, uncontrollable rage, or boredom. The shame-prone person recognizes shame issues and tends to repeat them. It is a sad dance moving between the experiences of being a victim and manifesting victimization behavior.

It is not unusual for a shame-based teenage girl with childhood trauma to compensate for the pain by excelling in academics. Then, at the height of her achievement, she has a child and becomes extremely emotional, labile, and depressed. She is terrified of not being a good mother. The birth of the child exposes her to the trauma and the shame (abandonment, rejection, humiliation) of her earlier life. If the shame is not worked through, it will be passed to her child and the shame cycle will continue.

2. Shame and Addiction

Addiction has genetic, environmental, constitutional, and behavioral factors. It is generally accepted that shame is a causative and an associated factor of addiction. The early childhood trauma of abandonment, rejection, and humiliation creates a deep protest of various hurt feelings such as sadness, anger, frustration, and despair. If the protests are unheeded, the hurt and shame move deeper into the heart with a superficial numbing effect.

As the pain deepens, the first schema begins and the individual seeks to medicate the pain with different types of addictions. The addict seeks gratification in compulsive attachments to the addictive object restricting choices and roles, e.g., drugs, money, sex, people. As addiction deepens, the addict becomes more attached and the behavior is covered up with lies and multiple deceptions. Addiction associations include:

- Unawareness of the thought and feeling processes
- Distortion and denial
- Dysfunctional relationships because of manipulation instead of intimacy
- Strong dependency needs
- Excessive guilt and powerlessness
- Living from crisis to crisis (strong self-absorption)
- Dishonesty (reconstructing reality)
- Low self-image and powerlessness over the addiction
- Unresolved loss or aborted grief creating a cycle of multiple addictions

Codependency is a form of addiction, an attachment to pleasing or controlling other people. Codependents medicate their pain by pleasing and controlling others. Caused by dysfunctional family systems, codependency stems from the family of origin and evokes enmeshment and over responsive care taking. As a result, they become martyrs or victims and chronic caretakers with compulsive behaviors such as overeating and workaholism.

Unable to stand alone, the shame-prone codependent craves attention and the support of others. Often extremely talented, codependents are only able to express themselves or state their views in an environment of total acceptance.

3. Interpersonal Relationships

Shame hinders interpersonal relationships. When one partner dominates or abuses the other, the shame-based person with poor boundaries finds it difficult to pull away. Conversely, some shame-prone persons who are hurt in the power-control area and have deep humiliation will become contra-dependent and develop rigid boundaries. They seek to control the codependent partner who has weaker boundaries.

4. Negative Vision of Ourselves

Shame is associated with a negative vision of self as seen through our own eyes. This negative vision determines how we see others and particularly how we expect others to experience and treat us. A negative vision of the self causes loneliness in shame-based persons. It is interesting to note that lonely people have the same amount of social contacts as non-lonely people. The difference is that shame-based persons tend not to reach out to their contacts or to reciprocate hospitality shown to them.

To be lonely is to be aware of an emptiness which it takes more than people to fill. It is to sense that something is missing which you cannot name. 'By the waters of Babylon, there we sat down and wept, when we remembered Zion,' sings the psalmist (137:1). Maybe in the end it is Zion that we're lonely for, the place we know best by longing for it, where at last we become who we are, where finally we find home![11] —Frederick Buechner

5. Mortification

Shame makes us feel like hiding or sinking into the ground, wanting to die — mortification. Shame is now! In the 1960s at the age of sixteen, a girl became pregnant. Her parents took her for a medical consultation. She was ashamed and apprehensive about seeing the doctor. Her fears were realized as the doctor berated her saying that she should be ashamed of herself for being pregnant. She had destroyed her parents' dreams for her.

When she told the doctor that she only had sex once, the doctor laughed at her and said no girl gets pregnant after having sex once. Even though forty-five years had passed, the woman told me, "I feel the same shame now as I felt then. I wanted to die, fall into a hole in the ground and disappear." There is no time in the heart. Shame is a painful melody playing the same tune over and over again and transcending time.

Shame destroys or dumbs down the possibilities of life and creates *dead living people*. The tragedy of life is not death, but that shame destroys so much of our life while we are still alive. The line by William Wallace in *Braveheart* comes to mind: "Every man dies, but not every man lives."

6. Self-Absorption

Self-absorption is a characteristic of shame and an impediment to relationships. Self-absorption is healthy in infancy and early childhood, but in adulthood it restricts life to personal concerns giving little or no attention to others. Deprivation of the basic instinctual needs of childhood leads to self-absorption and results in narcissism, defensive self-sufficiency, vulnerability, and arrogance.

7. Focus on Limitations and Avoidance of Potential

Shame encourages us to focus on our limitations and ignore our potential which produces triumphant mediocrity. Graves are filled with unwritten books, unfulfilled dreams, unsung songs, and undiscovered solutions to the problems of humanity. Our shame makes us believe that we are not good enough to contribute to the world. That is a lie.

8. Repetition Compulsion

Sucking us into ourselves, shame seduces us to live the repetition compulsions of our pain. It blinds and draws us toward the pain and hurt we know and fear. As a result, we often marry our childhood trauma and repetitively regenerate it through our children. Sadly, the hurt trail goes in circles and keeps returning to the same painful memories of shame. Shame never ceases to create the repetitive compulsion of the pain we fear.

One woman told me that when she was ten, her father became upset on Christmas day. He had been drinking and overturned the table set for Christmas dinner. She recalled the pain she felt scooping up the cranberry sauce, turkey, and stuffing off of the floor. She promised herself that she would never marry an alcoholic. Forty years later, sitting in my office on Christmas Eve, she said with tears in her eyes, "Dr. Allen, I am married to an alcoholic. How could I do what I said I wouldn't do?"

9. Living in the Gaze of Others

Ignoring the true self, shame encourages us to live and dance in the gaze of those people who are important to us. Even after they leave us or die, we continue to live in the make-believe world of their gaze. We feel insubstantial, irrelevant, and hidden as if we have no soul or life.

A famous film director with world acclaim said that his life was like a film playing on a movie screen. In his later years, the projector was off, the lights were out, and his life was a blank screen because no one was watching.

10. Passivity and Aggression

Bogged down by the burden of hurts and low self-image, shame encourages us to succumb to a bland passivity or an empty aggressiveness. For example, a lady came to my office who had just received a promotion. She said that she would not leave until we talked to her boss to tell him she did not want the promotion. She said the promotion would destroy her life because people under her were difficult and would shame and disobey her. Together we talked to her boss. She refused the promotion and told him she preferred to be what she called an ordinary worker.

11. Loss of Face

Shame creates feelings of disgrace and the desire to hide our faces. Overwhelmed by feelings of fear, distrust, and latent rage, we build walls that block us from ourselves and others. When we build these walls to hide the garbage, we also block out the beauty around us, the people, the flowers, and the trees.

Challenged by this psychotherapeutic insight, a reticent, young professional woman decided to break down her walls. She determined to travel and open her life to meet people of different backgrounds. To her surprise, within a few months she found the love of her life and married him, had a baby, and is extremely happy. Shame builds walls for protection, but they often become a prison!

12. Chronological Fatalism

Paralyzing us with fear, shame encourages a self-fulfilling prophecy by making us believe that nothing we do makes a difference. We suffer a sense of chronological fatalism. We magnify our problems, we always complain, and we see the glass half empty rather than half full. As a result, many of us rush into marriage, change jobs, or escape to new geographical horizons only to find that wherever we go, our shame goes with us.

As Shakespeare said, "The fault...is not in our stars, But in ourselves." Shame can only be counteracted by an intentional, deliberate, and counter-instinctive commitment to face the pain in our hearts. As one song says, "I have been to Nassau, Paris, and New York, but I have never been to *me!*" The antidote to chronological fatalism is faith. Faith is the light that brightens the darkness of our shame and despair converting our fear into the freedom of love.

13. Identification with the Oppressor

Oppressed or marginalized people feel cultural shame when they are excluded or disenfranchised by the broader community. Paradoxically, shame-based persons tend to identify with the oppressor because shame seeks union with the person doing the shaming. Sadly, they tend to treat other oppressed or down trodden people even more terribly than the oppressors. This phenomenon is well-documented in the history of revolution.

14. Learned Helplessness

Shame produces *learned helplessness*. It destroys passion, purpose, and perseverance. It creates paralyzing, inner-psychic structures. Although we could perform the tasks, a self-induced form of helplessness makes failure a self-fulfilling prophecy. As a result, we do not show up for our life. In fact, where we are...*we* are what is missing!

15. Dance of Seduction, Exploitation and Destruction

Shame is associated with a powerful dance of seduction, exploitation, and abandonment. For example, a shame-based young man is seduced to take cocaine. When he is high, he is encouraged to use more cocaine. As a result, he is exploited. He took cocaine and then cocaine took him. Eventually, he is overwhelmed and the cocaine destroys him.

16. Splitting Off and Inferiority

Shame encourages incompetent feelings and acts. There is often clumsiness or feelings of stupidity in the presence of persons perceived to be more distinguished or competent than ourselves. Shame splits off our adequate parts and projects them onto others making us feel inadequate and inferior.

Shame-based persons are vulnerable to being controlled and dominated by persons in power. Cultures and organizations also produce a sense of powerlessness. Shame encourages the splitting off of the adequate parts of their citizens which are projected onto the dictator making him or her even more powerful. Conversely, the shame-based authoritarian leader splits off his inadequate parts and projects them onto his followers thus making them feel inferior and impotent.

17. The Past-Future Prison

Shame encourages us to focus and dwell on the pain and hurt of the past and it also projects negativity and hopelessness regarding the future and causes us to ignore present opportunities. As a result, freedom is compromised and we settle for the comfort of the all too common prison of the status quo.

18. Suicide and Homicide

The triangle of depression, shame, and anger in intimate relationships is an explosive mixture often resulting in suicide, homicide, or both. As the shame-based person is isolated, the pain is magnified, and the perceived hope of anyone helping is minimized. Alienated and alone, the person walks into the darkness of suicide or homicide.

19. Comparisons

Encouraging comparisons and envy of others, shame leaves us sad, dejected, and discouraged. As a result, we lose our uniqueness and become what the psychoanalysts call *as if* persons. In other words, shame takes away our personhood and it is only *as if* we were persons.

20. Pathological Jealousy

Shame is jealous of the joys and successes of others. It cheers for their failure. This is known as the *crab syndrome* because crabs pull each other down when trying to escape confinement. The *crab syndrome* is manifested by disloyalty, jealously, anger, opposition, and sabotage.

21. Destructive Gossip

Shame is usually the root cause of gossip which produces betrayal, fragmentation, and destruction. For example, a talented young female left her well-paying job because of the gossip saying, "It's destroying me!"

The Healing of Shame

This book will deepen your understanding of shame and, as one therapist put it, shame busting. However, this is not a typical Christian *how to* book. Shame is difficult to treat. It is ubiquitous, evasive, deeply internalized, and associated with the wish to conceal. Unlike other emotions which are released with catharsis and weeping, shame is difficult to admit and discharge. Shame has little or no facial expression; you might even say it has no face. The only signs may be turning away or downcast eyes.

Reading this book indicates that you are serious about removing your shame masks and dealing with the underlying shame core, self-loathing, and organized hurt. I encourage you to work at this with others, a friend, spouse, or small group. There is shame-busting power in being accountable to others. However, if you are struggling, do not let shame itself keep you from going to a good therapist.

The Treatment of Shame

Christian integrity and medical ethics require me to state that, for some readers, confronting the shame core will require a skilled therapist who has faced and worked through his or her own shame. Therapy is often ineffective if the therapist's shame has not been faced and unmasked.

Developing a meaningful therapeutic alliance with a shame-based client takes patience, tolerance, compassion, and understanding. Be aware that the therapist sometimes becomes the disavowed object of hate, rejection, and disgust as the client releases deep-seated shame. Receiving this transference with love, self-containment, respect, and a non-judgmental attitude is no easy task.

The treatment of shame is complex and would require a book in itself to discuss it fully. However, following are eight suggestions that have been helpful in my experience. They are addressed to therapists, but every reader will benefit from them as a foundation for understanding the shame core. We will return to these eight shame busters in subsequent chapters.

1. Working Through

The shame-based person can work through the hurt trail with the aid of psychotherapy, psychodrama, role playing, equine therapy, therapeutic letters, etc. As they do, ripples of pain, sadness, hurt, and anger are released freeing the patient from the bondage of shame. Working through the shame core requires the development of a deeper awareness and consciousness of a loving therapeutic alliance. The shame-based client with deficits of trust may seek to sabotage the alliance with a mixture of negative, unstable transference feelings towards the therapist. Issues that challenge the shame core of the therapist can create a confusing medley of feelings.

By listening longer and deeper, I have learned that I have often responded defensively to compensate for my own shame issues. The following incident brought this home in a powerful way. One afternoon, a very attractive and highly qualified young lady came for an assessment interview. After hearing her list of achievements, I said, "You have accomplished a lot, congratulations." She became extremely angry and shouted at me asking, "Why does that matter?"

The truth is that she was shame-based and worked hard to compensate for her inadequacy. When I drew her attention to the compensation for her shame, she unleashed her anger on me. The more successful shame-based persons are, the angrier they become when complimented. When the therapist creates an environment of stability, consistency, and predictability, the therapeutic alliance, though fragile and labile, will slowly develop.

2. The Release of Affect

Confronting destructive anger is time consuming because of the underlying compounded resistance and defenses. Much understanding and patience is required to work through the resentment, bitterness, hardness of heart, and grudges. Care and caution are necessary because when shame-based affect or feeling is released, the therapist becomes the target. Therapists working with shame have to be willing to carry negative introjects and painful affects to allow patients to break through their bondage of shame as they open to the freedom of love.

Distinguished psychoanalyst Janet Gibbs claims we have to be very careful not to storm the barrier. Like the story of the Trojan horse, it is best to be invited to enter through open doors or to very subtly and wisely infiltrate barriers of resistance. She warns that shame-based clients can infuse the therapeutic relationship with different counter transferences dropping us into the pit of despair and making us feel deeply inadequate.

3. Surrender

Shame circulates around poles of anger and sadness. When facing the anger, we have to be aware of the sadness. Conversely, when dealing with sadness, we have to be aware of the anger. We need to give up control over the Ego Addictive False Self based on fear. This surrender is how we make the perceptual shift [chapter six] to our true self.

The perceptual shift is blocked if the therapist is lacking experience and has not established a therapeutic alliance bond based on mutual positive regard with the patient. The result is that the patient becomes stuck in the destructive cycles of shame and fear leaving the therapist with feelings of gross inadequacy. The patient may even sabotage the therapy. In my experience, our ability to help patients make contact with their deep shame is the determining factor for the length and effectiveness of the therapy. Only a loving, caring environment melts shame and encourages the perceptual shift. But real love is hard and truthful, not limited, evasive, or superficial.

4. Letting Go

As patients surrender, they have to decide to let go of hurt feelings whether they were caused by themselves, the perpetrator, or others involved in the shame scene. Letting go does not mean trying to change the person who has shamed us, but to accept what has happened. Letting go is releasing fear and opening to love. Letting go does not mean changing the past, but deciding not to let it strangle us. Letting go does not mean blaming others. Letting go is a willingness to face our truth regardless of how painful it is.

Letting go is forgiving the past and choosing to live in the freedom of the present and to grow into the future. Letting go is not being dogmatic about being right, but being willing to learn and grow in self-understanding. Letting go is not being forced into simplistic reductionist solutions. Letting go is, however, learning to live with the questions so that we can grow into the answers. Finally, to let go is to make the perceptual shift from the negative affect of fear to an attitude of love.

5. Forgiveness

Similar to letting go, forgiveness is the only process in life that can heal a wound from a past that cannot be changed. Forgiveness is the personal experience of leaving the prison of our hurt to work through our feelings so that when the painful memory comes to consciousness, it loses its sting and does not affect us. Forgiveness helps us to realize that we can have a tomorrow different from our yesterday. We come to realize in forgiveness that the enemy is not the other person. It is the doubt we harbor about ourselves buried deep in our soul.

We can choose to separate ourselves from the hurt and to know the freedom of our true being. This freedom liberates us to see even the perpetrators of our pain for what they are. They do not define our self-worth or our well being. We and we alone are accountable for our lives. Finally, forgiveness lifts the burden of life's changing circumstances. It allows us to let go of the past, enjoy the present, and grow into the uniqueness of our true self.

6. Gratitude

When we make the perceptual shift from fear to love, forgiveness follows. When we experience the healing of love, our defenses drop, pain is released, and we develop an attitude of gratefulness. Receiving a gift is one thing, but when we say thank you, we give of ourselves. Gratitude means that the shame core has been impacted and, like the butterfly leaving the cocoon, we experience a discovery or rediscovery of self.

Speaking of the journey to self, T. S. Eliot wrote, "We shall not cease from exploration and the end of all our exploring will be to arrive where we started... and know the place for the first time." At the end of Henri Nouwen's life, his last words were, "Tell them I am grateful." Gratitude is the crowning splendor of life lived as the *beloved of God*.

7. Laughing at Self

Laughing at self is a powerful antidote to shame. It is self-transcendent and allows a person a sense of mastery. It is a form of surrender in which a person realizes that his essential being – his true self – cannot be characterized by shame. Surrender is opening up to the consciousness in which the mystery of our life unfurls.

An elderly man who suffered much of his life with multiple hospitalizations for depression said, "My life is hopeless." After listening attentively, I asked, "Hopeless?" He said, "Yes, I feel hopeless." I asked again, "You are feeling hopeless?" "Yes", he said. I confronted him, "Isn't feeling hopeless different than being hopeless?" As the insight dawned on him, his sad face changed into a smile and then he laughed. If he feels hopeless and is not hopeless, his being is intact and there is hope.

8. Contemplative Prayer

Contemplative prayer is a powerful antidote to shame [chapter eight]. The ancient practice of Lectio Divina includes Scripture reading (*Lectio*), reflection (*Reflectio*), oral prayer (*Oratorio*), silent prayer (*Contemplatio*), and taking the experience into daily life (*Operatio*). This spiritual exercise calms and neutralizes the deep pain in our psyche. In silent prayer, the psyche releases the shame feelings of anger, hurt, fear, and despair. Contemplative prayer has blessed many persons including me.

The woman who was betrayed and shamed by her husband in the opening paragraph of this chapter found great release in prayer from her deep shame and hurt. The freedom and peace of surrender enabled her to call her husband and forgive him. Shocked, her husband burst into tears and apologized profusely for having hurt her so deeply and wanted to do anything to make it up to her. He was puzzled how his wife could be so peaceful and forgiving in the wake of such tragedy. She had released the hurt and was given the freedom of love and experienced the peace that transcends deep shame and hurt.

From Ashes to Beauty

John was a tough young man. John's mother loved him and did her best to give him a good upbringing. But John missed his father. He never understood why his father refused to acknowledge him. This was painful, but that is the way it was. John said the absence of his father left a hole in his soul.

John described to me a painful event which has stayed with him forever. As a teenager, he and a few neighborhood boys went swimming on Arawak Cay. They had a wonderful time jumping off boats and frolicking in the water. The time passed quickly, but in the midst of the fun, one of the boys asked if anyone had seen Tim. They all looked for him, but could not find him.

Suddenly, John said he saw the outline of a human figure on the white sand bottom of the ocean. It was Tim. John dived into the water and tried to bring Tim to the surface, but the body was too heavy. He just could not do it. He called for help from the other boys and some men who were nearby. Eventually they were able to bring Tim up. They placed him in the boat and gave him CPR to no avail.

Tim was dead. In shock, John asked, "How could this happen?" In John's own words, "I was blown away. I never saw a dead body. I could not believe it. My cousin Tim was dead." It happened so fast. What could he do? John said this event is indelibly fixed in his mind. It never leaves him. He said it is just like it is happening all over again as he told me about it. It never goes away.

John dropped out of school and fell into bad company in spite of his mother's warning to be careful. John did his own thing. He became an arrogant know-it-all. He used and eventually sold and stole drugs. After many misdemeanors, John was arrested for armed robbery and put in prison.

Prison was tough, it terrified John. Throughout his time in prison, John's mother faithfully visited him and begged him to change his ways. After leaving prison, John became more involved in drugs and developed a reputation for being ruthless.

As John's involvement in drugs deepened, he found that people did not trust him and shied away when he was around. He went from selling marijuana to selling cocaine becoming fully immersed in the drug world. John lived a dangerous life. Stealing drugs is lethal because there is only one law in the drug world – the gun – swift justice.

Then it happened. John stole a pusher's drugs. A contract was put on his life and he had to go on the run. He had no money, no job, and his life was in danger, John was in dire straights. He heard about the dump and went there to hide and live. The stench was awful and the environment terrible, but it was the only place that John felt safe. After being accepted by the men at the dump, John settled in. Apparently, finding the right place to sleep at the dump is very important because around 2:00 a.m., a group of one hundred stray dogs roam around the dump and attack anyone they see. This terrified John.

John adapted to the dump and made a living by selling and stealing drugs. Life on the dump was difficult. One morning while John was still sleeping, his friend went to look for food. John never heard the dump truck back up to where he slept. It dumped garbage on top of him. As the truck was pulling away, John's friend returned and shouted at the truck, "Stop! Stop! You just buried a man." The truck driver turned around and along with John's friend tried to dig him out. After calling John's name and digging feverishly for about five minutes, they heard John yelling, "Right here! I'm right here!" After digging and searching they found John buried alive under life's garbage. They took him to the hospital where he was treated and released after three days.

John returned to the dump and continued using, stealing, and selling drugs. Sadly, he stole a cachet of drugs belonging to the chief drug dealer. Again a contract was placed on his life and he had to run. He slept under a sea grape tree in an open park near the beach. During the day he slept and at night he begged his way around area restaurants until the police caught up with him. He escaped the police and slept on the roof of empty buildings at the market complex. The police caught up with him again, but John ran away. Distraught, he asked a man for help and was told to go to a church breakfast program for the homeless. At the breakfast, he was told to go to a homeless shelter, but there was no space for him there. Dejected and discouraged, he was eventually referred to the Haven, a drug treatment program.

John was welcomed and made to feel at home at the Haven. He did well for the first month and seemed very motivated, but his deep cravings for drugs caused him to leave the program and return to the dump. One day, John was helping a businessman empty his trash. John was surprised that the man knew he had been in the Haven. The man offered to take him back to the Haven, but John refused and ran away to the other side of the dump. When he got to the other side, the *Hound of Heaven* had another group of men there emptying a truck. Those men also begged John to return to the Haven to finish his treatment. They took him back and he buckled down and took his treatment program seriously.

John was motivated to learn. One morning, he read in the Bible that God loved him (John 3:16). John said this was a shocking statement to him, "God loves me". He had let everybody down, his family, his neighborhood, and his friends. He felt like an outcast. He was ashamed of himself. How could God love him? But he said that the love of God and the love he experienced in the Haven made him feel accepted and loved for the first time in his life.

When he realized that God loved him, he broke down thinking, "I do not deserve to be loved." God pierced his heart, bursting his shame core. John went to daily therapy at the Community Assessment Center. His treatment progressed and he eventually went to work. He worked hard and competently. John was an inspiration to fellow workers and the students at the treatment program. As of this writing, John has been clean and in therapy for ten years. He is married to a good woman who loves and supports him.

John now directs the Haven drug treatment center and he owns a small landscaping business. Recognizing the ongoing value of therapy, John still attends therapy at the Community Assessment Center. With deep humility, John says, "Even though I have been clean for ten years, I still have so much to learn."

During a television interview, John was asked what he considered the most painful experience of his life. Recalling the drowning of his cousin Tim, John said, "I still can't get over his body lying so still on the ocean floor. Diving in to get him, I was scared and when I could not lift him out of the water I felt helpless. I was a failure. This has haunted me all my life. I can never forget it."

This is a classic shame scene with the dead body and onlookers. The deep piercing sense of helplessness is indelibly imprinted on his heart and radiated waves of pain and fear throughout the journey of his life. Such shaming, painful experiences create powerful hurt feelings which challenge our hearts.

Bombarding our psyche, the deep scream for help is a protest falling on deaf ears. Eventually, if help does not arrive, our heart becomes numb and the pain is displaced and seeps deeper. Over the years the pain organizes and seeps into the sinews of our being. As the years go by they create a post-traumatic reaction involving:

- Intrusive symptoms (flash backs, bizarre reactions)
- Arousal symptoms (anxiety, fear, anger, sadness)
- Catastrophic changes in our heart producing withdrawal symptoms of isolation, fear, or even dropping out

These symptoms are so painful that the person seeks to medicate the feelings with addictions, e.g., drugs, alcohol, delinquency, and other destructive tendencies. Propelled on a journey of destruction, John ran from crisis to crisis until he had no where to escape – he was broken. John came to the end of himself. He experienced the reality the First Step in Alcoholics Anonymous: My life is unmanageable! I need a power greater than myself!

Chapter 2

The Shame of Arrogance
The March of Folly

Shaming another in public is like the shedding of blood.
—Talmud

Robert's dad died when he was three years old. He remembered playing with his older brother as the funeral cortege passed by. He had no memory of the next three years. He remembered high school and feeling empty and inferior as his friends talked of their fathers. They were rich and secure. He was poor. His mother worked long hours to make ends meet and he missed his father deeply.

When he attended the parties of his rich school mates, he was ashamed of his lack of possessions that provide the security and freedom to enjoy life. He hated his life. What he really could not stand was the deep hurt that surfaced in his heart reminding him of his dad's death and how powerless and helpless he was compared to his friends.

He went to college and tried to impress people by casting off the shroud of fear, insecurity, and shame that had haunted him. Then he walked through the lobby of the student union and shrieked in horror when he saw his own image in a mirror. Pierced by insecurity, he was ashamed of himself and felt like every eye was glued on him. He was ashamed of being ashamed.

Soon, however, Robert felt that he had arrived. He fell in love with one of the most beautiful girls on campus who responded in kind. He strutted around, chest out, enjoying life. She was his new insurance policy from shame.

Then one evening she broke off the relationship. He was crushed and overwhelmed. He was breathless as the horrible bolus of hurt and shame re-entered his heart. It was the same pain he felt at the death of his father and the same inferiority he felt with his wealthy friends at school.

At the end of the third year, his supervisor called him in and told him his grades were not up to par. Robert's heart sank when it was suggested that he take a year off to get his life together. How could he fail his hard working, widowed mother who had sacrificed so much to keep him in college? When he called his mother to tell her of his failure, she berated him. She shouted that he should be ashamed of himself. Indeed, he was terribly ashamed for letting his mother down. Robert took a year off and worked hard to get back into college. He succeeded and went on to be a success.

After college, he once again fell in love. They shared wonderful times together, but her abuse of drugs petrified him. When she took drugs, she became incoherent making him ashamed and again feeling like a failure. Why did she have to have a drug problem? Therapy helped him realize that he could not deal with the situation and he broke it off. Upset and confused, she accused him of ruining her life. Shaming him deeply, he experienced the same bolus of pain which had haunted his life in the past.

Eventually, Robert fell in love with an attractive woman whom he described as the girl of his dreams. After a short and exciting romance, the young lady left Robert and returned to her job in another country. Robert followed her and was deeply hurt when she ignored him and refused to see him. Robert felt helpless and powerless as the bolus of shame returned making him feel incapacitated, hurt, and afraid. He described his sense of abandonment, rejection, and humiliation as the same painful feelings that haunted his life since his father's death.

Robert's challenge was not to find another woman, but to face his shame, work through it, and experience his true self. He looked at me and said calmly, "I can deal with it on my own. I can handle it." He left abruptly and said he was not coming back to therapy. In a pregnant silence, I watched him leave. Coming face to face with the humiliation schema of his shame, Robert's Ego Addictive False Self defended against the humiliation with an arrogant attitude of denial. This compensation occurs in persons with a humiliation schema. It is the same as arrogance which is associated with the myth of invincibility.

Arrogance is a powerful manifestation of shame in modern culture. Janet Gibbs would often say in our class at the Chautauqua Institute, "Hubris (pride) is the last issue to be resolved in psychotherapy." In ancient Rome, whenever a general won a war, the victory parade showed off the general and the heroes of the war. But behind the general stood a slave whispering in his ear, *Sic transit gloria*, "All glory is fleeting" and *Memento mori*, "Remember you are only a man." These were reminders to the general to guard against arrogance with humility and realism.

Arrogance is overbearing, dogmatic, proud and claims much for the self with little or no consideration for others. Arrogance means doing things my way. "I am the master of my fate: and the captain of my soul" (William Ernest Henley, "Invictus").

Through the process of projective identification, the arrogant person splits off the disavowed inadequate parts of the self and projects them onto others creating narcissistic grandiosity and a sense of supremacy. The death of Robert's father was a powerful narcissistic injury which created shame which is the veiled companion of narcissism. Leon Wurmser observed, "Where the clamor of narcissism reigns, shame is always tacitly present. In a much deeper way shame is both the shadow and even the antitheses of love."[1]

Through the death of his father, Robert suffered humiliation from a deprivation of the instinctual need for power-control. Eventually, this deep sense of loss was compensated for by arrogance, an air of invincibility that gave him the feeling that he could ignore the shame and move beyond it. In my experience, each time the shame bolus appears, the Ego Addictive False Self develops increasing layers of protection to defend against the trauma. The illusion of invincibility becomes attached to the central passion and deeply influences the will. In the end, compensating for shame with arrogance [Diagram 4] fails and results in serious additional damage.

> Life batters and shapes us in all sorts of ways before it's done.... The original, shimmering self gets buried so deep that most of us hardly end up living out of it at all. Instead, we live out of all the other selves which we are constantly putting on and taking off like coats and hats against the world's weather.[2] —Frederic Buechner

Arrogance is a powerful defense and one of the prevailing faces of shame in modern culture. It can be found operating in business tycoons, media moguls, and political potentates. It is particularly prevalent in unrepentant advertising. For example, driving along a major highway, a bold advertisement for a hospital showed a woman saying, "I am a cancer survivor and I am here forever." How presumptuous! How arrogant! *Memento mori!*

On the eve of national elections in a developing country, the leader of the ruling party said, "As sure as the sun rises, tomorrow, we will be in power." The sun did rise the next day, but his government was out of power. Sadly, arrogance is the cause célèbre in many areas of modern life.

Arrogance alienates and builds walls between people. It claims victories unachieved and strides across the length and breadth of life like a mighty colossus with the illusion of permanence and invincibility.

Adam and Eve: The Arrogance of Disobedience

The Genesis story places Adam and Eve in the paradisiacal splendor of the Garden of Eden. Given all the luxuries of life, they experienced the freedom, joy, and beauty of their environment. In this primal splendor, Adam exclaims about Eve:

> This is now bone of my bones
> And flesh of my flesh;
> She shall be called 'woman'
> For she was taken out of man. —Gen. 2:23

Simultaneously, the spiritual institution of marriage was established: "For this reason a man will leave his father and mother and be united to his wife, and they will become one flesh" (Gen. 2:24). Enveloped in the glory and awareness of God's presence, "The man and his wife were both naked, and they felt no shame" (Gen. 2:25).

The word *shame* is derived from Indo-European origin and means *to cover*. Thus, in the glory of paradise, even though they were naked, they had had no need for cover, they felt no shame. They were clothed in the splendor and glory of God.

The one restriction God gave to Adam was to forbid eating of the Tree of the Knowledge of Good and Evil whose fruit was attractive to the eyes and pleasing to the palate. Then Satan, the deceiver, engaged Eve in a dialogue and challenged God's command. Satan seduced Eve telling her that they will not surely die as God said, rather, they will become as gods themselves. Notice the appeal to becoming like God.

This is the basic format of any major temptation, i.e., the idea that you can arrogantly do what you want without consequences. Like us, Eve fell for it. She ate the forbidden fruit and gave it to Adam. Suddenly aware that their disobedience cost them the glory with which God had clothed them, Adam and Eve now felt "naked and ashamed". Embarrassed by their nakedness, they covered themselves with fig leaves. When God came to the garden to walk in fellowship with his creation, Adam and Eve hid from him. This led God to ask two important questions: "Adam, where are you?" and "What have you done?"

It is significant that the ancient Judeo-Christian story of our origins would introduce the concept of shame as the human response to sin, failure, and disappointment. Throughout human history, shame has relentlessly pursued man and woman with a fury. Until recently, in spite of shame's pervasiveness, it was rarely discussed in the psychological literature.

Why is this? One argument among many is that we professionals were not in touch with our own shame cores and therefore have been blocked in helping others to work on their shame. Here is Sartre on the relationship between shame and self-identity:

> Consider for example shame...it is a shameful apprehension of something and this something is me. I am ashamed of what I am. Shame therefore realizes an intimate relation of myself to myself. Through shame I have discovered an aspect of my being....I recognize that I am as the other sees me.[3]

Michelangelo captures shame in a powerful way in his painting of Adam and Eve being banished from the Garden of Eden (See cover photo). Notice the pained look of shame on Eve's face as Adam hangs his head in disgrace. In Book 10 of *Paradise Lost*, Milton has Adam telling Eve that they "face a long days dying to augment our pain."

However, in the pathos of the story of Adam and Eve, there is a powerful message of redemption and self-acceptance. God tells Adam and Eve that the seed of the serpent will bruise the heel of their seed. But in a crescendo of victory, God tells them that their seed, representing the human race, will crush the head of the serpent.

Removing the covering of leaves from Adam and Eve, God clothed them in animal skins thus laying the framework for the healing of the human condition. God then shed the blood of animals to provide skins as a temporary and symbolic covering for Adam and Eve's *nakedness and shame.*

This was a prophetic foreshadowing of the death and resurrection of our Lord Jesus Christ, "The Lamb of God, who takes away the sin [and shame] of the world!" (John 1:29). It would be he who had no shame who would drink of the shame cup and die on the shame cross to liberate us from the curse of our own shame. Professor Mark Bailey of Dallas Theological Seminary describes this as the "greatest romance story ever told."

> The kingdom of the world
> Has become the kingdom of our Lord
> And of his Christ,
> And he will reign for ever and ever! —Rev. 11:15

Cain: The Arrogance of Jealousy

Cain was literally the first man born of woman and, understandably, the pride of his mother. At his birth, Eve excitedly proclaimed, "With the help of the LORD I have brought forth a man" (Gen. 4:1). Cain was a prized possession, an extremely entitled child who basked in the special gaze of his mother. One can only imagine Eve's joy as she delivered a male child. Is it too speculative to imagine that she in some way reflected God's work in creating men in that she has also created or gave birth to a male child? Abel, Cain's younger brother, was not as entitled. Abel's name means *after thought*. Unlike Cain, Abel was not the apple of his mother's eye. It may be that Cain was attached to his mother while Abel was more attached to his father.

In light of their experience and knowledge of God in the Garden of Eden, we may assume that Adam and Eve gave their children spiritual instruction in the worship and service of God. Would the first brothers not have heard the story of God's sacrifice of animals to provide skins to cover the sin and shame of their parents? Naturally, then, at the appropriate time, Cain and Abel carried out their religious obligation. Cain and Abel each made a sacrificial offering to God for repentance of sin and the healing of shame.

Cain, a farmer, a man of the soil, gave as his offering the best of his produce. Although the fruit and vegetables were fresh and luxuriant, the offering was rejected by God. On the other hand, Abel, a shepherd, sacrificed a lamb on the altar as his offering. Abel's offering pleased God and was accepted by him because it included the sacrificial shedding of blood as the antidote for sin.

Mortification is synonymous with the highest expression of love – giving our one life for another. Thus it is not surprising that love conquers shame. Abel's sacrificial offering was prophetic and symbolic of the sacrificial death of our Lord Jesus Christ for the redemption and salvation of the world. Jesus Christ "has appeared once for all at the end of the ages to do away with sin [and shame] by the sacrifice of himself" (Heb. 9:26).

The rejection of his offering shamed Cain and evoked a painful sense of abandonment, rejection, and humiliation. Angry and downcast, Cain was in a rage. God, in the first ever psychotherapy session, reached out in love asking Cain, "Why is your face downcast?" Anger and a downcast look (dejection) are two external characteristics of shame. Cain's deep hurt developed into a deep shame core that hardened his heart.

Cain's shame was compensated by the development of an Ego Addictive False Self manifest in self-absorption, high experience seeking, and self-inflation. One can only imagine the painful shame thoughts, shame voices, and shame whip that Cain was experiencing [Diagram 4]. Overwhelmed by shame, Cain placed himself on the shame cross where his self-hatred intersected his hatred of Abel.

Offering love and forgiveness, God told Cain that if he would provide the appropriate offering, it would be accepted. Sadly, imprisoned in his Ego Addictive False Self, Cain was unrelenting. God was saying, "Cain I love you, you are my beloved. It is your offering I did not approve of, not you." But true to the Ego Addictive False Self, Cain equated the rejection of his offering – his life situation – with the rejection of his personhood, his being.

Shame, with its painful thoughts, deceptive voices, masochistic whip, destructive behavior, and shame cross had catastrophic consequences for Cain. Operating deeply in his psyche, shame was the incubator for the murder of Abel. God warned an angry and downcast Cain to be careful because the eruption of his shame into destructive action was imminent. Evil was crouching at his heart's door and it desired to consume him (Gen 4:7). Once again, God encouraged Cain and reassured him that he could choose to master it.

As described earlier, once the shame core is challenged, the Ego Addictive False Self kicks in. The self-absorbed Cain wanted instant gratification and demanded revenge. Cain's shame anger became resentment (*re*: again, *sentro*: to feel), i.e., he was feeling the anger over and over again [Diagram 5]. Resentment then turned to bitterness and his heart became hardened. Shame produces a wave in the hardened heart that makes a person want to hide.

As Cain's shame deepened, so did his severe grudge against Abel. A grudge is a permanent psychological fixture across the heart that pushes us toward the destructive Evil Violence Tunnel [chapter three]. Deep shame and anger are portals for evil, i.e., negative energy (1 John 3:12). At this point, the problem is magnified and the hope of available help or resources is minimized. We are exposed to a crouching loneliness and a disaster in the making.

A similar development occurred in the heart of King Saul when David killed Goliath. Upon their return, crowds of women sang their praises, "Saul has slain his thousands, and David his tens of thousands" (1 Sam. 18:7). This shamed Saul deeply. Jealous and angry at David, the shamed king entered the destructive Evil Violence Tunnel. As a result, evil had a foothold and an evil spirit possessed King Saul's heart causing him to spend the rest of his life attempting to kill David.

Scripture warns us not to carry our anger. When anger becomes organized or prolonged, it makes the heart, the psyche, a stronghold for negative energy, a habitat for evil: "Do not let the sun go down while you are still angry, and do not give the devil a foothold" (Eph. 4:26:27).

Deceived and controlled by evil, Cain invited Abel for a walk in the field. As is often the case with the phenomenon of shame, Cain's murderous rage was not evident to Abel. Shame's internal dynamics are often covered up by *the fig leaves of deception* and external manipulation. Unaware of Cain's evil motives, Abel joins him in the field and is brutally murdered. Driven by shame's need to cover up, Cain buried Abel's body.

Even now, the *Hound of Heaven* again reached out to Cain, "Where is your brother?" Nonchalantly, Cain replied, "I don't know." Note the blatant lie. Cain then asked, "Am I my brother's keeper?" (Gen. 4:9). The shame-based Ego Addictive False Self reconstructs reality to defend itself and make us feel good. Cain's often quoted question, "Am I my brother's keeper?" reveals the rift in human relationships and the community fragmentation so common in modern culture. Cain's anger and shame blocked any brotherly compassion or empathic concern for Abel. Disconnected and lonely, Cain's shame and anger alienated him from his brother. Many millennia later, the same dynamic is ubiquitous in our society.

Reaching out in love once again, God asked Cain a simple but profound question, "What have you done?" (Gen. 4:10). This question hits us between the eyes. It is the same question that reverberates in our hearts each day forcing us to face our truth and examine the issues and dynamics of our inner life. Remember the questions that God asked in the garden when Adam and Eve were hiding in shame? "Adam, where are you?" (Gen. 3:9) and to Eve, "What have you done?" (Gen. 3:13). These are the two basic questions we must answer if we are to be delivered from our shame.

According to Buechner, these questions integrate biblical theology and psychology into a new discipline called Contemplative Psychology. These questions unmask our shame and force us to come out of hiding to face our pain. The question, "Where are you?" challenges us to face where we are and how we arrived there. So often our shame behavior compels us to take a back seat in life, avoid openness, and go into hiding. "What have you done?" breaks through our denial and projective defenses. This question forces us to face the pathos of our hurt trail or inner pain.

Exposing our pain to these two questions challenges us to examine the shame gap between what we expect for ourselves and the reality of what we actually are. This also applies to the margins or space in our lives. Our load outweighs our limit and shame becomes the driving force of our life and leads us to experience more pain. If allowed to continue throughout our life, shame will produce a vicious cycle of hurt, pain, despair, and more shame.

Reminding Cain that he cannot hide from the truth, God warned Cain that the very ground cried out with his brother's blood. The words of Jesus in Luke 8:17 are a harsh reality: "For nothing is hidden that will not be revealed, and nothing concealed that will not be made known and brought to light."

Unrepentant and unresolved, the wild fire of the shame of arrogance burns everything and everyone in its path. After resisting God's overtures of love, the critical point is reached and God speaks in judgment. Cain is put under a curse and is driven away from the ground which contains his brother's blood. Cain is told that the ground is cursed and will not yield crops thus affecting his livelihood.

This hurts deeply because male self-esteem is often dependant on his profession, on what he does to earn a living. Cain was told by God that he will be a restless wanderer on the face of the earth. Shame makes restless wanderers of us all. As the old spiritual says, "Sometimes I feel like a motherless child, a long, long way from home!" Shame (**S**elf **H**atred **A**imed at **ME**), that deep painful wound continues its devastation of alienation, restlessness, and destruction. It creates a society where strangers walk as friends and friends as strangers.

Notice the arrogance of shame. Instead of admitting his failure and confronting his wrong doing, Cain reels in shock from God's judgment and says, "My punishment is more than I can bear.... I will be a restless wanderer on the earth and whoever finds me will kill me" (Gen. 4:13). The painful inner voices of shame condemn us and create restlessness, fear, doom, and self-destructive behavior.

In spite of all of this, God's unfailing love continued to reach out to Cain. God reassured Cain that if any one sought to hurt him he would suffer vengeance seven fold. Furthermore, God told Cain he would place a special mark upon him to prevent anyone from killing him.

The story of Cain is our story. We all suffer from different degrees of shame. Like Cain, in our arrogance, we often defy God's love which is reaching out to us through nature, people, and situations. But there is a price to pay. If we refuse to bow in humility and to continue in our arrogance, then God will act in judgment. And this is the nature of shame, that protection from physical death does not prevent the agony of living: "Wherever I banish them, all the survivors of this evil nation will prefer death to life, declares LORD Almighty" (Jer. 8:3).

In spite of this, the *Hound of Heaven* continues to seek us in love. But entrenched in our Ego Addictive False Self, we hide and worship at the throne of self-absorption, high experience seeking tendencies, and arrogance:

> We would rather be ruined than changed.
> We would rather die in our dread
> Than climb the cross of the moment
> And see our illusions die.
> —W. H. Auden, "Vespers"

I once heard Derek Walcott, the West Indian Poet Laureate in literature, say in a lecture at the College of the Bahamas, "Self hatred is difficult to eradicate." These words resonated deeply within me for this has been what I have experienced on my own journey in the field of psychiatry over the past forty years. Like the apostle Paul, we cry out with echoes of Cain's words, "What a wretched man I am! Who will rescue me from [the painful shame of] this body of death?" But in the stillness of the moment, in the midst of the pathos and chaos of life, arise comforting words of hope, "Thanks be to God [who delivers us] — through Jesus Christ our Lord" (Rom. 7: 24, 25).

King Uzziah: Pride Goes Before a Fall

One of the saddest stories of the shame of arrogance is the saga of King Uzziah, the boy king. King at sixteen years old, he obviously felt insecure and had powerful fear and shame, i.e., rejection, abandonment, and humiliation. He was deeply religious and sought spiritual direction from Zechariah, the prophet who instructed him in the fear of God. According to Holy Scripture, as long as King Uzziah sought the Lord, he had good success.

King Uzziah was victorious in battle. He broke down the walls of enemy towns and rebuilt his own cities. His fame spread far and wide. The Ammonites brought tribute to King Uzziah and his reputation spread as far as Egypt (II Chron. 26:8). He built massive fortifications on the walls of cities. He also built towers in the desert and created an effective irrigation system to supply water to his farms and livestock in the hills and plains. He hired many people to work his vineyards and fields in the hills and fertile lands.

King Uzziah had an elite, highly trained strike force which was ready for battle twenty-four hours a day. He also had an army of over 307,500 well-equipped men trained for war. Most impressively, he invented canons that rolled along the wall shooting arrows and large stones. With all this and more, the fame and power of King Uzziah spread far and wide making him a super power (II Chron. 26:15).

In spite of this success, the fear of abandonment, rejection, and humiliation haunted King Uzziah. He tried to compensate for this fear by the developing a powerful Ego Addictive False Self whose center of gravity was in himself and not in God. Controlled by his self-absorption, high experience seeking tendency, or the desire to be right, King Uzziah developed the shame of arrogance and an invincibility manifested by deep pride. "But after King Uzziah became powerful, his pride [arrogance] led to his downfall" (II Chron. 26:16).

Worshiping at the throne of his own arrogance, King Uzziah usurped the duties of the priests. He was unfaithful to the Lord in seeking to establish his own rules on how God should be worshiped in the temple. King Uzziah defied the commandment of God that only the priest was allowed to burn incense on the altar of incense. In other words, in his narcissistic arrogance, he became like God. Recognizing the danger of this, Azariah and eighty other priests followed King Uzziah into the temple and warned him:

> "It is not right for you, Uzziah, to burn incense to the LORD. That is for the priests, the descendants of Aaron, who have been consecrated to burn incense. Leave the sanctuary, for you have been unfaithful; and you will not be honored by the LORD God." —II Chron. 26:18

Arrogance is a hard nut to crack. King Uzziah was presumptuous with an associated myth of invincibility. He became angry and took incense in his hand and proceeded to defy the priests who had confronted him. The shame of arrogance in Uzziah turned to rage as it usually does when confronted. King Uzziah had gone too far. Like Cain, God's offer of mercy turned to judgment and Uzziah was struck with leprosy.

The priests removed Uzziah from the temple and he lived in isolation in a separate house away from the city for the rest of his days. Oh, how the mighty have fallen. The shame of arrogance collapsed into powerlessness and disgrace. King Uzziah was excluded from the temple of the Lord and his son Jothan was put in charge of the palace. Once again, a great ruler falls victim to the shame of arrogance, a tune that plays repeatedly throughout history.

The Story of Haman: The March of Folly

Haman is perhaps one of the most quintessential representations of the shame of arrogance in literature. In ancient Persia, Queen Esther had been chosen to replace Queen Vashti who openly disobeyed King Xerxes' (also known as King Ahasuerus). He had ordered her to parade her body before him and his military brass during a drunken bash. A poor Jewish girl mentored by her Uncle Mordecai, Esther assumed her position with grace and charm. Uncle Mordecai was deeply committed and checked on her daily. He was her best ally and psychological coach.

Mordecai sought to ensure not only the safety of the queen, but he was also loyal to King Xerxes. His vigilance paid off. One day, while at the palace, Mordecai uncovered a plot by two of the king's guards to assassinate the king. Mordecai quickly informed Queen Esther who told the king. An investigation was held. Both men were found guilty and were executed immediately.

1. Haman Appointed Prime Minister

The king cleaned house after the conspirators were executed. Then he appointed Haman to the office of Prime Minister, the second most powerful position in the land. Haman grew up poor and struggled with the shame of his background and with the fear of abandonment, rejection, and humiliation. As a result, he developed a powerful defensive Ego Addictive False Self manifested by self-absorption, high experience seeking, and arrogance.

The king's officials, with the exception of Mordecai, all fell on their faces whenever Haman passed by them. Mordecai was a faithful Jew and he refused to bow down because only God was worthy of that honor. This deeply upset Haman and his anger burned against Mordecai.

2. Haman's Plan for a Jewish Genocide

Prime Minister Haman was insulted that Mordecai refused to bow to him because of his faith. In his fury, Haman planned the genocide of the Jews rather than deal with Mordecai alone. When he discussed the matter with the king, Haman said that a certain race of people throughout the kingdom had different laws and they should not be allowed to live. Haman offered the king a handsome sum of money for the right to lead the purge of the Jews.

King Xerxes approved Haman's plan for the genocide of the Jews and sealed his commitment to the plan with his ring. He even told Haman to keep the money. A few weeks later, Haman dictated letters to all of the king's secretaries and sent messengers to distribute them throughout the kingdom. He mandated that all Jews — men, women, and children — would be killed on a certain day. Their property was to be confiscated and given to their killers. The edict was signed by the king and made the law of kingdom.

As the edict was read, the Jews mourned, screamed, and bemoaned their fate. As the city was catapulted into panic and confusion, King Xerxes and Prime Minister Haman sat down and drank to their hearts' content. How callous, indifferent, and cruel, a powerful example of how arrogance is untouched by the pathos and pain of human suffering. It is the stuff of megalomaniacs and dictators.

3. Mordecai Moves into Action

Upon learning of his people's fate, Mordecai tore his clothes and went into deep mourning by wearing the traditional sackcloth and ashes. He went into the city crying bitterly while throughout the provinces the Jews joined him in prayer, fasting, and deep mourning.

When Queen Esther heard that Mordecai was in sackcloth and ashes at the palace gates, she sent him food and clothes, but Mordecai refused them. Then she sent Hathach, one of the king's men, to investigate the matter. Mordecai sent Esther the edict and told her to intervene with the king to save the Jews. The queen replied to Mordecai that anyone going into the king's court without a summons is doomed to die unless the king holds out his golden scepter.

4. Mordecai Replies to Esther

Upon receiving Queen Esther's message, Mordecai sent her a stern message:

> If you remain silent at this time, relief and deliverance for the Jews will arise from another place, but you and your father's family will perish. And who knows but that you have come to royal position for such a time as this?" — Est. 4:14

Queen Esther replied:

> "Go, gather together all the Jews who are in Susa, and fast for me. Do not eat or drink for three days, night or day. I and my maids will fast as you do. When this is done, I will go to the king, even though it is against the law. And if I perish, I perish." —Est. 4:16

Mordecai followed Esther's instructions. Esther went to the king who graciously received her and asked what he could do for her. She invited the king and Prime Minister Haman to dine with her. At the feast, the king again asked Esther her wish, but she only wished to dine with him and Haman on the following day.

5. Haman at Home

Haman rejoiced in his new found glory and wealth. His only problem was that Mordecai still refused to bow to him. In Haman's mind, that alone canceled out all of his accomplishments. Haman's wife told him that he should make a seventy-five foot gallows and hang Mordecai on it to solve his problem. Haman liked the idea and told his family that he had been invited to dine with the king and queen on the following day.

6. Mordecai Rewarded

King Xerxes read the kingdom records and realized that Mordecai was not rewarded for uncovering the plot to assassinate him. The king called Haman and asked him to think of a reward for a man he wanted to honor. In his narcissistic arrogance, Haman thought it was he who was chosen to be honored and designed a reward that he wished for himself.

Haman told the king to dress the man in clothes that the king has worn and put him on a horse which the king had ridden. Then let the man wearing the king's clothes be lead on the king's horse with people shouting before him that this is the man the king seeks to honor. The king was pleased with this idea:

> "Go at once," the king commanded Haman. "Get the robe
> and the horse and do just as you have suggested for

Mordecai the Jew, who sits at the king's gate. Do not
neglect anything you have recommended." —Est. 6:10

Bitter and dejected, Haman reluctantly carried out the
king's orders. Shamed and humiliated, he sought comfort
with his wife Zeresh. But having no comfort to give, she told
Haman that if Mordecai is a Jew, Haman's plan will fail
and that to continue to oppose him would be fatal.

7. Queen Esther's Feast

King Xerxes and Prime Minister Haman attended
Queen Esther's feast. During the wine course, the king
asked the queen what he could do for her. Queen Esther
told the king that her people, the Jews, were about to be
slaughtered and that she was terribly worried and upset.

> King Xerxes asked Queen Esther, "Who is he?
> Where is the man who has dared to do such a
> thing?" Esther said, "The adversary and enemy is
> this vile Haman." Then Haman was terrified
> before the king and queen. The king got up in a
> rage, left his wine and went out into the palace
> garden. But Haman, realizing that the king had
> already decided his fate, stayed behind to beg
> Queen Esther for his life. —Est. 7:5-7

The king was shocked to see Haman kneeling at the
queen's couch and accused him of trying to rape his wife. He
ordered the death penalty for Haman and hanged him on
the same gallows that Haman had prepared for Mordecai.
After Haman's death, the king gave his estate to Queen
Esther. She then introduced Mordecai to the king as her
cousin and foster father. The king took the ring which he
had given to Haman and put it on Mordecai making him
the Prime Minister of the Persian Empire.

Haman is one of the most tragic figures in ancient literature. Controlled by the shame of arrogance and greed for power, he needed total obedience. His fragile arrogance was punctured by Mordecai's refusal to bow to him. That humiliation was enough to make him plan the destruction of a whole race of people. But the gallows that he built for another was used for him. Arrogance is a mighty wall that stands for a season, but when it cracks, it brings down whole person.

Abraham: The Arrogance of Deceit

Abram (later Abraham) was a wealthy son of an idol maker from a celebrated family in the ancient civilization of Ur who worshiped the moon god Naauah. Abram was a devout seeker of truth. Ur was known for its ancient, but sophisticated, libraries and schools of learning. God called Abram to take his wife, Sarai (later Sarah) and leave Ur to journey to the Promised Land. God's call was connected to a promise: "Abram, fear not, for I am your shield and exceeding great reward" (Gen. 15:1).

Abraham left Ur with his wife Sarah who was extremely beautiful. In one source, Sarah was called the beauty given of Ur. Abraham's deeply spiritual nature was characterized by altar building. This signified his deep commitment to God as the *summon bonum* of his life, i.e., he sought to love God with all his heart, soul, and mind. Abraham was also characterized by his tent, a reminder that life is transitory regardless of our status in life or the number and value of our possessions.

Wherever Abraham and Sarah pitched their tent, they worshiped God with an altar. In the presence of the Holy Other, they lived out the reality that life is transitory. We are only pilgrims passing through this valley of tears. We need to travel with our altar as a witness to our personal relationship with God and our tent as a reminder that life is short and all glory belongs to God.

Abraham arrived to find a famine in the Promised Land. How disappointed, demoralized, and ashamed he must have felt. Abraham had a sense of abandonment, rejection, and humiliation as the shame rushed in. The question looming in his heart was how God could lead him from the civilization of Ur to this empty wilderness wasteland.

Have we not experienced similar travails on our own spiritual journeys? As the shame and anger embeds in the heart, the mind compensates with the development of the Ego Addictive False Self which seeks fulfillment through self-absorption, high experience seeking, and self-inflation. Just as Abraham, in the face of famine, turned toward Egypt, the land of plenty, we seek self-fulfillment.

Once in Egypt, Abraham, followed the dictates of his Ego Addictive False Self and tried to reconstruct reality by asking Sarah to tell Pharaoh that she was his sister and not his wife. Replacing his altar with his own addictive narcissism and exchanging his tent for the permanence of a place in Egypt, Abraham crossed the boundaries of shameful arrogance. Passing off his wife, Sarah, as his sister for the pleasure of Pharaoh, Abraham settled for materialistic wealth. He gave up his altar for his addiction to wealth and his tent for a mausoleum of betrayal and deceit in Egypt. Are we not also susceptible to the illusion of greener pastures even though it means betraying our deepest beliefs and values?

This is pure arrogance. Suffering the shame schema of humiliation, we seek power by doing things our way. God has called us to a Promised Land, but since things are not to our liking, we arrogantly do our own thing. We delude ourselves with the illusion of permanence and the myth of invincibility. It is almost inconceivable that Abraham, the patriarch of the world's three greatest religions, Judaism, Islam, and Christianity, could be so arrogant as to defy the living God who promised to be "his exceeding great reward."

As Abraham was settling into his new home, there was trouble in Pharaoh's harem. There was an eerie feeling that something was drastically wrong. A disturbed Pharaoh called Abraham and challenged him about whether he had told the truth? Was Sarah your sister or your wife? Convicted by the *Hound of Heaven*, Abraham admitted to Pharaoh that Sarah indeed was his wife. Pharaoh was angry about being lied to and cast Abraham out of Egypt.

Abraham was shamed by being caught in a lie. He retreated in dishonor and left Egypt. Shame ruptures our soul, splitting us apart, putting us at war with ourselves. It is so lethal that left to ourselves we can easily self-destruct. Many of us destruct in complete silence and desperation.

The greatness of Abraham is seen in the depth of his spiritual humility. He returned to Canaan, pitched his tent to the transitoriness of life and built an altar to worship God. He accepted his failure; he surrendered to God and made the perceptual shift [chapter six] from shame (fear) to love (worship of God). This is the challenge of greatness, to admit our arrogance and pride, accept our failure, and repent by humbly returning to our spiritual journey. Let each of us build an altar to worship the eternal God and pitch our tent to the transitoriness of life.

The word became flesh and *pitched his tent* among us. We have seen his glory, the glory of the One and Only, who came from the Father, full of grace and truth. —John 1:14

Chapter 3

THE SHAME OF FAILURE

THE SILENT KILLER

How lovely is your dwelling place, O LORD Almighty! My soul yearns, even faints, for the courts of the LORD; my heart and my flesh cry out for the living God. —Psalm 84: 1-2

The weary King David paused to look back as he trudged sorrowfully up the Mount of Olives, weeping with each step. Behind him, across the Kidron Valley, lay the city of Jerusalem, with its magnificent temple and palace from which he had suddenly been forced to flee. After years of great success at home and on the battlefield, David was facing the supreme challenge of his career. None of the enemies of Israel had ever succeeded in mounting a serious threat to his kingdom, but now it was being overthrown and his life was in mortal danger, not from an external threat but from his own beloved son Absalom!

Like David, most of us have tasted the shame and bitterness of failure. Failure may come in relationships, finances, career, health, or continual defeat in the grip of some secret compulsion. In this chapter, I present ten important characteristics of the contemplative life of David.

These ten shame-busting steps will bring healing from the shame of failure through the intimacy of contemplation. It is only through contemplation that we can move to ever-deeper levels of intimacy with God, ourselves, and others.

Contemplation often has a soft ring to it. It conjures up a vision of witless dreamers building castles in the sky, denying the blood and guts of everyday living. And yet, David is described as Israel's greatest king, a consummate warrior, leader, musician, and poet (1 and 2 Samuel).

Contemplation opens us to the vision of God's love and is validated by courage, compassion, and uncompromising commitment to intimacy. David was far from perfect. He made wrong decisions and suffered the consequences of his actions, yet through his mistakes, David sought deep contemplation and intimacy with God. He is the only God "a man after my own heart; he will do everything I want him to do" (Acts 13:22).

Absalom was David's pride and joy, a son who, like his father, was attractive and highly gifted: "In all Israel there was not a man so highly praised for his handsome appearance as Absalom. From the top of his head to the sole of his foot there was no blemish in him" (2 Sam. 14:25).

Absalom did, however, lack David's character. In time, his arrogant and ruthless side surfaced. He coveted the throne of his own father. He schemed to win the affection of the people by assuming the trappings of royalty, riding through the streets of Jerusalem in a majestic chariot with fifty men running before him. He would sit in a prominent place at the city gate and hear grievances, exclaiming: "If only I were appointed judge in the land! Then everyone who has a complaint or case could come to me and I would see that he gets justice" (2 Sam. 15:4).

Like any good politician, Absalom employed an intensive public relations campaign to promote his cause. Some politicians kiss babies, but Absalom, in a slavish demonstration of mock deference, kissed the hands of those who came to him. Flattered by the aspiring king who deferred to them, the populace flocked to Absalom. We read that, "He stole the hearts of the men of Israel" (2 Sam.

15:6). When Absalom felt he had garnered sufficient popular support, he made his move.

It is amazing how gullible parents can be. It seems that David did not suspect that his son was planning to usurp his very throne. And so, when Absalom asked to be allowed to go to the city of Hebron for a spiritual retreat, David readily agreed, perhaps thinking, "At last Absalom is showing an interest in spiritual things!"

What a brutal shock it must have been to be told that Absalom was leading a rebellion against him and that all Israel seemed eager to follow. Hebron was but a day's hard march away and David realized he had no choice but to flee for his life. David came face to face with the painful shame of failure in his family, work, and personal life.

Ten Shame-Busting Steps for Overcoming Failure

1. Recognize the Problem

Each of us needs to do what David did when his world collapsed: face up to the reality of life. He was no longer king and there was no use pretending. Absalom had overthrown him. The naiveté with which David glossed over his son's faults dissipated as he warned his followers, "Come! We must flee, or none of us will escape from Absalom. We must leave immediately or he will move quickly to overtake us and bring ruin upon us and put the city to the sword" (2 Sam. 15:14).

We are all tempted to fall back on certain typical defense mechanisms which prevent us from facing up to the truth. One of these is denial, as in: "Oh, my little boy, Absalom, would never do anything like this!" It is a good thing David did not delude himself because the results could have been fatal. Denial prevents hurts from being dealt with and those hurts are often passed to succeeding generations. We damage our dear children in the ways we ourselves were damaged. "Hurt people hurt people." The first step to breaking the power of shame is to face up to the deep hurt in our hearts.

Another natural defensive reaction is projection. Projection allows us to be caught up in the endless *if only* cycle of introspective wishful thinking: *If only* Absalom were more loyal; *If only* I had not married her, I would never be in this mess; *If only* I had never met him, this would not have happened; *If only* I had never have taken this job. Projection puts the blame squarely on someone else's shoulders.

I once had complications set in after having a couple of wisdom teeth removed. I was not able see my dentist so I bought an over-the-counter medication to ease the pain. I found that this topical medication did indeed relieve the pain as advertised, but it did so only briefly. I had to apply it continually to keep the pain at bay. Projection is like that medication. It temporarily makes us feel better. It blames others, circumstances, employers, the government, or even inanimate objects, anything and anyone but ourselves.

Projection can never produce healing. Healing only comes when we take responsibility for the wounds in our hearts. We may be the cause of only a very small part of the hurt we have suffered. We may have no responsibility at all for the wounds that were caused in us as children, but as adults we have the responsibility to work through the resulting hurt and pain. Healing begins when we own up to our responsibility.

2. Face Reality

David was devastated by the news of Absalom's revolt. His response was to face up to the reality of his situation and take action even though it meant the embarrassment of open flight from his own son. Perhaps, as he fled across the Mount of Olives, David pondered the defeats of some of his illustrious forefathers. It is enlightening to see how many of the great men of faith in the Bible experienced significant failure in their lifetimes. Moses, for example, fled Egypt at the age of forty in fear for his life after killing an Egyptian. He spent the next forty years as a humble shepherd in the desert. He must have thought his career was just about over. Then, at eighty, God called him to lead the children of Israel on their epic journey out of Egypt to the Promised Land.

Putting things in perspective means facing up to the reality of our situation however unpleasant it may be. For David, it meant flight into the desert. It was the last thing he would have envisioned, but his very life was at stake. We also have to gain the proper perspective when facing serious problems. It means being willing to abandon the ineffectual, half-hearted remedies that we have been desperately hoping might be sufficient to bring the needed change. Our situation may require that we, like David, take drastic action. This might mean a change of employment or geographic separation from a dysfunctional family, an abusive spouse, or fellow drug abusers.

3. Don't Go It Alone

At critical times of his life, David surrounded himself with faithful friends who helped and supported him. As a young man fleeing for his life from Saul, he gathered a band of loyal men around him in the wilderness. Here again, many years later, David did not find himself alone. One of those faithful friends was Ittai the Gittite who accompanied him on his flight from Absalom. When David tried to dissuade him, Ittai replied, "As surely as the LORD lives, and as my lord the king lives, wherever the lord my king may be, whether it means life or death, there will your servant be" (2 Sam. 15:21).

Often, it is not pain itself that we find so unbearable, but rather the lack of love and support we experience during our suffering. Friendship and community are vital for helping us through our difficulties. No man is an island; each of us, without exception, needs friendship. We may have been hurt and lonely for so long that we even try to tell ourselves we do not need anyone else, but deep inside we long for a friend.

How do we find a friend or a support group, a community to stand with us? We find them when we come out of hiding and seek healthy relationships. It is a hard first step to take. The shame of failure and fear of rejection are powerful inhibitors that can keep people in their shells for a lifetime. Others are not attracted to us when we are withdrawn. We give the impression of being unfriendly, disinterested in others, and we suffer further rejection as others in turn avoid us.

Taking the risk of opening ourselves up breaks the vicious cycle that only leads to deeper loneliness. It begins the process of unleashing the healing forces within our hearts. I can hear the protest: "But I lack the natural charisma or attractiveness of a David. How can I find friends?" Finding a good friend is one of the most essential yet most difficult tasks in our modern, isolated society.

Some people have great difficulty finding friends because they are not friendly. They do not show genuine interest in others, but appear to be interested only in finding a *pin cushion* in whom they can stick their troubles. Friendship is a two-way street. If we take the time to listen genuinely to others, then we will find other people with a willingness to give us the support that we need.

One of the most rewarding ways to find friendship is belonging to a social group. Many of us get into trouble in the first place by "looking for love in all the wrong places." We desperately seek friendship, but only in the social groups where we think we can find acceptance. Rather than true friendship, we find ourselves trapped in harmful, self-destructive, or illicit behavior. Unhealthy communities are characterized by non-mutual relationships and by being seductively easy to enter, but complex or difficult to leave.

Perhaps the best way to begin to find a supportive community is to rediscover your own family. Spend time together; begin to rebuild broken relationships and nurture one another. Work on renewing your relationships with your relatives, especially if you are single.

Another place to find supportive community is in a friendly and open church. Religious communities are ideally suited to meet both our spiritual and our social needs. Choose carefully, however, religious communities that are not friendly have hurt some people. Other good sources for finding friends are groups organized around contemplative prayer, AA, NA, and other such support groups.

Groups like these provide a focus and have the potential to unleash God's unfailing love which is a powerful antidote to shame. You might have a few false starts on your road to finding a friend, but do not give up! Remember the twin rules of being friendly to others and avoiding unhealthy social communities and, in time, you will discover genuine friendship.

4. Contemplate God

The practice of contemplative prayer calls us to solitude in companionship with God. The wonderful thing about being in relationship with God is that we do not have to play God ourselves. We recognize the existence of one who is greater than we and is ultimately in control. We no longer have to pretend to be in control of everything.

Contemplation is a shame buster. It opens us up to the vision of God's love and commits us to the mission of God's love in the world. Life is not hopeless because there is someone who cares. We can be vulnerable and move into intimacy in the confidence that he is watching over us and guiding us.

As David fled over the Mount of Olives, he felt the hand of God upon his life. Zadok and his fellow priests started to follow him carrying the Ark of the Covenant. They were turned back by David who told them: "Take the ark of God back into the city. If I find favor in the LORD's eyes, he will bring me back and let me see it and his dwelling place again" (2 Sam. 15:25). However, he hastened to add that if God should reject him, "then I am ready; let him do to me whatever seems good to him" (2 Sam. 15:26). In the contemplative experience, we live *in* God, *for* God, and *under* God's influence.

David was broken, he did not know how it would all end, but he trusted in God. When our world is shattered, we need someone to help us out of our despair, to give us hope. The God of the Bible represents what many of us have lacked in our earthly families, stability, consistency, and predictability. In Psalm 23 David pictures God as a caring shepherd who lovingly guards his sheep: "The LORD is my shepherd, I shall not be in want. He makes me lie down in green pastures; he leads me beside quiet waters" (Ps. 23:1-2). When more trouble threatened to overwhelm David, he threw himself unreservedly into the care of his shepherd.

God is consistent in his loving, merciful, and just nature, but we can never predict how he will act. Our ways are not his ways (Is. 55:8), but still we can trust him as Job did: "Though he slay me, yet will I hope in him" (Job 13:15). This does not mean that Job expected God to act cruelly towards him. Far from it, Job is saying that whatever happens, he can rely on his Maker. Hear afresh God's word to the patriarch Abraham, "Do not be afraid....I am your shield, your very great reward" (Gen. 15: 1).

5. Express Yourself

David seemed to have the ability to express his feelings openly, a trait which helped earn him the love of his people. But David's wife, Michal, felt uncomfortable with any expression of emotion. Years earlier she became greatly offended when she saw David celebrate the arrival of the Ark of the Covenant: "As the ark of the LORD was entering the City of David, Michal daughter of Saul watched from a window. And when she saw King David leaping and dancing before the LORD, she despised him in her heart" (2 Sam. 6:16).

David fled from Absalom and once again he did not hide his emotions: "David continued up the Mount of Olives, weeping as he went; his head was covered and he was barefoot" (2 Sam. 15:30). Expressing yourself means being real. If we are hurt we do not have to pretend, but are free to express our feelings to God, regardless of how painful.

Our culture has taught us to expect our leaders to control their emotions and maintain a "stiff upper lip" in the face of adversity. Instead of weeping with others, we try to change the subject to something more comfortable or, failing that, offer empty platitudes like "Don't worry about it," or "Just hang in there."

A gentleman once told me that when his wife died during a church service, his fellow church members sought to comfort him with pious admonitions and a litany of Bible verses. But the only balm for his intense grief came later when he arrived back home. His Haitian gardener came to him crying and showed by his tears how sorry he was to hear about the woman's death. Many of us have difficulty facing our feelings and we forfeit the healing and cleansing tears that flow when the emotional dams in our hearts are released. Not so David! He made no effort to conceal the pain he was feeling as he covered his head and wept bitterly. He set the example for those with him, for we read: "All the people with him covered their heads too and were weeping as they went up" (2 Sam. 15:30).

David was able to face his feelings and, by so doing, he was demonstrating his great love for his son Absalom. Grief and love may seem to be opposite feelings, but in truth, they are connected. Grief is called the *healing feeling* because the depth of our grief indicates the depth of our ability to love. We cannot have one without the other. We must allow ourselves to feel the pain when our world is broken and those we love hurt us.

6. Repent

Repentance is not a common concept in the modern world. In essence, it means changing our attitudes and opening our hearts to God. The Greek word for repentance, *metanoia*, literally means *to turn*. David's attitude, as he walked up the mountain with bare feet and a covered head, was one of open repentance. In his pain, he opened his life to God (2 Sam. 15:30).

King David's dream of power and respect as a king with a cohesive and loving family was shattered when his son Absalom usurped the throne and threatened his life. Abandoned, rejected, and humiliated, King David faced his past failings, accepted defeat, and humbled himself before God in repentance. Trusting only in the mercy of God, he turned away from his false self-defenses of denial and projection. These only create the illusion of security, power, and invincibility. David chose reality over illusion. He was vulnerable and left with only his true identity as a person *Beloved by God*.

Jesus had an amazing saying that runs contrary to our aggressive, power-oriented culture: "Anyone who will not receive the kingdom of God like a little child will never enter it" (Luke 18: 17). That is repentance, to open up our inner child to God. It means becoming vulnerable as a child, asking him to touch us so that we can respond to his love as a little child would. Like a trusting child, we need an inner flexibility so that we can bend as we go through the inner turning of repentance. Mature adults bend rather than break when they come to a point of change in their lives.

Often there is another dynamic that prevents us from opening up to God in our time of deepest need, that of transference. *Transference* means attributing qualities from a significant person in our lives onto others, in this case, God. For better or worse, our human parents and other authority figures become our models for our understanding of God. If those human relationships are marred and we are angry about them, those feelings are displaced onto God and can profoundly affect how we relate to our heavenly Father.

Instead of seeing God as kind and loving, we may envision him as cold, distant, or someone to be feared. Our woundedness causes us to turn away from God rather than to accept his unconditional love. Life is meant to be an adventure and we should cultivate a childlike enthusiasm for learning. As painful as tragedies are, they can be the optimum time for growth. Suffering forces us to face ourselves – both our strengths and our weaknesses – and to confront the issues in our lives. Repentance can turn a crisis into an opportunity for profound transformation.

7. Seek Help – Find a Hushai

When David came to the top of the mountain, his friend General Hushai came to meet him. Hushai was in mourning, "his robe torn and dust on his head" (2 Sam. 15:32). This may seem odd to us, but Hushai was showing his shock and sorrow over David's misfortune. He was, in effect, saying to his king, "I love you. I am loyal, committed, and willing to help."

David was in desperate need of assistance. He devised a plan whereby Hushai returned to Jerusalem and frustrated Absalom's plans to pursue and capture him. David was not afraid to ask for help when he needed it and neither should we. Having the humility to seek help means not living in denial, but facing the real in all that is real in the presence of the Real. This might also mean seeking professional help when needed.

When we are looking for someone to help, we need a Hushai. Look for someone who is able to show genuine love and concern, someone like Hushai with a heart of humility and gentleness. The book of Proverbs advises us: "A man of many companions may come to ruin, but there is a friend who sticks closer than a brother" (Prov. 18:24).

8. Face Resistance – Beware of Shimei

As David continued, he was accosted by a rascal named Shimei. Shimei cursed David shouting, "Get out, get out, you man of blood, you scoundrel! The LORD has repaid you for all the blood you shed in the household of Saul, in whose place you have reigned. The LORD has handed the kingdom over to your son Absalom. You have come to ruin because you are a man of blood!" (2 Sam. 16:7-8).

Like David, we all suffer from the internal Shimei syndrome which kicks us when we are down, condemning us in the midst of our defeats. When we try to confront the issues of the heart and seek intimacy, the accusing voices chime in: "What are you doing this for? You can't do that! You'll never amount to anything." Along comes projection:

"If you'd been a better parent he would not have turned out like this" or "If you weren't such a poor excuse for a wife, he would not have left you."

The Shimei in our lives can be external as well. Those who have suffered misfortune know all too well how so-called friends can gossip behind our back and remind us to our face of our failures. Few injuries are more painful than being hurt by someone when we are already as low as we can get. Once burned, twice shy. It is no wonder that so many – even in our churches – no longer reach out for fear of encountering another Shimei, a *Job's comforter*.

One of David's soldiers, Abishai, decided enough was enough and asked permission to lop off the scoundrel's head. But David would have none of it. He told Abishai, "My son, who is of my own flesh, is trying to take my life. How much more, then, this Benjamite! Leave him alone; let him curse, for the LORD has told him to. It may be that the LORD will see my distress and repay me with good for the cursing I am receiving today" (2 Sam. 16:11-12). This sense of forbearing and understanding at a time when we are being maligned is a true shame buster.

This reveals the spiritual depth of David who had lost everything, but listened patiently as a nobody openly humiliated him. David refused to exact revenge upon Shimei. He knew that he might deserve some of what Shimei was saying. David faced Shimei's resistance. He did not allow his shame to either excuse or accuse him. He trusted his future to God, to the Love that will never let us go and the Face that never turns away.

Meanwhile, in Jerusalem, General Hushai arrived at the court of Absalom just as Ahithophel, another of David's former counselors, was advising the new king on how to deal with David. Ahithophel recommended that he himself be given a strong contingent of soldiers with which to pursue David immediately.

It was sound counsel and Absalom was inclined to accept it, but decided to ask Hushai's advice first. Hushai subverted the advice of Ahithophel by appealing to Absalom's innate narcissism. Should another lead the attack against David? "No!" counseled Hushai, suggesting that Absalom should wait until the next day and then have the honor of defeating his father himself, thus establishing his right to David's throne! Absalom accepted Hushai's advice and the extra time allowed David and his men to escape (2 Sam. 17:5-14). As a footnote to this incident, Ahithophel showed his rigidity in dealing with rejection by tragically going out and hanging himself (2 Sam. 17:23).

Ahithophel's co-dependence with the Party in Power (PIP) proved fatal. When David ruled, Ahithophel sided with him, but when the PIP changed he quickly changed his allegiance. When the new PIP rejected him there was nowhere left to turn which caused him to despair. It is the same with us when we entrust others with our Identity card and give them authority over our Dignity, Meaning, and Value. Disillusionment follows as others fail us.

9. Take Appropriate Action

That evening Hushai secretly sent word to David of Absalom's plans to pursue him the next day. David took action immediately and he and his men escaped that very night. David also devised his battle plan. Shame makes us wait in passive acquiescence. David overcame all of his shame voices and acted with God's guidance.

After we have isolated the problem and faced our hurts, grieved and done the work of repenting, there comes a time for action. Sometimes, instead of making plans and setting goals for self-improvement, we hold back, fearful of taking that first step. Shame does this, it makes us passive. It is like trying to walk on water like Peter did without stepping out of the boat. We cannot realize the changes we desire unless we are taking concrete steps. Even if we suffer some initial setbacks, we cannot help but succeed in the end if we persevere. What steps are you taking right now to help bring change into your life?

My wife, Vicki, is painfully aware of my own shortcomings in this area. Her friend's Dutch husband can fix anything. If the washing machine breaks down, she just calls her husband and he is there in a minute to fix it. But when our washing machine breaks down and Vicki calls me, my response is: "Well, how do you feel about it?" We can talk ceaselessly about what has gone wrong and how we feel about it, but sooner or later we have to take action and fix the washing machine.

Another pitfall is setting goals that are unworkable. At first David unrealistically insisted on leading his men into battle against Absalom, but he was older and his fighting days were over. Besides, David's men doubted that he had the resolve to do battle against his own son and they prevailed upon him to stay back. David accepted the pleas of his generals. He was willing to listen to good advice. In the same way, we need to listen to good advice and be practical in our objectives. Many goals are not attained because they bear so little resemblance to reality that we never seriously attempt to accomplish them. It is better to set a modest, workable goal rather than a grandiose scheme that does not have a prayer of being realized.

Absalom soon found himself in a situation for which he had no strategy. After the battle began he was riding on his donkey through the thick of the forest when his famed long hair became ensnared in the branches of an oak tree. His mule continued on leaving Absalom hanging between heaven and earth. We feel helpless when sudden tragedy strikes and the bottom drops out. Absalom had not prepared himself for such an eventuality and was paralyzed when the unexpected occurred. This was his downfall.

10. Be Compassionate

Absalom was spotted by one of David's soldiers who told his commander, Joab. Joab had a long and turbulent history and would eventually himself fall to the sword (1 Kings 2:34). He was angry when he learned that the soldier had not killed Absalom when he had the chance. The soldier had spunk, stood up to Joab and replied, "Even if a thousand shekels were weighed out into my hands, I would not lift my hand against the king's son. In our hearing the king commanded you and Abishai and Ittai, 'Protect the young man Absalom for my sake'" (2 Sam. 18:12). Joab brushed aside what the soldier said; grabbed three spears, and rushed off to kill Absalom.

David, ignorant of what had happened, waited eagerly for news of the battle and especially of the fate of his son. When the messenger arrived, he had only one question: "Is the young man Absalom safe?" (2 Sam. 18:32). David was a powerful warrior and a great king, but he was also a father. Despite Absalom's act of rebellion and treachery, David loved his son as he loved himself. He was overcome with grief and went into his private chamber where he lamented, "O my son Absalom! My son, my son Absalom! If only I had died instead of you, O Absalom, my son, my son!" (2 Sam. 18:33).

The final step of shame busting is the intimacy of compassion.. We may go through the first nine steps only to fail at the last, compassion. When we begin to understand the dynamics of our pain and who has hurt us, it is easy to turn on those responsible and seek vengeance. A lack of compassion towards those who have hurt us can generate enormous anger and resentment. True healing means being willing to say to the parent, husband, wife, child, or friend who hurt you, "I forgive you and I still love you." Sometimes, due to self-loathing, we need to say this even to ourselves.

David's soldiers could not understand his grief. After all, the rebellion was over and the treacherous Absalom was dead. Joab castigated him for showing remorse over the very one who had betrayed him and caused such turmoil in the kingdom. But he did not understand the powerful sense of intimacy that allowed David to weep for the one who hurt him. David's love for Absalom was such that he had no choice but to grieve deeply for him.

Compassion is the death blow to our Ego Addictive False Self and shame core. Are we compassionate towards our families, ourselves, our neighbors, and the world? Compassion expands our capacity for intimacy even in little things. How do we respond when someone makes a mistake that causes us a minor headache? Do we feel anger and self-righteous indignation or do we see ourselves in the faults of others and offer the same compassion we would desire to have others show us? Perhaps we feel both anger and compassion and can learn to act only on the compassion.

Conclusion

Our lives are like the clear blue waters of my native Bahamas. When the strong winds of failure disturb the waters, the clarity is gone. The beautiful fish and coral like the beauty of our lives can no longer be seen against the white sandy bottom of God's love. We feel ashamed and ugly, failures at life.

The shame of failure destroys our intimacy with God. Practicing the ten shame-busting steps calms and settles us. The waters become transparent again, the white sandy bottom can be seen clearly, the beauty of our life is restored. The shame of failure itself is destroyed and intimacy with God sweeps away the shame-producing false expectations of ourselves and others.

The story is told of a little boy who lived in a camp on the shores of the Mississippi River. One day he was sitting with a lonely drifter on the riverbank when a big steamboat came into view. "Come over here!" the little boy called out. The man laughed. "Don't waste your time. That boat has better things to do than come over here and see you!" But the boy persisted and, to the man's surprise, the steamboat started moving toward them. He watched with amazement as the huge boat pulled up to the bank and lowered its gangplank. As the young boy climbed aboard he turned to the incredulous man and said, "I told you it would come. You see, the captain is my daddy."

Life has a captain; it can be the Ego Addictive False Self or our heavenly Father. We may not be able to bring back a relationship that we have lost or a love betrayed to which we entrusted our meaning, dignity, and value. What we can do is open ourselves to God's love which melts away the false self and brings healing to the hurt, dark, and destroyed places in our hearts.

God's love transforms the shame and chaos of the inner self and gives "beauty instead of ashes" (Isa. 61:3). May God's love help us as we move from shame to intimacy so that, like that little boy, we will realize: "It'll come, because the captain is my daddy."

> Our Father in heaven
> Hallowed be your name,
> Your kingdom come,
> Your will be done,
> On earth as it is in heaven. —Matt. 6:9-13

Chapter 4

The Shame of Anger
The Evil Violence Tunnel

Of the Seven Deadly Sins, anger is possibly the most fun. To lick your wounds, to smack your lips over grievances long passed, to roll over your tongue the prospect of bitter confrontation still to come, to savor to the last toothsome morsel both the pain you are given and the pain you are giving back – in many ways it is a feast fit for a king. The chief drawback is that what you are wolfing down is yourself. The skeleton at the feast is you.

–Frederick Buechner

One day while walking to my car after a busy clinic schedule, I was grabbed by a woman who screamed, "Dr. Allen, help me, please, help me!" She said she had just visited her husband who was dying of cancer in the hospital. In his death bed confession, her husband told her he had done something terrible. He told her that about five years ago, in a state of drunkenness, he had signed their house, which was in his name, over to his mistress.

Regretful, he said he would like to change it back to his wife before he died. I took the woman in my car and we rushed to a lawyer's office and asked that he immediately come with us to the hospital. Upon arriving at the hospital, we learned that the woman's husband had died!

Screaming at the top of her voice, the woman cried bitterly, "I am angry. He betrayed me. I can't take it. How could he do this to me?" Settling down a little, she said, "Dr. Allen, I can't live with this, this is too much for me."

A year later I was reading the obituary column in the newspaper and there was a picture of her and an announcement of her death. Stunned, I sat quietly for awhile reflecting on my experience with her. A heart attack may have killed her, but I could not help thinking that she had died from a broken heart. The shame of anger and betrayal is lethal leaving its victims dead or discarded on the wayside of life, *the living dead*!

Anger is one of the most powerful emotions in our modern culture. Anger is an emotion that can be used for constructive, positive action as when we are angry at an injustice. Jesus' anger in the temple is a clear example of this (Matt. 21:12-13). But anger can also have negative consequences when it is allowed to linger and block our ability to love.

Anger is a natural and normal reaction and in some circumstances there is nothing wrong with it. The key issue is how we manage anger. The news media are filled with stories of road rage, air rage, and yacht rage. Columbine and numerous other instances of children acting violently, blood-filled video games, and many other examples indicate to us that our modern culture is saturated with anger. Anger is the leading cause of intimacy dysfunction among couples, families, friends, churches, synagogues, political parties, and other social groupings.

When we approach fifty, many of us face shattered dreams and live with the painful reality of what might have been. We must then choose either to live the rest of our lives in a state of shame, anger, and frustration or recognize our failures and losses and learn to grieve the pain and open up to a life of faithfulness and gratitude.

In order to understand the deep parts of the heart, to experience the love of our true selves in God, we must deal with our anger. If we do not, it will contaminate every area of life and impede spiritual growth. We must overcome shame and experience a reformation of emotions. Only then can anger become a positive motivating force to fight injustice and other wrongs of the world.

I have been struck as a consulting psychiatrist by the increasing number of people of all ages who have come to me with issues associated with anger since the turn of the century. Anger takes many forms. It may present as a disgruntled or complaining attitude, violence, hatred of others, self-hatred, intimacy dysfunction, depression, a grudge against a family member, or personal betrayal.

Anger prevents us from moving away from the defensive Ego Addictive False Self to the true self based in love. It disrupts our relationships and requires us to find the will to face our deep hurts and deal with the *shame of anger* that paralyzes us. If we are unable or unwilling to address our anger, it will destroy us.

The Causes of Anger

Anger is usually associated with hurt that has its origin in childhood. Children are fragile. They find it difficult to process or grieve pain. Much of the hurt and anger of our childhood trauma is repressed and does not present itself until we are provoked as adults. Adult anger is often a delayed reaction from childhood. Anger has many causes. Here are the four most prevalent sources of anger.

1. Deprivation of Instinctual Needs

All children have three basic instinctual needs [chapters 1, 2, 5]. First, *survival-security*; will I survive and, if so, how secure will I be? Second, *affection-esteem*; who will love me and how will I feel about myself? And third, *power-control*; will I have some autonomy over my life? Life is wounded and we have all been damaged or betrayed, especially as children. This deprivation causes us to react out of hurt and anger and to compensate by intensifying the instinctive need and making it more pronounced.

Childhood deprivation in an area of instinctual need results in a compensating behavior. Children who are hurt in the *survival-security* area feel abandoned. *Abandonment* leads to anger and then to a compensating need for security through people or things. Children who are hurt in the *affection-esteem* area feel rejected. *Rejection* creates feelings of anger and a compensating need for affection by self-soothing through pleasing people or addictions. Children who are hurt in the area of *power-control* feel humiliated. *Humiliation* produces anger and a compensating need for power through the control of self or others [Diagram 1].

The deprivation of these instinctual needs is associated with hurt and anger in childhood. The feelings of abandonment, rejection, and humiliation form the shame triangle that can continue for the rest of one's life. The compensations become ends in themselves and the shame cycle repeats and anger results when something interferes with these compensations.

The brain deals with deprivation by developing a defensive Ego Addictive False Self. This mind-produced self creates three complex and illusory emotional programs for happiness: self-absorption (narcissism), high experience seeking (feeling good), and self-inflation (pride). Thus, anger results both from the deprivation of basic instinctual needs and whenever there is any kind of interference with whatever is being used for compensation.

2. Fatigue and Stress

Anger is commonly associated with fatigue and stress. Time pressures, long hours, the burdens of family life, and ever-new technologies that allow the office to accompany us everywhere, leave us fatigued, stressed, and angry. On this subject, I particularly recommend Sigmund Freud's classic *Civilization and its Discontents*[1] and Ann Morrow Lindbergh's *Gift from the Sea*.[2]

3. Illness

Anger is associated with a number of physical, psychiatric, and neurological illnesses. Depression can be seen as anger acting inwardly toward the self in repressed rage. Depression can also be understood as anger expressed outwardly toward others. Anger is also associated with bipolar disorder and some types of epilepsy.

Diabetes and hypertension may also have anger associated with them. Traumatic injuries, especially head injuries, may result in anger. Anger has a range of possible causational factors which must all be considered when assessing its origin.

4. Loss

One of the most common causes of anger is loss. All life involves *change*, all change involves *loss*, and all loss involves *pain*. Loss is ubiquitous. We lose everything in life, our youth, our hair, our jobs, and, ultimately, our lives. Loss is a constant in life and always evokes a powerful grieving process. Loss has two poles, an anger pole and a grief pole.

When we lose something or somebody we love, we are both angry and sad. In our culture, many of us get stuck at the anger pole when we experience a loss. The anger pole makes us feel empowered and self-assertive which gives us the illusion of power. At the same time, anger blocks our ability to open ourselves to the love around us. We then become isolated and disconnected from community.

Opposite the anger pole is the grief pole. There we experience deep feelings of sadness and loss and sometimes even a sense of impotency. But the grieving process is healing. Its cathartic nature opens us up to love and gratitude. In grief we seek the security that only God can give us. Jesus said, "Blessed are those who mourn for they will be comforted" (Matt. 5:4).

We have all been hurt in childhood and have a lot of crying to do. The next time we become angry it may be helpful to see if we can move from the anger pole to the grief pole and accept the grieving or sadness in our heart. It is in grief, not anger where we find the gifts of liberation and hope.

Anger Sets Off a Cycle of Shame

The causes of anger must be faced if our anger is not to turn to shame. The shame of abandonment, for example, causes anger which in turn causes us to do things that cause us even more shame. George was abandoned by his father when he was a child. As an adult, he found security in being a self-absorbed book collector. He was angry about being abandoned and got angry if it was suggested that he stop collecting books. His anger drove him to continue even though it was depriving his family its financial security.

Hurt is synergistic and has a post-traumatic effect. As we articulate and work through our hurt, we are liberated. Psychotherapy and contemplation both deal with the emptying or the clearing of the heart, the unloading of unconscious shame. In psychotherapy we talk or give words or images to release our shame. In the silence and stillness of contemplation, we open ourselves to the significant words and images that release our shame [chapter eight].

Although controversial, the careful exploration of our unconscious dream life can also be effective. Scripture tells us that God spoke in significant ways to his people through dreams, but he also provided an interpreter. It may be wise to get help to understand the deeper meaning of our dreams. Our subconscious is often manifested in dreams when we are unable to face the painful issues of life in a purely conscious state. Our dreams are sometimes trying to share with us a deeper side of our hearts or our true selves.

God often reaches out to us in our dreams. Say a simple prayer before sleep to ask God to clear our hearts or psyches and to speak to us in our dreams. Recording dreams in a diary helps us to see what God is doing in us. Please, note that only God, the dream giver, knows the dream. Dreams are a gift; so let us accept them in love with a willingness to learn.

The Dynamics of Anger

Anger can be understood as a post-traumatic effect resulting from the repressed anger of childhood and is built upon by hurtful experiences in later life. In other words, much of the anger we feel today results from the hurt we experienced yesterday or in our early childhood. There are a few important issues which may help us to clarify and understand the process of anger in our lives. When we become angry, our bodies experience a physiological change called Diffuse Physiological Arousal (DPA) in which blood pressure and pulse rise, our breathing becomes shallow, and our bodies prepare for the fight or flight reaction.

Aroused males have a much more difficult time self-soothing or calming down than females. In fact, males tend to settle down best after they have sought revenge. All this wear and tear from the anger response and the inability to self-soothe takes its toll and may help to explain why men die younger than women. When we become extremely angry we stop using our higher brainpower and behave much more instinctively. When we are unable to benefit from the use of our cortex, we find it difficult to learn from previous experiences or to use our rational faculties effectively. As our anger increases, we become less human in behavior. We act without wisdom or guidance. In such a state, we can be dangerous to ourselves or others.

As DPA occurs and our pulse rises ten per cent above normal, our intelligence drops, leaving us retarded and irrational. In a 2002 seminar at Harvard Medical School on coping with difficult children, the professor stressed that we have to connect with the child before the anger becomes so intense that the IQ drops significantly. He said it is possible to still work with a child who has lost five to ten IQ points, but as the anger rises and IQ drops by thirty points, it is almost impossible to communicate. Now the angry person is in a state of functional retardation and is unable to discuss things from a rational perspective. In my experience, you cannot really talk to an overly angry person. The time to talk things over is after the anger has subsided.

When another person's anger is increasing in a heated discussion, we can help the situation by listening empathically and taking a calm approach. Yet because of our codependency and desire to please, we persist in trying to reason with an angry person even though it is a waste of time. This leads to useless escalation of the argument and to destructive behavior. This is why men in particular can become extremely violent when they are angry.

Imagine a man who becomes very angry. His pulse and blood pressure rise and he looses much of his reasoning power. Now he is already acting in a subnormal or retarded state and then he goes to a liquor store or bar and has a drink. Reduced reasoning powers combine with decreased inhibitions from alcohol to create a volatile mix. This explains why so much violence is domestic. The Police Commissioner of the Bahamas has said that in one three year period, fifty percent of all murders were related to domestic or relationship violence. It is usually the ones we love the most that make us the angriest. One person said, "I've never thought of divorce, but I must say I have thought of murder!"

Anger causes us to lose a sense of the present. Our minds are attached to the hurts of the past and we are caught in a past-future prison. This is because the hurts of the past can project painful images onto the screen of the future and make us ignore or avoid the present. A problem may be quite easy to resolve, but while we are angry we are divorced from the present and caught up in a past-future prison and we miss the opportunity to find a resolution.

Anger is often the root cause of intimacy dysfunction and, consequently, the cause of the breakdown of many marriages, families, and friendships. We find intimacy and growth in relationships more difficult as anger becomes more widespread. The spiritual journey is an antidote to destructive anger and allows us to open ourselves in love to our true selves in God.

Four Stages of Anger

While it is useful to talk about the four stages of anger, we must keep in mind that they do not occur in a neat, sequential pattern. The following discussion should be used only as a framework for thinking about the difficult issues of anger. In my experience, the four stages of anger offer an outline helpful in understanding and appreciating the power and destructiveness of the anger process.

1. Hurt

The first stage of anger is always the hurt which occurs primarily in childhood. Children are very sensitive to hurt which is often completely unintentional. For example, a child is sucking at its mother's breast; the telephone rings and the mother leaps up, the breast slips from the child's mouth. The interruption is unimportant to the mother, but for the child, it registers as an experience of rejection or abandonment. Children are extremely vulnerable to pain because they are unable to process or grieve it. As a result, it is repressed and expressed later in life.

2. Anger

In the second stage, hurt becomes anger. As anger increases, it may move into a strong affective response known as rage. Rage is often the reaction to a shaming or humiliating event. In rage there is a powerful DPA and, generally speaking, a person is unable to think clearly and can become violent. As time goes on, if the anger is not addressed, it moves into our hearts or psyches and becomes resentment.

Resentment comes from two Latin words, re (again) and sentir (to feel). When the anger goes into our hearts and becomes resentment, it means we feel it again and again. The anger becomes like a vacuum cleaner, scooping up all the hurts of life and creating a major bolus of resentment.

Resentment has a powerful effect on our lives. In fact, when we resent others, we give them power to control us. We give them our Identity card and control over our Dignity, Meaning, and Value. We take them on vacation with us. We take them to bed with us. We spend our every waking hour thinking about those we resent. Resentment hurts the heart and gives control to another person or situation. Another dynamic not generally recognized is that as resentment becomes embedded in our hearts, we become addicted to it and it dictates our lives.

Resentment produces roots of bitterness which extend into all aspects of our lives, possibly affecting our bodies in the form of headaches, low back pain, and illnesses such as depression. It influences relationships both close and casual. Bitterness gives life a sour taste and all events, regardless of how positive, are seen from a negative perspective. It may be a beautiful day, but for the bitter person it is too hot; it may be a lovely party, but the bitter person complains that the music is too loud. The bitter person sees negativity in every part of life and, because life is wounded, they usually find the hurt. A bitter person can brighten up a room just by leaving it.

Many young people have experienced the loss of the nuclear family, extended family, and community. This hurts deeply and causes the roots of bitterness to spring up in their hearts. What a joy to visit persons in a nursing home who are grateful, working through their anger and hurt, and who still have a positive view of life. Contrast that to others who have become hard-hearted, angry, and bitter. The physical circumstances may be similar, but their past experiences and outlook on life are very different.

3. Grudge

Unaddressed anger moves on to form a grudge. A grudge is a bitter feeling that becomes embedded in a person's heart and usually occurs between two people who were once close to each other and had a painful falling out. A grudge means there is a permanent hatred, a separation, and isolation. Grudges occur between spouses, siblings, children and parents, genders, races, faith communities, and nationalities. Grudges can also be transgenerational, in essence, passed down from generation to generation.

A classic example of a grudge is found in the story of John the Baptist (Mark 6:21-28). Salome, the daughter of Herodias, danced so beautifully at King Herod's birthday party that he promised her a gift, anything up to half of his kingdom. Salome could have chosen to ask for great wealth.

Instead, she went to ask advice from her mother, Herodias. Herodias had a grudge against John the Baptist because he spoke out against her affair with King Herod. She had caused John to be imprisoned in a dungeon, but she still was not satisfied. Acting on her grudge, Herodias told Salome to ask King Herod for the head of John the Baptist on a plate. Against his will, but bound by his promise, King Herod had John the Baptist beheaded and his head brought to Herodias on a plate.

It was not an axe that killed John the Baptist, it was a grudge. Grudges kill the life in our hearts, destroy our families, poison our communities, and create intimacy dysfunction. Most sadly, they destroy the possibility of a deeper calling to the mission of God's love in the world. If we seek to move to a deeper spirituality and love, we have to deal with the grudges in our lives.

Grudges result from the hardness of our heart. This may be described best by Jesus' parable of the sower. Jesus taught that while the farmer was sowing seed, some of the seed fell on stony ground, it failed to grow, and the birds ate it. This illustrates that the seeds of love cannot penetrate our hardened hearts. The forces of evil, represented by the birds, neutralize the love that does exist. Long-term, unaddressed anger hardens our hearts making room for evil. Evil brings us to the final stage of anger.

4. The Evil Violence Tunnel

Grudges harden the heart and open us to the Evil Violence Tunnel. When possessed by evil, we experience murderous rage and other destructive forces. Evil destroys the essence and quality of life and brings darkness, despair, disharmony, and the death of hope. Anger that becomes a grudge is devastatingly destructive. It degrades the person and deteriorates into a portal for evil. "'In your anger do not sin.' Do not let the sun go down while you are still angry, and do not give the devil a foothold" (Eph. 4:26-27).

After David killed Goliath, the women shouted, "King Saul has killed his thousands, but David has killed his tens of thousands." A jealous and angry King Saul nursed his hurt allowing his anger to organize in his heart. As a result, an evil spirit – negative energy – entered King Saul. There it festered and he developed a very severe and murderous grudge against David. Saul spent the rest of his life trying to kill David (I Sam. 18:6-72).

I have witnessed this phenomenon in young men and women addicted to cocaine. At certain points, they were very aware of the force of good on one hand and the force of evil in the Evil Violence Tunnel on the other. They freely accepted responsibility for the choices that were theirs and theirs alone.

One addict who had killed three times said he was very aware of the conflicting forces of good and evil. When he killed, he would always choose the force for evil entering the destructive Evil Violence Tunnel. While his mother was visiting him in prison, she said that she had been praying he would choose the force for good. Shocked by this, he found himself praying to God for forgiveness and mercy.

Maladaptive Expressions of Anger

We all have anger and we each express it in some form or other. Many, however, have only maladaptive and destructive ways of expressing anger. Following are a few destructive styles; you may be able to add others!

1. The Bomber

Bomb throwers are very pleasant and kind and have a long fuse. When they do explode, however, it is usually at home, frightening the spouse, terrifying the children. After the explosion they feel much better and may even want to throw a party while everyone else is shell shocked.

After one such explosion, an angry father and husband did not understand why his family could not enjoy the pizza he brought home. To him the explosion was over and forgotten, but the family was walking on eggshells, terrified of another explosion. This has a terrible effect because children tend to be egocentric and blame themselves for the parents' behavior.

2. The Scorekeeper

The scorekeeper does not react immediately when hurt or angry, but keeps score. When the anger does burst out, it brings up issues that happened today, last week, last year, maybe ten years ago. Even though we may try to reach a rational understanding with the scorekeeper, angry outbursts continue.

One lady brought me a little black book in which her husband detailed everything she had done wrong over three years. With the pain of realizing that she was in a relationship with someone who was putting a magnifying glass on every mistake she made by recording it, she went into a nervous collapse.

3. The Velvet Harpoon Champion

The velvet harpoon champions seem pleasant on the surface, but at a church event, well dressed and smiling, they might ask, "Have you gained a few pounds?" If you react, they retort, "Oh, did I make you angry?" Their words appear innocent, but they pierce our hearts with their harpoons of shame.

Often we do not feel the hurt immediately. Later, lying in bed at home, we wonder, "How could they say or do that to me?" When we see them next, their lovely smile disarms us and we find ourselves vulnerable again to their barbs. Finally, we get the message and we protect ourselves by avoiding them and their velvet harpoons.

4. The Deep Freeze

This person becomes quiet, distant, and cold when angry. A pilot shared that when his wife makes him angry, he does not speak to her for two weeks. At the end of two weeks, he claims she is pliable and submissive. This terrible, destructive stonewalling is more common in men. The result is hurt, resentment, and intimacy dysfunction.

5. The Gang Fighter

Gang fighters are unable to express anger alone and feel empowered to express it only when surrounded by certain friends. They might ignore a person they know well or act out in a destructive or negative way which is extremely painful.

6. The Guerrilla Fighter

Guerrilla fighters express anger in a passive-aggressive way rather than expressing it openly. This tactic includes gossiping. Gossip is nothing more than talking behind the backs of others and it is a form of guerrilla fighting that is very destructive to relationships.

7. The Persistent Complainer

Persistent complainers can never find anything good to say. As their name implies, they are always complaining. They are never grateful and can find a negative side to everything. They have learned that by expecting nothing, they will never be disappointed!

8. The Button Pusher

Button pushers convince us of their confidence and loyalty; they encourage us to share our secrets with them and promise to keep things confidential. When they are not with us, however, they share our secrets with others. Such hurts may continue for a lifetime. In addition, many use drugs, alcohol, and various forms of psychological defenses to express anger. All are maladaptive and destroy intimacy.

Anger Management

We will experience hurt and anger as we move toward authenticity. We need to manage the anger to keep it from developing into a grudge and entering the Evil Violence Tunnel. This requires us to be focused and willing to deal with our anger. I have found these five steps are often helpful.

1. Keep an Anger Diary

No matter how slight the incident, write it up. Look at what causes it, how it is expressed and if there is any connection to your early childhood. A diary helps us think things through. It speaks back to us. It is a powerful way of understanding the inner workings of our hearts. A diary clears our hearts of anger and opens us to a deeper form of God's love.

2. Know What Makes Me Angry

Different circumstances make different people angry. Some of us have been hurt through criticism, disappointment, and rejection. Others have been hurt by abandonment or shame, but we have all been hurt somehow. It is vital to know what makes us angry.

3. Know How I Get Angry

We each have our own ways of behaving when we are angry. Some of us become tense, others quiet, some noisy, others shake and go red. If we know what makes us angry and how we behave when angry, we are better prepared to deal with anger.

4. Take Timeout

When we are angry, it is important to recognize the fact and take timeout to self-soothe. Self-soothing occurs in stillness or contemplative prayer where we quiet ourselves, focus our intention on God and consent to his presence and his unconditional love. This is calming and renews our perspective.

Women self-soothe more quickly than men. Men are sometimes unable to self-soothe until they have sought revenge. But revenge can have very serious consequences. Some seek to self-soothe by drinking, but this creates havoc because, as the anger increases, our ability to reason decreases and alcohol destroys our inhibitions. This creates a walking time bomb.

5. Say an Anger Prayer

Anger can be so overwhelming that we forget we are the beloved of God.. We forget that the anger is just a feeling, not our defining character. A simple prayer like "Lord God, have mercy on me" can remind us that this transcendent God loves us.

God made us in his own image and anchors us in our God-given personhood. Prayer allows us to face and deal appropriately with the shaming incidents of our lives. Being forgiven does not mean that we forget, but when these incidents return to consciousness, they no longer have the power to hurt us, they are but are empty shells.

Healing the Shame Within

After I gave a talk on anger, Maria approached me to say that she was very angry. I asked about her life and she told me that when she was six years old, her mother died of cancer. It was a very painful time, but she had little memory of the circumstances. She recalled, however, that her mother asked her to go and live with a friend who also had a little girl. She remembered this as being very painful. She felt betrayed because the woman tended to favor her own daughter and would treat Maria unfairly. As a result, Maria left her mother's friend and returned to live with her father and grandmother.

I asked Maria to tell me more about the events surrounding her mother's death. She remembered standing outside a church with a crucifix. She felt very sad and cried for Jesus, but she was also crying for herself. I asked her if she would spend the next evening writing a letter to her mother at the time she was dying. At first, she rebelled and said she could not do it, but the next day she brought back a few lines she had written and cried profusely.

She said she felt blocked when she sat down to write. The pain in her heart was so heavy that she just cried and cried. The few lines she wrote went something like this, "Dear Mom, I am sorry you died. I wish you could have gotten better and been my friend to help me in life." Then she just stopped and sobbed.

When asked if she could recall more, she said that her mother was in the hospital for some reason, but when things became worse she moved home to die. I asked Maria to write a letter to herself as a six year old at the time of her mother's death. She found this difficult and began to cry. She could not do it. I begged her to try. The next day she brought a short letter and told me what happened. She had started to write the letter, but found it too difficult. She was able to write only a few lines by imagining that she was high on the balcony of an eight-story building looking down on a little girl age six sitting in the garden below.

The letter went something like this: "Dear little one, I am sorry that your mother died. It is very sad and life will be hard for you, but you must try your best." The paper was stained with tears and while reading it, she wept profusely. Despite her tears, Maria felt it was quite impossible to get in touch with the pain of what had happened.

The next day I lectured on getting in touch with our pain through appropriate grief processes and mechanisms. It is only then that we can release the pain in our hearts and open up to love, gratitude, and a new enthusiasm for life. After the lecture, six-year-old Pricilla, a girl whom I knew, ran to me. I scooped her up into my arms and found myself walking toward Maria.

Maria made the connection between Pricilla and her own six-year-old self and it caused her to run from the building screaming. Pricilla's father sensed what was going on and was very supportive. After a short time, Maria ventured back into the building and approached us like a frightened child. She slowly touched Pricilla's arm and then quickly withdrew. Soon she gave Pricilla a hug and started crying and crying. It was touching to see the healing bond between them.

The next day Maria explained that when she saw little Pricilla, she was able to get in touch with the memory of herself as a little girl for the first time. She saw how vulnerable she was, how difficult it must have been to lose her mother at such a tender age. Now she understood that the memories were too painful and had been repressed. She also said that after she cried, she found herself feeling lighter, freer, less bitter, and less angry as her heart emptied of grief and hurt.

A few months later I received a letter from one of Maria's friends who said that Maria's life was now very different. Our week of work had a powerful effect on her and, when she returned home, she made a point of apologizing to the people she had hurt.

This is no quick fix because she will have to continue to work through the issues of the hurt in her heart for the rest of her life, but her life has changed. She is now less angry, more peaceful, and having a positive impact on her local community.

Coping When Others are Angry with You

Perhaps the greatest challenge in any relationship is coping when the other person is angry with us. Many of us have been wounded by people who were angry with us or whom we perceived to be angry with us. Here what I call the "Abigail response" is relevant, simple, and effective in dealing with these situations.

Abigail was married to a man named Nabal, an obnoxious and cantankerous alcoholic. He was extremely rich and very proud of his accomplishments. David was in hiding from the jealous rage of King Saul not far from their farm (1 Sam. 24-25).

Hungry and tired, David asked his men to go to Nabal's farm and ask for food and water. This was a reasonable request since David's men had protected Nabal's sheep from thieves. Nabal was enraged, "Why should I take my bread and water, and the meat I have slaughtered for my shearers, and give it to men coming from who knows where?" (1 Sam. 25:11).

The men returned to David and told him of Nabal's response. The desperate state of his men made David viciously angry. He organized four hundred men into an army and set off to destroy Nabal and his family. His men were dropouts and vagabonds who could not make it in the armed forces of King Saul. Tired, hungry, and frustrated, they had little self-control and were unpredictable which only made them even more vicious and destructive.

One of Nabal's workers saw David and his army approaching. Petrified, he ran to Nabal's wife, Abigail, to tell her. He explained to her the situation and shared how David's men had requested food and water from Nabal, but were refused. The worker explained that David's men had been very kind to them in helping to protect the sheep. He apologized for coming directly to Abigail, but said that he had no choice because Nabal would lose his temper and they would all die. Abigail's response to this situation illustrates ten principles which will help us cope with other people's anger. The ten principles follow below.

Conflict Resolution

1. Develop a Sense of Identity

The most effective quality to exhibit in dealing with an angry person is a sense of one's own identity, a sense of being somebody. People without a sense of identity are seriously threatened by people who are angry with them. The anger is perceived as a threat, as being unloved. They feel guilty, ashamed, and will do anything to please or conform to others wishes.

This is particularly true of codependents who have their identities outside of themselves and spend their lives trying to please or conform. Abigail lived at a time and place where women had fewer rights than men, yet she had a sense of herself. Her husband's staff knew she could be depended upon to deal effectively with difficult situations.

A sense of one's true identity involves a unity of personality with a core of unchanging stability. This allows a person to be proactive and creative in times of crisis. However, with the breakdown of the family and the fragmentation of society as a whole, maintaining a secure identity is difficult. In an ever-changing world, people need an unchanging core.

Faith in what the theologians call an immutable God gives us an unchanging core in changing times. Abigail had faith and a clear sense of identity. She was proactive; she was responsible and dependable and based her decisions on values rather than feelings or circumstances.

2. Recognize the Problem

Abigail immediately sensed the gravity of the situation. There was no time for shame voices, such as, "This can't happen to me" or "He must be exaggerating." She did not use projection or blaming thoughts like, "It is Nabal's fault" or "Nabal created this mess, he'd better get us out of it." She did not use magical thinking and say, "Everything will work out" or "David is a godly man, he will not hurt us."

She did not use religious sentimentally, "Don't worry, God will handle this" or "We are devout Jews, God will not let anything happen to us." No, Abigail broke through all of those defenses and recognized the danger to herself and her family. She knew that if she did not act, there would be bloodshed.

3. Act Immediately

Abigail acted fast and with a clear sense of herself. She responded immediately and effectively. She ordered her workers to prepare donkeys laden with food. The food included two hundred loaves of bread, two jugs of wine, five sheep, grain, raisins, and two hundred cakes. She sent them ahead and followed behind on her own beast.

4. Listen Empathetically

Abigail met David and his men as they came down the mountain. Abigail and her men listened as David spewed out his anger about her husband. This empathic listening is a way of allowing the angry person to express intense feelings. It involves listening objectively. She listened to an angry David so that he could empty himself of his powerful angry feelings.

Angry people are so full of their own feelings that it is a waste of time to explain or talk to them while they are still angry. Once they have expressed their anger, it is more feasible for them to hear what you have to say. It requires restraint and patience to let angry people express their anger. It requires a sense of security in oneself to be able to stand there patiently and be shouted at.

We must learn to listen in order to understand others. I once heard a parent say, "I can't understand my son because he never listens to me." If he really wanted to understand his son, he would have been the one listening. Abigail did just that. She stayed there quietly listening as David vented his anger.

5. Show Respect

An angry person is essentially a hurt person. "Hurt people, hurt people." So following the hurt trail may enable one to cope more effectively with the anger. Hurt threatens a person's self-esteem and they feel undervalued and disrespected. Abigail knew that showing an angry David genuine respect would go a long way towards helping him feel better about himself. After listening to him, she dismounted her donkey, bowed down and called David, "My lord." This too is not easy when someone is angry with you.

Humility and respect help soothe the hurt in an angry person. It also allows for more effective healing of the hurt after the anger is expressed. We have become much too careless about manners and simple decency. Saying "You are welcome," "Thank you," and "Please," helps develop positive attitudes in others and in ourselves.

6. Admit Responsibility

Although Abigail was not the one who rejected David's request, she admitted her share of the responsibility. So often, we put all the blame on others and are unwilling to take responsibility. In fact, anger can be eased by admitting responsibility. This attitude facilitates the mediation and resolution of the problem. It takes a clear sense of self and identity to be secure enough to take responsibility and admit wrongdoing.

7. Be Honest

Abigail admitted to David that Nabal was a difficult man because of his temper and drinking. She acknowledged the hurt and rejection meted out to David and his men by her husband's selfishness. She was honest and honesty along with a willingness to take responsibility allows the hurt to be brought into the open. Anger can then be expressed more freely and problems resolved more easily.

8. Be Kind

Seeing the frustration of David and his men, Abigail gave them a gift of food and drink. As simple as it sounds, kindness goes a long way. A gift at the right time can have a truly healing effect on a person who is distraught or angry. "A gift given in secret soothes anger" (Prov. 21:14).

9. Seek Forgiveness

Abigail gave David a gift and then asked for his forgiveness. When she said, "As the LORD lives, forgive me," she was practicing transcendence. Forgiveness is the process of giving up the hurt and roots of anger. It is hard to give up a hurt that has been riveted to your soul. However, the realization that God forgives us lays the basis for us forgiving each other.

Appealing to the Lord's grace, Abigail asked David to forgive her as God had forgiven him. To ask forgiveness is to admit wrongdoing and a sincere desire to change. We may not feel that it was right for Abigail to ask for forgiveness in this situation. But in times of serious conflict, healing may only be possible when we ask forgiveness for our part even if it is only ten percent and the other party is ninety percent at fault. This takes courage.

10. Affirm Others

Abigail told David that he is fighting the battle of God and that he will be king someday. Humbly she said that when he is king, he would not want it on his conscience that he had destroyed a whole family of innocent people. Thus she affirmed the goodness of David's cause and the eventual success of his battles.

She appealed to his sense of justice and the kind of king he would like to be. Angry people are hurting and in need of affirmation. By affirming David, Abigail healed the wound and resolved the crisis. David was extremely impressed. In fact, he extolled her discernment and thanked her for saving him from taking vengeance.

Conclusion

The often painful journey toward authentic faith requires a total commitment to brutal honesty in how we deal with our anger. We must learn to face all or our unprocessed hurts and resentments. By the grace of God, we have to break up the unplowed ground of our hearts which harbors all of these deep hurts and resentments, some of which took place years ago.

Contemplation is a powerful shame buster [chapter eight]. Once again, David helps open our hearts and sets us on the path to a deeper contemplative experience.

> Search me, Oh, God and know my heart; test me and know my anxious thoughts. See if there is any offensive way in me, and lead me in the way everlasting. —Ps. 139:23-24

Our hearts and minds are constantly fragmented between work, home, family, friends, and our own selves. My mother would come home from work and say, "Let me catch myself." I always wondered what she meant. Now, as an adult, I understand that the pressures of the day spread our hearts thin over many activities and concerns. That moment after work to compose herself allowed my mother truly open up to her family in love. Just a brief moment of contemplation and stillness defragments and calms the heart and mind. Contemplation produces the undivided heart that David prayed for in Psalm 86:11: "O LORD.... Give me an undivided heart, that I may fear your name."

Anger is a brutal gift of love. Anger invites us to face the false self, to hear our heart calling us to come home. Surprisingly, anger can be a pathway to contemplation. When we take time to explore the deepest parts of the heart in contemplation, we are in the presence of God who is the true foundation and fulfillment of our being. The deeper we go, the more we open up to the One from whom we came, the One in whom we have our being, the One whose Love will never let us go and whose Face will never turn away.

Chapter 5

Shame and the Dance of

Idols and Pseudo gods

I have seen
The old gods go
And the new gods come.
Day by day
And year by year
The idols fall
And the idols rise
Today
I worship the hammer
> —Carl Sandburg, "The Hammer"

Recently, my family saw an off-Broadway production in New York called *The Little Shop of Horrors*. The play struck me powerfully because it seemed to illustrate some of the dynamics of how pseudo gods are developed in our lives. The play is about a young clerk who works in a flower shop. He is a loser. He is a failure at his job. A young lady once fell in love with him, but he was unable to respond to her love because of his low self-esteem.

The young clerk was despondent and about to give up. He walked to Chinatown and bought a magic plant from an old Chinese man. He took the magic plant back to the flower shop where he worked, but it failed to thrive. The sorry condition of the plant made him feel more of a failure.

One day, while working near the struggling plant, he accidentally pricked his finger and the blood dripped onto the plant. The plant was suddenly rejuvenated and started to thrive in a dramatic way. Apparently, the plant lived on human blood, so the young man gave more of his blood to the plant.

The plant grew luxuriant and became quite a hit in the store. People from all over flocked into the store to see the plant and overnight the young man became a success. He became valuable to his boss. Now he was making a lot of money and all because of his magic plant.

Meanwhile, the magic plant demanded greater supplies of blood. The young man had to give more and more of himself for the plant to flourish. He did so; he believed it was worthwhile because the plant had brought him fame, wealth, success and power.

However, a dilemma developed when the young man grew weaker and weaker. No matter how weak he felt, the plant still said, "I want more." In fact, the words of the plant are, "Feed me. Feed me." The young man recognized that he was going under because he was giving so much blood. In desperation, he broke his value system – he murdered a dentist (who had been somewhat unkind to him) and used the dentist's blood to feed the plant.

The plant, still not satisfied, demanded more blood. The play ends with the plant demanding so much of the young man's blood that it finally kills him. Even after its owner died, the plant still screamed, "Feed me! Feed me!"

The plant is a symbol of the power of the idols we create and worship. We give our blood and our time to our idols. We change our values to feed their insatiable appetites. Ultimately, we are lead into the dance of the idols and pseudo gods, the dance of seduction, exploitation, and destruction [Diagram 6].

Worshiping the Creature Rather than the Creator

Human beings are made in the image of God, the *imago dei* (Gen. 3:1). We all need to either worship God (authentic faith) or to convey god-like status to a person, situation, thing, or problem. The goal of human existence is to search for ultimate meaning. As a result; we worship whatever we consider to be the ultimate. According to Diarmuid O'Murchu, M.S.C.:

> Anything to which we are deeply committed can become a 'god'. Money, power, possessions, pleasure, scientific certitude and religious dogma are among the leading gods of our age. Insofar as none of these can bring us ultimate happiness or fulfillment, they are false idols. We worship them not out of love, but out of an unconscious need for power.[1]

An idol or pseudo god is formed when we give ultimate status to that which is not ultimate, e.g., money, sex, people, problems, etc. The young man in the play, overwhelmed by shame, failure, and powerlessness, gave his magic plant ultimate status. Worshiping at its shrine, he gave his life for it. Succumbing to the dance of the false gods, the young man was seduced by money and power. As he gave up his blood and forsook his values (killing the dentist), he was unmercifully exploited. Finally, he was destroyed as he gave up his own precious blood to the plant. The dance of seduction, exploitation, and self-destruction is characteristic of the worship of pseudo or false gods.

We are warned that when we have knowledge of God and refuse to honor him and worship him with gratitude, our thought processes become distorted as our minds are darkened by the loss of the eternal light. As a result, we dumb down and, instead of being wise, we become foolish and exchange the glory of the immortal God for a lie. We worship the creature rather than the Creator.

As we turn away from the true God, we become vulnerable to such destructive thinking as, "I am what I do," "I am what I possess," "I am what I feel." Initially, it gives us a sense of comfort and power, but the truth is we are only building a house of cards. Eventually, when I cannot do what I do, have what I possess, or feel the way I am supposed to feel, I am destroyed. "The idols fall and the idols rise."

Authentic Faith

As paradoxical as it may seem, in spite of suffering and even feeling anger at God, faith is still possible. Fyodor Dostoyevsky poignantly displays this dilemma of faith in his book *The Idiot*.[2] One character, dying of tuberculosis, is angry at the universe which he believes is deaf to his excellence, his beautiful soul and, most of all, to the great service he potentially might have done for humanity. On his deathbed, he struggles between the pathos of his belief in nothingness on one hand, and faith in the beauty and goodness of life on the other.[3]

Watching the devastation of the recent earthquake in Haiti, one is overwhelmed by the darkness, hopelessness, and destruction. Yet, in the despair and chaos of the situation, children were singing, "Jesus Loves Me," adults were singing, "How Great Thou Art," and others were reaching out to God in prayerful lament.

In such a disaster, what did they have to sing about? Could it be that they were witnessing to the presence of God which transcends the tragedy and pathos of life? The Haitians became Christ figures presenting to the world the shattering reality that earthquakes may destroy people, life, and buildings, but it cannot destroy authentic faith.

Is that what Job meant when he shared his faith by saying, "Though he slay me, still will I trust him" (Job 13:15)? According to Peter Kreeft, authentic faith involves belief (intellectual) and trust (cognitive-emotional). We may say we believe in medicine, but it also takes faith to say, "I trust my doctor."[4]

Faith is not some sentimental mumbo-jumbo. It does not come cheap. Like life, it is a gift from God. Gerald May, my mentor and colleague, describes it this way, "After twenty years of listening to the yearning of people's hearts, I am convinced that all human beings have an inborn desire for God. Whether we are consciously religious or not, this desire is our deepest longing and our most precious treasure. It gives us meaning."[5]

The Evolution of Idolatry

Shame is now understood to be the *Master Emotion* and has surfaced powerfully in our modern culture. Why is this? We are not sure. What we do know is that addictions have become the flagship of modern illness. Shame (**S**elf **H**atred **A**imed at **ME**) is the deeply painful conscious and unconscious feeling which is medicated by addictions. Our inner shame self-manifests abandonment, rejection, and humiliation. Our shame is compensated for by the development of the Ego Addictive False Self involving self-absorption, high experience seeking tendency, and self-inflation. The evolution of pseudo gods or idols has a psychodynamic process similar to addictions. Scott Peck wrote of modern idolatry:

> One way of looking at addictions is to see them as forms of idolatry. For the alcoholic the bottle becomes an idol. And idolatry comes in many different forms, some of which we have become quite accustomed to recognizing. There are also nondrug addictions, such as addiction to gambling

and sex. The idolatry of money is another.... To put things in perspective, therefore, it is important for us to keep in mind that there are innumerable kinds of idolatries or addictions. Many addictions can be far more dangerous than the addiction to drugs, such as, the addiction to power, the addiction to security. In some ways, drug and alcohol addiction may be among the least destructive of addictions or idolatries in terms of the overall cost to society.[6]

According to Erich Fromm, "A pseudo god or idol represents an object of central passion, a craving for power, possessions or fear."[7] The passion represented by the idol or pseudo god becomes a supreme value in a person's life. Compare this to the temptation offered Eve in the Garden of Eden. Satan entices her to power if only she will eat the forbidden fruit, "You will not surely die.... Your eyes will be opened, and you will be like God" (Gen. 3:4).

From time immemorial there lies in the heart of human beings a desire to transcend the pathos, fear, and tragedy of life by projecting our will and passion to deify or empower different aspects of our lives, such as, people, money, situations, religion, family, drugs. When we do not worship God in authentic faith, we do not worship *nothing*. Rather, being in the image of God, we create our own gods.

The psychodynamic-spiritual process outlined below is not written in stone. The stages do not necessarily always occur in the same sequence. But they do offer a conceptual model for thinking about this complex subject.

Stage I – Feelings of Inadequacy

Life is wounded. As a result, we all have some hurt or deep shame core that creates feelings of inadequacy. We also have adequate parts, so, when we say life is wounded, we do not mean that there are no positive aspects to our existence. Nevertheless, as we look deeper into our hearts and nature, we see the woundedness of life leaving us with a sense of inadequacy. As Karl Rahner said, "We must live with the insufficiency of all things and realize in the end that all the symphonies of life remain unfinished."[8]

Stage II – Feelings of Satisfaction

The deeply felt inadequacy of our shame core is compensated for by a series of neural and psychological processes that create the Ego Addictive False Self in our own image. This false self is an illusion which defends against memories of childhood hurt, shame, and fear. It involves our central passion and seeks power through self-absorption, high experience seeking, and self-inflation by attachment to objects or experiences in our environment. This sense of being empowered becomes an end in itself and creates a temporary sense of self-satisfaction or well being that defends against our feelings of inadequacy.

Stage III – Elevation to Pseudo god Status

Through the process of projective identification, our disavowed adequate parts are split off and projected onto the attached object. As the attachment deepens, our ego boundaries break down and we become fused to the idol or pseudo god. Reminiscent of the both early mother-infant birth fusion and romantic attachment fusion, projective identification creates a sense of oneness and rapture.

Through the powerful psychological defenses of denial, rationalization, and magnification, the attached object assumes ultimate status and is elevated to being a pseudo god or idol. It becomes our meaning for life and raison d'être. As in addiction, the process of withdrawal and tolerance occurs. Withdrawal occurs because the idol requires constant attention. A decrease in the amount of attention produces withdrawal symptoms such as anxiety.

Tolerance occurs in that the idol requires increasing involvement and participation to produce the same sense of satisfaction to fight the boredom and lack of meaning. In euphoric recall, all negativity or doubts about the idol are repressed. This leaves a pervasive sense of euphoria and well being. Euphoric recall of the past is projected onto the future which creates an illusion of permanence.

Stage IV – The Dance of Idols and Pseudo gods

1. Seduction

As in *Little Shop of Horrors*, the idol seduces us by providing a sense of adequacy, relative self-satisfaction, and empowerment. We undergo both the reconstruction and the constriction of reality which produces the illusion that the idol is omnipotent in our narrowed world. Isaiah warned Israel of the same thing, "For we have a lie as our refuge and falsehood as our hiding place" (Isa. 28:15).

As the seduction deepens, we internalize the false god and it becomes an idealized self object transference relationship empowering us as we worship at its shrine. Similar to addiction, seduction is enhanced because of withdrawal and tolerance. The idol depletes our energy. Our drives and persona are dominated by the desire to possess and be possessed more fully by the idol. As the seduction grows, we hand over our Identity card to the idol giving it authority over our Dignity, Meaning, and Value.

2. Exploitation

We create the idol and then the idol controls and abuses us. Essentially narcissistic, when we worship the idol, it is only a projection of our Ego Addictive False Self which is not the totality of our being. This idol or false god worship diminishes the totality of the person leading to exploitation, dehumanization, and dependence on the idol. According to Fromm, the person experiences "the shadow and not the substance of the self."

3. Destruction

As the power of the false god increases, it robs us of our essential self. Surrendering more of ourselves to the idol, boundaries weaken and our energy resources become depleted. We collapse under the strain of destruction and abandonment by the idol that made us feel all powerful. The young man in *Little Shop* collapses and dies while the magic plant, his idol, begs, "Feed me! Feed me!" Often, when we collapse, the false god, the house of cards collapses as well. "The gods rise and the gods fall!"

God created us in his image for union and fellowship with him. When we fall short of God's holy standard, our deep narcissism alienates us from God, others, the cosmos, and our own self. Nevertheless, the *Hound of Heaven* sought reunion with us by sending his Son who is "the radiance of God's glory and the exact representation of his being" (Heb. 1:3). Through the incarnation, Christ emptied himself and became one of us. He accommodated himself to our limitations, but without sin.

Idolatry and the Three Temptations of Christ

In the beginning of his ministry, after fasting for forty nights and wandering in the wilderness, our Lord was severely tempted by the Evil One. These temptations are the building blocks of all false idols which we raise up by seeking to make them ultimate and to replace the living God. These temptations challenge our basic instinctual human need for survival-security (safety), affection-esteem (acceptance), and power-control (adequacy) to produce shame out of abandonment, rejection, and humiliation.

1. The Temptation to Security through Self-Satisfaction

In the first temptation of Christ, our Lord is asked to turn stones into bread. This temptation seeks to provide our Lord with a foolproof survival-security program with the promise of protecting him from any feeling of abandonment. Rejecting the Evil One's offer, our Lord replied that humanity cannot live by bread alone. We must feed our souls by the Word of God which is spirit and life. Time and again we resist this truth and often end up feeding on the crumbs of our abandonment, anger, and anxiety.

God is our survival and security. "My soul finds rest in you, O God, and you alone" (Ps 62:1). He is our basic mirroring self object transference. His Holy Spirit (object) dwells in us, relates to us (self), and produces a mirroring self object relationship which gives us acceptance, fortitude, and encouragement.

2. The Temptation to Esteem through Self-Centeredness

In the second temptation, Satan offered our Lord a rejection-free life. He promised universal affection and esteem if Christ would only do something spectacular, e.g., perform a James Bond leap from the pinnacle of the temple. Refuting the Evil One's challenge, our Lord told him, "You shall not tempt the Lord your God" (Matt. 4:7 AKJV).

In resisting the temptation of the miraculous, our Lord reminds us that it is he who is our twinship self object relationship. This provides us with an empathic connection and understanding that heals our sense of rejection and makes seeking affection in the spectacular unnecessary.

3. The Temptation to Power through Self-Glorification

In the final temptation, our Lord was promised the kingdoms of the world if he would bow down and worship the Evil One. The Lord brushed away this temptation to power and control, chastising the Evil One saying that only God is to be worshiped. The Lord gave us this same power over temptation when he formed an idealized transference through the presence of his Spirit in us. This allows us to neutralize the humiliation in our hearts that results from our failures, sins, and negative habits.

Pseudo god's (Idols) and the Three Temptations of Christ

The modern pseudo gods may be summarized as six processes: narcissism, materialism, the sacredness of the affect, conformity, the illusion of permanence, and the bane of the extraordinary. All of these processes can be pseudo gods in themselves, but they are also a part of the dynamic process of the development of pseudo gods or idols. The six modern pseudo gods may also be related to the three temptations of our Lord. These temptations recur over and over again in our time and lives. We lose awareness of them to our own peril.

I. The First Temptation – Relevance

Satan told our Lord that since he was the Son of God, he should turn the stones into bread to satisfy his hunger. Our Lord replied that humanity "does not live on bread alone, but on every word that comes from the mouth of God" (Matt. 4:3-4). This is the temptation of relevance.

Satan used the seduction of relevance to tempt Jesus with a title, *Son of God*, and with self-indulgence, *stones into bread*. Relevance corresponds to the compensation dynamic of self-absorption and gives rise to the powerful pseudo gods of *narcissism* and *materialism*.

A. Narcissism

According to the classic Greek myth, Narcissus was a handsome young man. He was the heartthrob of all the nymphs who constantly threw themselves at him, yearning for attention. The arrogant, beautiful Narcissus ignored their overtures and was totally absorbed in himself. Looking into a pool one day, he fell wildly in love with the image he saw reflected in the water.

Obsessed with his own image, Narcissus tried in vain to initiate a relationship with the image. But when he reached out to make contact, the water rippled and the image disappeared. He begged the image of this handsome youth to stay, it refused and went away. Rejected and forlorn, Narcissus became increasingly depressed. Wasting away from unsatisfied desire, he was transformed into a flower which bears his name.

What is fueling the development of narcissism in our culture? No doubt the breakdown of the family and the resultant poor nurturing of children create what may be called a *functional attachment disorder*. The lack of the ability to give and receive love causes intimacy dysfunction which creates a society where strangers walk as friends and friends as strangers.

The increasing incidence of child abuse and neglect is another factor. When children are hurt, they withdraw into themselves. The inability to cope with the pain leads to the repression of the real hurt self and the development of a shame-based, false self involving self-absorption, pride, and high experience seeking tendencies. Likewise, a child may be traumatized by being overindulged. Giving too much to a child creates narcissistic entitlement and an attitude that says, "The world owes me."

Narcissism is a powerful false god in its own right and a major factor in the creation of all other false gods. In modern culture, narcissism is associated with three pseudo gods: *problems of living, appearances,* and *leadership.*

1. Problems of Living

Life is hard. Economic downturns, war, terrorism, and natural disasters have created a plethora of individual and societal problems. These problems attached to our central passion have become magnified and larger than life. As a result, we often find ourselves bonded to them. Our disavowed adequate part is projected onto them and is magnified. Soon we find ourselves worshiping at their shrine as they suck the life blood out of us. The apotheosis of problems in our personal, professional, and family lives strikes at our hearts and we are overwhelmed by them.

It is important to remind ourselves that in authentic faith, God is bigger than our problems. As paradoxical as it might sound, we often do not need the solution to our problems, but to bow them before God so that they are put in the proper perspective. God is the alpha and the omega, the beginning and the end (Rev. 1:8). He is with us regardless of our situation. "If God is for us, who can be against us?" (Rom. 8:31). "God is our refuge and strength, an ever-present help in trouble" (Ps. 46:11). "Cast all your anxiety on him because he cares for you" (1 Peter 5:7).

2. Appearance

Our culture invests a lot of psychological energy in having the right look, e.g., thin, tall, sharp features, the right weight, etc. Our whole worldview is often dependent on the gaining of one pound, having the right body size or shape, or the right look. It is all relative, after having twenty-two plastic surgeries on her face, a woman queried, "Does my nose have the right look?" Our true hope must be to come to authentic faith and see ourselves as the *beloved of God* and experience being fully accepted as we are.

3. Leadership

The pseudo god of narcissism is very common in leadership. The narcissistic desire to *lord it over* other people creates a deep restlessness and craving. Although made in the image of God, human beings are flawed which runs counter to our desired positive self-image.

> Freud called into question some deeply held beliefs such as the unlimited perfectibility of man and his inherent goodness. Freud made us aware of our ambivalence and our ingrained narcissism with its origin in infantile self centeredness, and showed us its destructive nature.[9]
> —Bruno Bettelheim

Leadership is a special calling. On the one hand, leadership can be servanthood as our Lord demonstrated in washing his disciples' feet (John 4:13). Conversely, leadership can be reduced to putting others in servitude. This authoritarian leadership belittles, shames, and disempowers people. Authoritarian leadership is the result of narcissism. The leader splits off his or her disavowed inadequate parts and projects them onto the followers. The followers split off his or her adequate parts and projects them on to the leader.

This endows the leader with the superhuman power of an evil dictatorship. This occurs in the church, politics, medicine, and business and is a prevalent dynamic in our culture. Like all pseudo gods, this powerful seduction leads to exploitation and destruction. Whenever one dictator leaves, another often rises until the cycle is broken. It takes a special person to hold power without giving into the malignant narcissism of jealousy, partiality, and control.

B. Materialism

Materialism is the visible god. It is one of the most powerful idols in our culture. On the surface, materialism is an obsession with status symbols, shopping, driving for success, collecting, hoarding, or owning the right toys. But on deeper reflection, materialism is the tangible evidence we use to replace the intangible, the *Holy Other*.

"Faith is the substance of things hoped for, the evidence of things not seen" (Heb. 11:1 KJV). The pseudo god of materialism reverses this implying that you can only believe what you see and you possess only what you can touch. Therefore, we worship the temporal and ignore the invisible. In our culture, the pseudo god of materialism is manifested by possessions, the repression of beauty, and technological innovation.

1. Possessions

In our consumer culture, it is so easy to *become what we possess*. This has serious consequences because when we lose what we posses, we are nothing! The recent economic downturn has affected many of us because of the loss of income, jobs, houses, and other resources. This has been particularly hard for men who get their self-esteem from their work. In one case, a young woman said that when she visited her boyfriend, she found a hangman's noose in his living room. When she confronted him, he said that things are tough and if he does not get another job and recoup his financial losses he would kill himself. The young lady was shocked and burst into tears.

Money is a powerful pseudo god and a jealous mistress. Money is seductive, controlling, exploitative, and very destructive. Money can make slaves of us all and destroy families, relationships, and even cherished values. One gentleman told me in a session that although he had a few million dollars, he did not feel safe. I asked him how much he would need to feel safe. He said twice as much, but after thinking for a second, he said maybe even that would not be enough. The fact is that enough is never enough. The greed dynamic wreaks havoc on all of our personal and societal life. Like the magic plant, it sucks our blood and eventually destroys us.

> Jesus said, "No one can serve two masters. Either he will hate the one and love the other, or he will be devoted to the one and despise the other. You cannot serve both God and Money." —Matt 6:24

2. The Repression of Beauty

Another way the pseudo god of materialistic reductionism presents itself is in the repression of beauty. Rushing along on our busy schedules, we find little time to appreciate the beauty around us. This blindness is compounded by the fact that the hurt stored in our hearts leaves little space for beauty and love.

Beauty is often repressed because we are addicted to the internalized images of external objects. When a child sees a rose, he feels its petals, is mesmerized by its appearance, and is fascinated by its smell. When adults see flowers, however, we are fixated on our own internalized images of them and do not really see them. We miss the beauty and meaning of the flower because we leave little space between seeing and labeling.

With the breakdown of the family, the neighborhood, and the surrounding community, our children are forced to face the ugliness and pathos of society. Overcome by hurt, resentment, and fear, it is difficult for them to appreciate beauty. How does a young child who watches his father shoot his mother appreciate poetry or music? How do young children who grow up with crack addiction and violent crimes learn to appreciate a sunset or a rose?

One man stated that every night after he watched the 11:00 p.m. news he became depressed and found it difficult to sleep. In the morning, he found he was irritable and unable to function effectively. Seeing the connection between the two, he stopped watching the news. Now he sleeps better and is less troubled the following day.

That may demonstrate a simplistic dynamic, but I wonder if it is not something we should consider. Would we not see more of the beauty of life if we minimized our exposure to the ugliness and the hurt thrown at us by the news media, unpleasant conversations, and shocking films, novels, and music? I am convinced that it is possible for that negativism to fill our hearts and make it too difficult for us to appreciate love and the beauty around us.

> People who have lost the sense of their identity as selves also tend to lose their sense of relatedness to nature. When a person feels the self inwardly empty as is the case with so many modern people, he experiences nature around him also as empty, dried up and dead.[10] —Rollo May

Gertrude Stein intoned, "A rose is a rose is a rose." That may be true in one sense, but in the spiritual realm, a rose is not just a rose. In a way, the rose becomes a symbol of God's love to us. A rose points to the Creator. We may nurture the rose, we may care for the rose, but we cannot make the rose. To appreciate a rose, we cannot just stop at the physical. We have to go back and look at what the rose means symbolically, what it means spiritually. As we see the rose, it reminds us of God's creativity and love.

> The world is too much with us, late and soon,
>   Getting and spending, we lay waste our powers;

Little we see in Nature that is ours.
We have given our hearts away, a sordid boon![10]
—William Wordsworth

My friend Debbie grows the most beautiful roses that I have ever seen. On two occasions she has given our family some of those roses and they have ministered to us dramatically. They bloomed magnificently for days, filling our home with their message of life, love, and hope. It was lovely to enjoy their scent and beauty. Even deeper was the awe we felt at the mystery of the roses as they reminded us of the One who created them. The roses become a spiritual statement, saying to us during our time of trouble and conflict that we are the *beloved of God*.

3. Technology

The rationalistic, scientific approach to life is similar to materialism. Scientific rationality and technology can be powerful means to enhance the dignity of human life. There are, however, intended and unintended tragic consequences when technology and scientific inquiry are seen as ends in themselves. A scientific mode of thinking can become a religion amounting to another pseudo god.

Brian Appleyard makes a case that science has become a dominant faith of our time, but unlike traditional faiths, it is unable to address questions of meaning and purpose. He states, "Science works but it has split truth from meaning. Its enforced neutrality about issues of meaning and purpose is spiritually not neutral at all."[11]

Technology has become the predominant force in science and, with its purely materialistic perspective, it can be a very powerful pseudo god. In medicine, my particular field, we see technology having a tremendous impact. To make matters worse, we are beginning to see that the scientific method in medicine has developed its own religious perspective. Hence we see the dilemma of modern technology. In fact, our technology has been so successful that we are now confronting such critical questions as:

- Who should be born? (Prenatal diagnosis and treatment)
- Who should live? (Technological maintenance of life)
- How long should we live? (Quality of life)[12]

Who should make these decisions? Is it possible that our technological developments have moved so fast that they have outdistanced our ethical decision making? Now we are faced with the possibility of cloning the human embryo. Questions about biomedical technology strike at the heart of our basic value system.

Technology can serve humankind as a means of enhancing personal dignity. We cannot, however, allow it to become a pseudo god where it becomes an end in itself and thus destroys human beings. The growth of technology is out pacing our ability to relate face to face with each other. In spite of burgeoning communication technology – email, Facebook, MySpace, Twitter, smart phones – loneliness is increasing in our culture. In fact, studies from 1992 to 2004 show that we have one-third fewer close personal contacts with whom we can share our hearts.

The technological revolution is a massive pseudo god. Husbands, wives, children, friends, and business associates communicate by cell phone, email, and text messaging. Internet pornography is growing exponentially. Facebook is threatening communication between couples. One wife sued for divorce after the husband refused to give up nightly communication with a woman on Facebook.

II. The Second Temptation – The Spectacular

In the second temptation, our Lord was challenged to jump from the pinnacle of the temple – the temptation of the spectacular. The idea was that the leap would be so spectacular that people would be impressed and believe in him. Responding in authentic faith, our Lord told Satan, "It is also written: 'Do not put the Lord your God to the test'" (Matt. 4:5-7). It was a solemn warning against substituting a pseudo god for true faith.

Since the sixties, society has believed and taught that feeling high is good and feeling low is bad. Feeling good has been internalized as a prevailing value leading to the sacredness of the affect which is associated with the modern idols of *addiction* and *conformity*.

A. The Sacredness of the Affect in Addiction

Addiction is the modern disease. In Freud's day, repression was widely pervasive and resulted in multiple hysterical phenomena which were healed by the sharing of repressed memories. Now, with everything out in the open, sex, lifestyles, personal preferences, there is less repression. Instead, we seek emotional balance through attachment to substances, people, feelings, and situations.

1. Drug Addiction

In my many years in crack cocaine research and treatment, I have heard addicted men describe it as an idol, a god, or the antichrist. The high is stronger than the mother-child bond. Crack cocaine is the drug that feminized drug addiction. The mother is the one who holds the home together and children feel deeply hurt and abandoned when the mother leaves them for her beloved crack.

Crack addiction is powerful. A doctor who was addicted to crack cocaine lost his family, medical practice, and his health. He was reduced to an empty shell of a man. Before he died he told me, "The best thing that happened to me in my life was crack cocaine." It seduced, exploited, and eventually destroyed him, yet he still worshiped it.

2. Relationship Addiction

After the attraction phase of a relationship, the ego boundaries break down and create a powerful fusion that is associated with a euphoria that defines the relationship. Inevitably, when the ego boundaries snap back into place, the couple experiences a loss of euphoria. This produces a crisis when the couple projects their individual shame and hurt experiences onto each other.

This phase destroys many relationships because the fusion and euphoria to which they have become attached or addicted are gone. Our culture worships the fusion and euphoria of relationship addiction. We use excessive energy trying to re-capture them with money, possessions, etc. Relationship addiction seduces, exploits, and eventually destroys relationships and often the people in them.

3. Thoughts and Feelings

Human beings are guided by their thoughts and feelings. Shame-prone persons tend to become addicted or attached to particular negative feelings and thoughts. We are often unaware of these attachments and addictions to forms of thoughts and emotions.

Addiction to our stream of thoughts is one of the most powerful addictions of modern culture. Our thoughts form an incessant internal dialogue which plays twenty-four hours a day. Thinking is good, but when it becomes excessive, it blocks our appreciation of reality making it difficult to be present in the now. Like the body, the normal division of cells produces growth, but excessive cell division produces cancer. So often our attachment to past negative events projects pictures of the future on the screen of the mind. The end result of these constant negative thoughts is a past-future prison blocking us from the power of the now.

We also become addicted to feelings such as anger. One woman consulted me and said she would talk with me about anything – spirituality, family, lifestyle, etc., but if I even tried to interfere with her anger toward her husband, she would fire me. After ten sessions, she rushed into my office and said, "You are interfering with my anger towards my husband. Last night at dinner my husband appeared innocent as a little lamb with his cute little dimples. He started to look lovable." Looking me straight in the eye she shouted, "You are messing with my anger towards my husband. You're fired!" and slammed the door. Could it be her hurt, medicated by her addiction to anger, empowered her to cope? In this regard anger becomes idolatry.

B. The Sacredness of the Affect in Conformity

Conformity is a powerful dynamic in modern society contradicting authentic faith and encouraging idolatry. We all want to fit in and be part of the predominant group.

1. Codependency

Codependency is the phenomenon in which we seek empowerment by pleasing people. In the deep hurt of our hearts and feelings of insecurity, we give our life blood to please people with the hope that they will love or empower us. Codependents have a hard time saying no because of guilt or the fear that they will be unloved. It is a powerful pseudo god that saps our energy, seduces, exploits, and eventually destroys us.

Terrified of her husband, Tara did everything to please him by spending much time and energy on her cooking, housekeeping, and appearance. She believed that if she pleased him, he would love her and never leave her. When displeased with Tara, her husband would leave home and check into a hotel. Distraught and hurt, Tara would go from hotel to hotel in the area trying to find him. Oppressed, depressed, and shamed, Tara worshiped at the throne of codependency. Giving up so much of herself, Tara suffered burnout and became depressed. Her desire to please was destroying her. She eventually went into therapy and broke the codependency cycle.

3. Denominational Tribalism

The idol of conformity has played a major role in religious denominational tribalism with one group teaching that they are superior to the other. According to Diarmuid O'Murchu, the Reformation in the sixteenth century drove both Catholics and Protestants into theological enclaves:

> Protestants preserved an exclusive allegiance to the Word of God, paving the way for a rather cerebral, intellectualized, dehumanizing quality of religion, while Catholics developed a strong sacramental and canonical (legal) approach which became a measuring stick, who was and who was not, deemed to be in and out of the Catholic church.' Continuing O'Murchu claims that in these artificial confines, theology became an ideological criterion for allegiance to one camp or the other. Thus it was only a matter of time until theology assumed an idolatrous significance.[12]

Our God is real and yours is not is the cry of denominational tribalism. Authentic faith calls us to hear afresh the prayer of our Lord before his passion, "That they may be one as we are one" (John 17:22). The plethora of denominations detracts from the power and effectiveness of

God's mission of love in the world. We often worship our theology or our desires rather than God. When his wife died, C. S. Lewis said he had to change his idea of God in order to worship God as he truly is, not as Lewis imagined him to be. God is the great iconoclast, the idol breaker.

4. Worshiping the Family

We also see the pseudo god of conformity working in families. In fact, the family can become a pseudo god itself when we isolate ourselves from the rest of society in order to preserve family unity and closeness. We shut out the rest of the world, elevate family to pseudo god status, and then find that things never work out as well as we had hoped.

Sometimes the kids do not perform brilliantly or even acceptably. Sometimes a financial crisis occurs robbing us of our house, our possessions, and the easygoing lifestyle that made family life so good. Sometimes sickness or death intrudes. Crises dispel the illusion of invulnerability and leave the idolized family reeling.

We also see family idolatry when parents actually fuse with their children. When that happens, the children's performance at school or in sports activities or in musical performances affects the parents' self-esteem. One only has to watch parents at a Little League game to see this tendency in action. When our kids become an obsession, we become fused to them. When they do poorly, we become anxious and upset. When they do well, we feel better. There can be a powerful connection between the performance of the child and the emotional state of the parent.

Within some families, there is a conformity issue related to being part of the *right* kind of family. Those people who are *in* feel superior to those who are *out*. This dynamic influences prejudices and even cruelty to others outside the group. It extends beyond families into clubs, organizations, schools, ethnicities, nationalities, races, and political affiliations.

> Idolatry...comes in forms we are not accustomed to recognize as readily. One is the idolatry of family. Whenever it becomes more important to do or say what will keep the family matriarch or patriarch happy than it is to do or say what God wants you to do or say, we have fallen prey to the idolatry of family. Family togetherness has become an idol and often a most oppressive one.[13]
>
> —Scott Peck

III. The Third Temptation – Power

In the third temptation of Christ, the Evil One took our Lord up on a high mountain and promised to give him all the kingdoms of the world if he would bow down and worship him. Our Lord counters by saying, "'Worship the Lord your God, and serve him only'" (Matt. 4: 9, 10).

Out of this temptation comes the dynamics of pride and power as compensation for the humiliation schema of shame. These are the foundation of two modern idols: the *illusion of permanence* and the *bane of the extraordinary*.

A. The Illusion of Permanence

Like all idols, the pseudo god of the illusion of permanence uses denial and rationalization to give us a false sense of confidence.

1. The Idolatry of Change Without Transition

Change in life is inevitable, but we often have great difficulty with transition. Change is the external movement of events, such as, going from employment to retirement. Transition is internal, meaning that even though a man might be officially retired, his heart is still at work every day. As one doctor said after moving to a retirement home, "The bottom has fallen out of my life. I don't know how to live without practicing medicine. I feel powerless."

2. The Idolatry of Worshiping the Status Quo

Unconsciously, we become so accustomed to the way things are that we are seduced into believing that things will always be as they always have been. This happens in regard to sickness and health, wealth and poverty, power and powerlessness. Life involves change, all change involves loss, and all loss involves pain. Nevertheless, we plan our lives with little thought and prayer for God's guidance or will. We worship the status quo with the illusion that we are the masters or victims of our fate.

> You do not even know what will happen tomorrow. What is your life? You are a mist that appears for a little while and then vanishes. Instead, you ought to say "If it is the Lord's will, we will live and do this or that." —James 4:14

Our Lord reminds us of the rich man who, after rebuilding his barns, said to himself that he would spend the rest of his life enjoying his wealth, but he was told, "Tonight your soul is required of you" (Luke 12:13-21).

3. Chronological Fatalism

Experience without faith is fatalism. We see things in *Chronos* (chronological) time in the material world. We forget that God's grace interrupts life "in the fullness of time", i.e., *Kairos* time. When we live only in *Chronos* time and ignore the grace of *Kairos* time, we create a powerful chronological fatalism.

This leads to a sense of boredom, not because we have nothing to do, but because we believe nothing we do makes a difference or has meaning. Life is always open and not deterministic. To have an authentic faith means to invite God to intervene in all aspects of human life.

> Holy, holy, holy is the LORD Almighty;
> the whole earth is full of his glory. —Isa. 6:3

B. Bane of the Extraordinary – Power and Invincibility

1. The Idolatry of Dreams

Dreams are good, but a dream can also be idolatrous. A doctor who was a very bright and industrious academic lived for his dream of winning a Nobel Prize in medicine. When he reached his fifties and did not see how his dream could be realized, he felt like a worthless failure. He turned to alcohol and became self-destructive. In authentic faith, we bow our dreams to God's providence. God may say "No" to our dreams, but always "Yes" to what is good for us.

2. Workaholism

Workaholism is a prominent idol of modern life. It robs us of the time for inner reflection; it blocks us from truly being present to ourselves, our families, and others. Workaholism often keeps us occupied with our careers which are temporary at the expense of our vocations which are eternal and redemptive. Recognizing this dilemma is rare, but I know of a man in his fifties who was offered a lucrative job traveling around the world. Considering his calling to family and faith, he turned it down, saying, "This job is good for my career, but it is terrible for my vocation."

Workaholism is a powerful idol, a jealous god. Seducing and exploiting us, it eventually destroys us. There was once a man who was a great doctor. In fact, he died of a heart attack on his way to deliver a baby. His loss was deeply grieved. A few months after his death, his daughter consulted a psychiatrist who told her that her father was a great doctor. To the psychiatrist's surprise, the daughter said, "He may have been a great doctor, but he never had time to be my daddy."

3. Idolatry of Control

In competitive societies which glorify the Ego Addictive False Self, we seek power by control. At a prestigious competitive medical school it was found that, in order to get ahead, certain students were stealing other students' lab books to sabotage their studies. Similar stories occur in business, politics, and even religious and charitable groups. Worshiping at the throne of power and control is seductive, but it exploits others and eventually destroys us.

Summary

Our Lord was victorious over all of the Satan's temptations. He did not need the compensation of an Ego Addictive False Self as a defense against the deep pain of shame. Unlike us, our Lord did not have a hurt trail of shame and yet he was abandoned, rejected, and humiliated on the cross. He suffered shame, but whose shame did he die for if not his own? The answer is that he suffered for our shame once and for all giving us the power to walk in victory over shame.

Because Jesus our Lord lives, we can now face life with courage, hope, and patience. Most of all, we can now say in the words of the famous composer Johann Sebastian Bach, "Come thou sweet death" and with the apostle Paul:

> O, death where is your sting
> O, grave where is your victory?
> —I Cor. 15:55 AKJV

Moses and the Idolatry of the Golden Calf

Feelings of Inadequacy

When the children of Israel left Egypt to journey to the Promised Land, God warned them not to worship other gods. The journey in the wilderness was treacherous and difficult. In the words of T. S. Eliot, "They had a hard time of it." Moses had felt from the beginning that he was inadequate for the job. The lack of food, the difficult mountain trail, and the interpersonal conflicts led to much complaining and dissatisfaction. The people had a negative attitude and berated Moses for bringing them out of Egypt. Slavery, they said, was better than dying in the wilderness.

God called Moses to Mount Horeb for fellowship and to present to him the Ten Commandments. These were the theocratic blue print of the rules and boundaries for the nation of Israel. The commandments are constitutive imperatives upon which all the laws of society are based. Moses was transformed by this close communion with God and is the only man ever recorded to have seen God and lived. It was said that "The LORD would speak to Moses face to face, as a man speaks with his friend" (Ex. 33:11).

The Rise of the Golden Calf

With Moses absent, the people felt abandoned, rejected, and humiliated and succumbed to shame. Angry and fed up, they followed the dictates of the Ego Addictive False Self with its self-absorption, high experience seeking behavior, and self-inflation. They asked Aaron to make them a god because *this Moses* had disappeared. The angry mob overwhelmed a codependent Aaron who chose to please them. He told them to bring him the gold earrings from their sons and daughters and he melted them in fire and formed a Golden Calf.

Seduction

The people danced and sang around the Golden Calf in celebration praise to the god whom they claimed led them out of Egypt. What a delusion, splitting off their central passion from the living God they projected it onto the Golden Calf which, though lifeless, was endowed with superhuman characteristics. David cried out, "How long, O men, will you turn my glory into shame? How long will you love delusions and seek false gods?" (Ps. 4:2).

Feeling good in a party atmosphere is seductive and compensates for fear and insecurity. This sense of feeling good is a predominant dynamic in the development of idolatry. We pay a heavy price for desecrating God's image.

> Although they knew God, they neither glorified him as God nor gave thanks to him, but their thinking became futile and their foolish hearts were darkened.... They exchanged the truth of God for a lie, and worshiped and served created things rather than the Creator — who is forever praised. Amen. —Rom. 1:21, 25

Exploitation

The people were worshiping the Golden Calf and Aaron built an altar to God in front of it and called for a festival to worship Jehovah on the next morning. The people rose early to make sacrifices and offerings. After worshiping they sat down to eat and drink. Then they arose and engaged in revelry – dancing and sexual immorality.

Confusion resulted because the people had lost their way and were trying to use the worship of God as a back up to the worship of the idol of the Golden Calf. God has made it clear: "I am the LORD; that is my name! I will not give my glory to another or my praise to idols" (Isa. 42:8).

We have exchanged the glory of God for the desires of the shame-based Ego Addictive False Self. We thus create our own emotional programs for feelings of empowerment or happiness. When our allegiance to God is mixed or confused, we are exploited and become lost. Jonah 2:8 warns, "Those who cling to worthless idols forfeit the grace that could be theirs."

> Thou has made us for thy self and we shall ever restless be until our rest is found in thee.
>
> —St. Augustine

Intercession

God, the all seeing one, was revolted by the peoples' idolatry and hedonistic lifestyle of drunken revelry and sexual immorality. Calling them stiff necked and rebellious, God threatened to destroy them and promised Moses, his faithful servant, to make of him a great nation.

Showing deep compassion and servant leadership, Moses interceded for the people. He reminded God that if the people were destroyed, the Egyptians would say that God delivered the people only to destroy them in the wilderness. Moses also asked God to relent because of his promise to Abraham, Isaac, and Jacob to make their descendents as the stars in the sky.

God relented and promised not to destroy the people. It is humbling to conceive that the eternal God, our refuge and strength, is willing to listen and respond to the prayers and requests of mortal man.

Destruction

Moses came down from the mountain to find the people worshiping the Golden Calf. He was revolted by this counterfeit god. He had just been in the presence of the true God, the Holy Other. He became enraged and confronted the people about their loyalties. Many died as the camp was purged of idolatry. When false gods are shattered, there is always much pain, disillusionment, and destruction: "Do not be deceived. God cannot be mocked. A man reaps what he sows" (Gal. 6:7).

Conclusion

Moses encouraged the people to repent and returned to the mountain to once again intercede for the people. Admitting to God that the people sinned greatly in worshiping the idol, Moses, willing to sacrifice himself, asked God to destroy him and save the people. In his mercy, God relented again saying that he would destroy only those persons who sinned against him. Then God told Moses to march on with the people to the Promised Land with the assurance that an angel would guide them.

Growing in the knowledge of God takes commitment. Facing the pathos of life, we become hurt, afraid, and our Ego Addicted False Self seeks to create false gods involving self-absorption, the desire to feel good, and pride. But there is only one God. All other gods will rise and they will fall. In the darkness of seduction, exploitation, and destruction, we often suffer the fate of the gods we worship.

The tragedy of this story is that we often forget the goodness of God and project our central passion on an idol or pseudo god attributing to it the blessings given by God.

> Our world today is rampant with idolatry....All forms of idol worship tend to be self-validating and self-perpetuating, resistant to change, and consequently deaf to the call to conversion, growth and new life.[14]

The wise men in T. S. Eliot's "The Journey of the Magi" returned to their kingdoms forever changed after seeking and worshiping the Christ child saying:

We returned to our places, these Kingdoms,
But no longer at ease here, in the old dispensation,
With an alien people clutching their gods.
I should be glad of another death.

John warns us about pseudo gods, "Little children, keep yourselves from idols" (I John 5:21). This is not easy. Authentic faith in the true God requires vigilance, faithfulness, and loyalty. It means letting go of our Ego Addictive False Self to surrender to God and to rest in his abiding and unfailing love. In so doing, we experience our true identity as the *beloved of God*.

Chapter 6

Surrender: Making the Perceptual Shift

There is something within you that remains unaffected by the transcendent circumstances that make up your life situation, and only through surrender do we have access to it. It is your life, your very being, which exists in the transcendence of the present!

—Eckhart Tolle

After a lecture on surrender, Sandra said she would like to share a story with me. Curious, I sat down as she recounted a recent visit to Nepal. Sandra was so impressed by the grandeur of the mountain scenery that she decided to take an elephant ride up the mountain to see the view. Seated in a chair on the back of the elephant, Sandra was overwhelmed by the breathtaking scenery as the elephant began his trek up the mountain. Seeing mountain peaks covered in snow alongside deep ravines bursting with luxuriant vegetation was an unforgettable experience.

As the elephant ascended the mountain, Sandra said that she noticed the ground of the steep winding slope was wet from earlier rain making the trail muddy and slippery. As the elephant trudged up the mountain, it felt as if his feet were slipping in the mud. Sandra was terrified. No longer able to concentrate on the beautiful scenery, she became extremely worried about the elephant slipping down and catapulting her into the deep ravine. Sweating and panicky, her heart pounded and her breathing became shallower and faster as she was overcome with fear.

She felt that each step of the elephant brought her closer to what was her unavoidable fate, being thrown over the mountain into the deep ravine. When she practiced the relaxation techniques from her study of Yoga, she became still and began to breathe mindfully. After breathing deeply and slowly for about fifteen minutes, Sandra began to relax. Her heart slowed down and she became less tense. She started to enjoy the splendor of the beauty around her. Most of all, the fear which paralyzed her started to melt away.

A relaxed Sandra was again able to appreciate the scenery. The fear was disappearing and as she became still, she experienced a new sense of peace and freedom. Though the danger was still there, her sense of relief outweighed the fear of danger. This is the meaning of surrender: to let go of fear, resistance, and negativity, and open up to the peace and freedom of love.

Finally relaxing and enjoying the beauty of the scenery and the epiphany of the moment, Sandra was startled to feel the tail of the elephant brushing against the bottom of her feet. She again became afraid and lifted her feet to avoid upsetting the elephant. No matter where she tucked her feet the elephant found them and hit them with his tail.

Determined not to upset the elephant, she pulled her legs up farther, but again the elephant's tail found her. Sandra continued her deep breathing and tried to relax again. As her mind cleared, she realized the elephant was communicating with her, "Relax lady, I've climbed this mountain hundreds of times. I know what I am doing."

At that point, Sandra surrendered and opened up to the grandeur and beauty surrounding her. "I found myself feeling more and more filled with peace, love, and joy. Peace because I felt safe, love for the wonderful elephant carrying me, and joy for the beautiful scenery of God's creation." Sandra said she felt especially grateful for discovering how to let go of her fear and surrender to the moment.

Could it be that when we surrender, we enter the inner rhythm of life where we experience the oneness and interrelatedness of all things?

Definition of Surrender

The word surrender is derived from the old French word *surrende* – *sur*: over and *rende*: to give back. To surrender is *to give over* to true love as opposed to being controlled by our defensive Ego Addictive False Self which functions on fear, negativity, and resistance (Diagram 7).

The true self is the unchanging, self-reflective, conscious being in which the events of our lives unfurl. For example, we do not see a tree or have a thought or feeling. We are the consciousness in which the tree or the thought or feeling appears. Surrender does not transform our circumstances, it transforms us to act appropriately, to *change*, *improve*, or *withdraw* from the situation at hand.

When our situation is intolerable, and no action is possible, when we surrender to our essential being (true self) in love, the inner resistances of fear, guilt, shame, and inertia peel away leaving a positive perception. Surrender is an inner phenomenon in which we choose to accept the truth of our life as it is, not as we want it to be. The true self emerges when we chose to cultivate gratitude, art, music, spirituality, psychotherapy, and stillness.

Surrender is experiencing life in the now. The now is not what is happening presently, but like our true self, it is the consciousness or awareness in which the present occurs. As long as fear and its associated feelings contaminate our life situations, we are blocked from using our full resources and find our lives anchored in and controlled by the past. The negativity of the past blocks out present opportunities and contaminates our view of the future. Consequently, we live in an all too familiar scenario, the past-future prison. Surrender opens us up to the presence of our being to experience peace, freedom, and love.

Surrender has many negative connotations implying defeat, retreat, or giving up, but contemplative surrender is different. This is the surrender that eliminates the mental resistance, negativity, and fear that clouds our judgment. It opens us to our true self. Our true being, created in the image of God (*imago dei*), is anchored in the *Eternal Love*. This kind of surrender transcends the circumstances of our lives. Surrender is our small *i* being part of the great *I am*.

When things go wrong, as they often do, our mental judgment produces inner resistance and negativity which creates a painful gap between the rigid expectation of our mind and the reality of what *is*. Surrender is accepting the situation in the present – the unaffected now – apart from negativity, anger, or despair. Surrender is an inner phenomenon with external faces of peace, freedom, and courage. When we surrender, we create positive action as opposed to negative action from fear and resistance.

Non-surrender has psychological and physical effects. Psychologically, non-surrender strengthens our Ego Addictive False Self and blocks us from oneness with others and ourselves and from the interrelatedness of all things. Physically, non-surrender makes our body rigid and unresponsive due to stress preceded by resistance, anger, and negativity. Relaxation techniques, stretching, and exercise facilitate surrender by releasing fear and tension.

Surrender separates our life situation from our being. It liberates our sense of being so that we act in a more focused and effective way. Sometimes surrender is its own reward allowing us to see more clearly. Connecting us to the source and ground of being, surrender results in peace and joyful celebration. In so doing, we see what needs to be done and take positive action.

The Psychodynamics of Surrender

The quality of our present state of consciousness determines our future. Surrender is the most important thing we can do to initiate positive change. Surrender disconnects our fear, negativity, resistance, and anger from our present situation and allows us to experience a new level of consciousness.

It was the regular weekly group therapy session and emotions were running hot because a cadre of lawyers was weighing in with advice on how to help Joan deal with a complex divorce case. As the lawyers gave an abundance of advice, Joan became more frustrated and confused and began crying profusely. The more the lawyers explained, the more Joan became confused and did not understand. Flushed, sweating, and overwhelmed, Joan started to sink like the Titanic under the heavy load of legal jargon.

As the group moved into chaos, Shirley, the female co-therapist said, "Stop! Quiet! Joan needs to surrender!" She encouraged Joan to quiet herself and breathe slowly and deeply. Puzzled, one of the lawyers said sarcastically, "I guess this will help her in court." After about five minutes Joan said, "I feel much better!" This was miraculous. Joan became relaxed and empowered. What happened? Joan surrendered. An overwhelming amount of advice frustrated, angered, and confused her. When she stopped and calmed down, the fear and resistance disappeared. Joan became more positive about her situation. Joan had surrendered.

Surrender is similar to allowing a stirred up pond to settle down. As the water calms and the particles settle, the pond clears up allowing us to see to the bottom. Surrender allows us to experience the meaning of our life more clearly and brings the full complement of our resources to confront our problems.

Our mental judgment, emotional negativity, and the pressures of other people cloud our perspective on life. We expend a tremendous amount of energy trying to reduce the chasm between what we or others expect of us and what we actually are. Surrender frees us from this shame gap and allows us to face life as it is. For example, while traveling in the Serengeti plains in Kenya, our car got stuck in the mud in the middle of a jungle populated by lions and elephants. Fearing, complaining, and bemoaning our fate only created resistance. We had to surrender and accept the reality of our situation. Surrender is not resignation. After a period of breathing mindfully, reflection, and prayer, we were at peace and were eventually rescued by a passing driver.

We are created in the image of God with an Identity grounded in him with the Dignity, Meaning, and Value he bestows. Surrender allows us to face life with a positive attitude. Sometimes we are not always able to solve our problems. Surrender places them in the proper perspective as our heavenly Father gives us new hope and courage.

In our woundedness, we often treat problems as ends in themselves. We embellish them with fear, anger, anxiety, and negativity creating perhaps a greater issue than the problem itself. By increasing awareness, surrender converts insurmountable problems into challenges which can be addressed. Surrender opens us to a power beyond ourselves. Did the sun not rise this morning and set this evening without help from you or me? As they say in Alcoholics Anonymous, "My life is unmanageable and I need a power greater than myself."

The Ego Addictive False Self is formed as an illusion to defend against inner pain and shame. The Ego Addictive False Self is based on fear. It counteracts anxiety and the pain of abandonment, rejection, and humiliation with programs of happiness using pride, self-absorption, and high experience seeking tendencies.

Surrender returns power and control of life from the Ego Addictive False Self which is based in fear to the true self which is based in love. This is a simple, but not easy task. We must learn to surrender in order to live in the constant awareness of the true self. Otherwise, we live in the dance between the Ego Addictive False Self and the true self. Surrender does not mean that we never find ourselves at the pole of our Ego Addictive False Self, but we must not stay there – surrender, surrender, surrender.

Surrender is not denial or resignation. It means we let go of our fears, negativity, and hopelessness to allow our true self – our being – to regroup and become refreshed to face problems. Surrender brings us the awareness and resolve not to confuse *being* with circumstances. Our life situation is not our being. Our being is not and cannot be characterized by I am *rich*, I am *poor*, I am *sick*, I am *well*, etc. Regardless of my life situation, *I am*.

Surrender is letting go of our life situation to become open to the true essence of being and its connectedness to the *Eternal Being*, the unfathomable mystery. As we open to our essential being, we open to God who is all powerful and all knowing. Then we can say with Paul, "If God is for us, who can be against us?" (Rom. 8).

The burgeoning pressures of life so deeply burden us that it is becoming more difficult to show up for our lives. One man told me, "I have a great life, but I have not been able to show up for it." We often feel alone, disconnected. We idolize our fears, problems, and life circumstances. By worshiping idols, we lose the ground that is already ours (Jonah 2:8). Like Peter walking on the water, when we lose the awareness of that love, we lose courage, become overwhelmed, and sink. Only in surrender can we walk on the water in the midst of life's waves and wind.

It simply cannot be repeated enough: surrendering means letting go of fear and opening to the *Eternal Love* that *has been* before, *is* during, and *will be* after our lives. When we surrender, we become the *i* to his great *I Am*.

The old George Matheson hymn reminds us of the Love that will never let us go:

> O Love that will not let me go,
> I rest my weary soul in thee;
> I give thee back the life I owe

Characteristics of Surrender

In my experience, a number of components make up the process of surrender: awareness, choice, the perceptual shift, humility, prayer, breathing, attitude, gratitude, and letting go.

A. Awareness

So often in the hustle and bustle of daily experience, our life is filled with negativity, anger, fear, and resistance. Burgeoning reports of bad news often leave us frustrated and depressed. We are constantly challenged and overcome by stressful lifestyles, urgent time pressures, and ever increasing demands.

> No one sees a flower
> No one makes a friend
> To see a flower takes time
> To make a friend takes time
> And we have no time.
> —Georgia O'Keefe

Nevertheless, peace is possible through awareness, but awareness is only possible in surrender. Many of us do not come to awareness without the challenge of illness, tragedy, or suffering. As one man said, "I did not learn stillness until I suffered illness." We must live in the awareness that surrender is possible. There is love in fear, peace in the storm, hope beyond despair, a "balm in Gilead".

Rushing into my office, an overwhelmed young lady said her life was impossible. Increasing financial burdens, a broken marriage, and having to bring up three little children made her life unmanageable. Shouting at the top of her voice she said, "I can't do it. I just can't!" Listening to her express her fears and the pathos of her life, I felt her pain. I asked her to join me in breathing mindfully. After a period of deep anxiety, she started to relax and became peaceful. She was able to surrender.

I asked her if she had anything for which she felt grateful. She shared that she was very thankful that her children were healthy and doing well in school. As peace entered the room, we accepted the gift of surrender. The problems were the same and the challenges remained, but she had a new perspective and determination. In the Scriptures, Jesus reminds us that worry cannot heal our lives. He encourages us to live in his kingdom of love where we will receive his promised revitalization and hope.

B. Choice

Surrender is a choice. We can choose the tyranny of our circumstances by continuing to live in fear and negativity or we can choose to surrender to God, the source of love and the ground of our being. Choice is cataclysmic. It can make the difference between living in hell or heaven.

Victor Frankl was imprisoned in the concentration camps of Germany. In his memoirs, he said that when he discovered that he alone was responsible for his choices, he chose to live with a positive attitude. At that point, he became free and his captors were imprisoned.[1] We, too, can choose to surrender or be destroyed.

To surrender is to choose freedom from the shackles of despair and to open up to the eternal freedom of love. Positive attitudes keep us focused and present. Negative attitudes are destructive and produce ongoing negativity, anger, fear, and despair. Positive attitudes encourage us to be proactive, to focus on what can be done and knowing what cannot be done.

C. Making the Perceptual Shift

Essentially there are two basic feelings – love and fear. All feelings tend to encompass or are connected with one of these two. The perceptual shift moves our point of view from fear to love [Diagram 8]. The deeper our shame, the harder it is for us to make the transition from fear to love. Surrender makes the perceptual shift from fear, resistance, and negativity to the freedom of humility, peace, understanding, and compassion. The insight of this dynamic has blessed my life and many others. It is a conscious, simple, and a reliable way to practice surrender.

How do we make the perceptual shift? First, it is important to be aware that anger and relaxation, negativity and gratitude, find it difficult to exist together in the same heart. Relaxation brought on by mindful, diaphragmatic breathing blows out old air and inhales fresh air. Inhale slowly to the count of four and exhale slowly to the count of four with a gap between inhalation and exhalation. This leads to relaxation. After about five to ten minutes, the heart and pulse slow down and our higher brain center prepares for action.

Repeating the Jesus prayer is helpful, "Lord Jesus Christ, Holy Son of God, have mercy on me." It helps to further relax to focus on someone who loved us, e.g., a parent, teacher, rabbi, priest, friend, etc. Relax in the deep warmth of their love and let it move deeper and open you to presence and self-acceptance. Let the warmth of their love bless and encourage you. When people ask me why this is important, my simple answer is that all love is God's love.

Prayer is the discipline of the moment. When we pray we enter into the presence of God whose name is God-with-us. To pray is to listen attentively to the one who addresses us here and now. When we dare to trust that we are never alone, God is always with us, then we can gradually detach ourselves from the voices that make us guilty or anxious and thus allow ourselves to dwell in the present moment.[2]

–Henri Nouwen

C. Gratitude

Expressing gratitude opens us to love. Gratitude is a portal into the unmanifested. Gratitude frees us from our Ego Addictive False Self. Gratitude opens our hearts to the experience of love which is our true identity. I was shocked when a deeply hurt female cocaine addict said, "Dr. Allen, in the crack house, I have come to realize that the addict who is grateful for one day sober, soon surrenders and moves on to sobriety."

Expressing gratitude for life, family, job etc, frees us to be who we are. Gratitude is the humble acceptance and acknowledgement of God's love for us. Surrender prevents complaining and empowers us to act positively with gratitude. Without gratitude there is no surrender and our negativity leads to despair and frustration. Even if we are successful in addressing the problem, we are left empty, unsettled, and looking for the next problem because our consciousness is identified with thought and problem solving.

It may also help to visualize a place or space in which we feel safe, still, loved, and at peace. For me it is a quiet beach in the Bahamas, for you it may be a mountain or national park, etc. As these experiences come together, we automatically find ourselves making the perceptual shift from fear to the love and peace of surrender.

D. Humility

Humility is a prerequisite for surrender. But it is also the result of surrender. Surrender is only possible if there is an intentional desire to be humble. Humility is opening up to accept who we are and not who we wish to be, acknowledging where we are and not where we wish to be. The Ego Addictive False Self with its self-absorption, high experience seeking tendencies, and pride (control and arrogance), defends against our deepest hurt or shame. It blocks us from experiencing who we are (true self), it catapults us into a defensive retinue of wishful illusion of being anything but who we actually are.

The road to humility is strewn with the stones of humiliation. Humiliation drives us to humility and opens us to surrender. Waves of humility usually precede surrender. Sadly, we often have to be broken. I do not say this lightly because much pain is involved.

George was a cocaine addict who was in and out of trouble. Arrogant, difficult, and abusive to staff, he did not take his treatment seriously. One Friday afternoon, George rushed into the clinic. Unkempt, dirty, broken, and shamed, he cried out, "I get it. I am killing myself. Please, help me!"

Upon entering treatment, George was a different person. Working his program, George did very well and he never looked back. He has been clean for over twenty years; he is married and has a successful business. Humbled and broken, George reached bottom. He came to a place where his only choice was to surrender.

E. Letting Go

Change is an external phenomenon, a situational shift, e.g., moving from house A to house B. Transition, on the other hand, is an internal phenomenon that takes place in our hearts. We may make the physical change from house A to house B, but in transition it is possible for our heart to still be at house A. In transition we have to let go of how things used to be and take hold on the way they are. In between letting go and taking hold again, there is a chaotic but potentially creative neutral zone where things are not the old or new way.

We do not usually resist change because change just happens. We resist transition because it is emotional and slow moving. Resisting transition occurs because we find it hard to let go of that part of our heart which is embedded in how things used to be. Transition takes longer than change and requires letting go of negativity, resistance, and fear. It lingers in the neutral zone until a replacement reality forms. The letting go of transition involves *disengagement*, *disidentification*, *disenchantment*, and *disorientation*.

1. Disengagement

Disengagement means giving up the old reality to open to the new, breaking away from former roles and activities. Psychological disengagement is particularly difficult because human beings are adaptive and we find it hard to say goodbye. When we do say goodbye, it is fraught with sadness, anger, resistance, regret, and obstinacies. But if we cannot say goodbye, it is hard to say hello.

2. Disidentification

Disidentification is difficult. It means letting go of that part of us embedded in the old way. Disidentification leaves us with many painful feelings because a piece of our old self, our heart, is left behind. It sometimes takes years to release it. It takes time for a new identity to develop. The process is slow and often chaotic. But no transition is complete until our identity is fully in the new paradigm.

3. Disenchantment

Letting go means giving up the blessings and nurture that we received from the old way. This is hard because human beings are creatures of habit. It is hard to give up what has blessed and nurtured us. We have to let go of the old reality with its assumption, e.g., "this relationship is for life" or "my health will last forever." As strange as it seems, we all tend to have our illusions of permanence. Change and transition mean we have to leave the old reality and open to the formation of the new.

4. Disorientation

Having disengaged, given up our identity, and let go of past enchantments, we find ourselves disorientated. Our actions are detached leaving us confused and insecure. This leads us to a zone of chaos. The zone of chaos is painful. But if we can be creative, we move into the new paradigm. As the process of transition progresses, the zone of chaos decreases. Sadly, this zone of chaos discourages many persons and they never move into transition.

Transition is like a trapeze artist waiting for the new baton. To grasp the new baton he has to let go and be suspended in midair for a few seconds. Only then can the acrobat grasp the new baton. If we do not have the faith to let go, we are condemned to the old reality. Surrender requires the patience, faith, and time to not only go through change, but the more difficult process of transition.

John's Fight to Surrender

John was an alcoholic who became violent when he drank. It sometimes took up to ten policemen to hold him down. The police often had to lock him up. Upon release, he would do more of the same. One day when he was drunk, he attacked his mother and was committed to a State Hospital.

In a dark corner of his room, he saw the pain and suffering of the people around him. John felt ashamed of his behavior. He sobered up and came to his senses. John said that as he thought about his life, all he could see was shame, darkness, and destruction. Overwhelmed and afraid, John prayed and promised that if he ever got out, he would stop drinking alcohol and would change his life.

John attended individual and group therapy and AA regularly. For awhile it looked like he had turned his life around. Unfortunately, after being sober for six months, he relapsed again around Christmas. He fought against the deep shame with its negative thoughts and voices and persisted in group therapy and AA. Sober, but restless, John's life was dull and empty. John was miserable. Worst of all, the shame voices were vicious, "Nobody trusts you." "You know you are a failure." "You can't make it."

John berated and beat himself with the shame whip and hung on the shame cross for the painful memories of hurting so many people. He was driven back to alcohol – his shame behavior. It seemed hopeless, but John began attending contemplative prayer each Sunday. John told us he was fed up because he had made a mess of his life.

Through contemplative prayer and AA, John became sober. Miserable and tormented by his shame, John said, "I finally get it, I have to surrender." Sitting in the silence and healing of contemplative prayer, John let go of his past and his fear of the future and surrendered to God's love. John said surrender is a decision he has to make hour by hour and day by day. Sober for over five years, he said, "I have seen hell and I do not want to go back."

John has surrendered his shame and fear and along with attending his AA group, he is an ardent participant in our contemplative prayer group. Whenever I am late or missing, John chastises me saying that I should know better. He has taught me that my life, too, is unmanageable and I need a power greater than myself. Like John, many of us have come home late to the love of God, but it is never too late to surrender.

> How late I am to love you, O beauty so ancient and so fresh, how late I came to love you! You were within me, while I had gone outside to seek you. Unlovely myself, I rushed towards all those lovely things you had made. And always you were with me, and I was not with you... You called, you cried, you shattered my deafness. You sparkled, you blazed, you drove away my blindness. You shed your fragrance, and I drew in my breath, and I pant for you. I tasted and I now hunger and thirst. You touched me, and I now burn with longing for your peace.
>
> —St. Augustine
> *Confessions*, Book 10:22

CHAPTER 7

Ecce Homo: Behold the Man

Because of the tender mercy of our God, by which the rising sun will come to us from heaven to shine on those living in darkness and in the shadow of death, to guide our feet into the path of peace.
— Luke 1:78-79

*E*cce Homo is the Latin phrase used by Pontius Pilot in the Vulgate translation of John 19:5. He utters them shortly before his crucifixion when he presents Christ to a hostile crowd, wearing the crown of thorns, The King James Version translates the phrase: "Behold the man".

Ecce Homo: Unto Us a Child is Born

It was an ordinary Thursday morning, all seemed calm and peaceful. My cell phone rang and on the other end was my niece Jewel who worked closely with me in community outreach. An attorney by training, Jewel has a deep empathic connection with people who suffer. Jewel said that during the early morning hours a family had been robbed at gun point. Because the family was poor and had no money, the bandits grabbed the one-month-old baby and held the child for some form of ransom. The father jumped the assailants to rescue the child, but was shot dead in the process. The father had sacrificed his life for his child.

Jewel and I arrived on the scene a few hours later. All was calm, but the blood was still on the floor. The mother explained what happened while the baby lay sound asleep. We gazed intently at the baby's face radiating harmonious epiphanies that struck deeply in our hearts. We were mesmerized by the beauty, peace, and innocence of the baby's face and could not help but see the father as a Christ figure who sacrificed his life for his child.

Throughout history many individuals in war and peace have sacrificed their lives to create hope and provide a better life for others. We must learn to be grateful for those who made the way for us. The story of Jesus is one of sacrificial giving to liberate us from the shackles of shame.

> For you know the grace of our
> Lord Jesus Christ, even though he
> Was not shame prone, he became
> Of no repute (ashamed) so that we could be
> Free from shame. —Author's paraphrase Phil. 2:5-8

For unto Us a Child is Born

Watching the little baby sleeping so peacefully, I found myself focusing on the birth of the baby Jesus.

> For to us a child is born,
> To us a son is given,
> And the government shall be upon his shoulders.
> And he will be called
> Wonderful counselor, mighty God,
> Everlasting Father, Prince of Peace —Isa. 9:6

The scene changes to the hills of Bethlehem where shepherds, the victims of institutional shame, tended their flocks at night. Disenfranchised and ostracized by society, shepherds earned a meager living. It was to these shame-prone persons that the angels announced:

> Do not be afraid. I bring you good news
> Of great joy that will be for all the people.

Today in the town of David a Savior
Has been born to you; he is Christ the Lord.
—Luke 2:10-11

A great company of the heavenly host appeared and affirmed the message praising God and saying:

Glory to God in the highest, and
On earth peace to men
On whom his favor rests. —Luke 2:14

The annunciation of the birth of Christ is a perceptual shift from fear to love. All feelings can be reduced to fear and shame or love and compassion. The message of Christmas is to let go of fear and shame and open up to love and compassion. The angels' words have offered hope and encouragement for shame-based human beings throughout the years. T.S. Eliot's "The Journey of the Magi" reminisces on the meaning of Christ's birth.

This set down
This: were we led all that way for
Birth or Death? There was a Birth, certainly,
We had evidence and no doubt. I had seen birth and death,
But had thought they were different; this Birth was
Hard and bitter agony for us, like Death, our death.
We returned to our places, these kingdoms,
But no longer at ease here, in the old dispensation,
With an alien people clutching their gods.
I should be glad of another death.

Poet William Wadsworth Longfellow of Cambridge, Massachusetts, lost his wife in a fire at their home in 1861. The Civil War started shortly after that tragedy and his son was badly wounded in the battle of the Potomac. Longfellow traveled to Washington, D.C. to take his son home where he eventually succumbed to his injuries.

Christmas in Cambridge was always bright and beautiful with the ringing of church bells and the laughter of children in the Longfellow home. But the fire, the tragic loss of his wife, the Civil War, and the death of his son left a gaping wound in the Longfellow home destroying the joy and meaning of Christmas.

Years later, on Christmas day, while sitting in his study, Longfellow heard the ringing of the Christmas bells and found himself writing a now familiar Christmas carol.

> I heard the bells on Christmas Day
> Their old, familiar carols play,
> And wild and sweet
> The words repeat
> Of peace our earth, good will to men!

Describing the Civil War he continues:

> Then from each black, accursed mouth
> The canon thundered in the south,
> And with the sound
> The carols drowned
> Of peace on earth, good will to men!

Bowed down by the shaming pain of despair he continues:

> And in despair I bowed my head;
> "There is no peace on earth" I said:
> "For hate is strong,
> And mocks the song
> Of peace on earth, good will to men!

Then, as if ignited by the holy fire of love, Longfellow is grasped by the revelation of the meaning of Christmas as the perceptual shift from fear to love. As the bells pealed more loudly and deeply, Longfellow wrote:

> Then pealed the bells more loud and deep:
> "God is not dead; nor doth he sleep!
> The Wrong shall fail,
> The Right prevail,
> With peace on earth, good will to men!"

In essence then, the coming of Christ reaffirms the importance of our commitment to love and encourages a deeper spirituality involving the vision and mission of God's love in the world. The reality of the Christmas message was brought home to me in the annual Christmas celebration at Yale Divinity School. The choir processed with lighted in darkness from the chapel along the balcony, down the steps, and into the quad.

In an atmosphere of deep reflection and inspiration, the choir prepared our hearts for the Christmas story told by the now old and distinguished Martin Luther scholar Professor Roland Bainton. Small in stature and weak with age, Professor Bainton shared the Christmas story with great gusto and conviction.

He described Mary as a poor peasant girl with little to look forward to in life, Professor Bainton said she was chosen to be involved in the battle of the spheres. The armies of the Evil One were lined up for battle awaiting the arrival of some great warrior from heaven with an army of trained soldiers to establish God's kingdom on earth.

With a twinkle in his eye, Bainton said, "To the Devil's surprise, God dropped on him a little baby." How do you fight a baby? Leaning forward he said, "This is a mystery. And don't forget that at Christmas, great things often come in small packages."

With sober voice and deep reverence the good professor continued, "The Son of God came to earth as a weak little baby, fragile and helpless, but forever giving hope to the oppressed, the small, the weak, and hurting parts of ourselves. He ended his lecture with the exclamation, "Great is the mystery of Godliness!"

The Journey

The life of Christ is the journey toward the healing of our shame and hurt as foretold by the prophet Isaiah:

> He was despised and rejected by men,
> A man of sorrows, and familiar with suffering.
> Like one from whom men hide their faces
> He was despised, and we esteemed him not.
> Surely he took up or infirmities
> And carried our sorrows,
> Yet we considered him stricken by God,
> Smitten by him, and afflicted.
> But he was pierced for our transgressions,
> He was crushed for our iniquities;
> The punishment that brought us peace was upon him
> And by his wounds we are healed. —Isa. 53:3-5

Dante captured it well when he said, "His will, our peace." Throughout his earthly journey, Christ's life was punctuated with intimations of death and sacrifice. John the Baptist exclaimed at the beginning of Christ's ministry, "Behold the Lamb of God which takes away the sin of the world" (Jn. 1:35).

Challenging the Establishment

It was the Sabbath, a time to worship God and rest from work. The religious elite were gathered as usual in the synagogue and seated in their respective places of eminence with pride and confidence in their religious traditions and beliefs. Shocked by Christ's claim to be the Son of God and his teaching that the Sabbath was made for human beings and not human beings for the Sabbath, the religious leaders plotted to entrap him as a heretic.

Entering the synagogue, our Lord was confronted by a man with a withered or injured hand. Tradition has it that the man was a carpenter and was injured at work and was unable to provide for his family. Hearing of Jesus' reputation as a healer of the poor and the dejected, the man came to the synagogue to worship God hoping against hope that he would be healed. The scene was set and the face off began with the religious leaders questioning in their minds whether Jesus would respect their religious tradition. Would he refrain from healing on the Sabbath or disrespect their ancient traditions?

Facing the same challenges in our daily experiences, we should question whether our religious practices are an end in themselves or means to faithful service to God. In the midst of the hustle and bustle of life, it is so easy to make an idol of our faith and forget, in the closing words of the film *Ushpizin*, "There is God and there is only God."

Jesus paused, recognized that he was being tested, and asked the man to stand up in front of the synagogue. Challenging his detractors, Jesus asked, "Which is lawful on the Sabbath: to do good or to do evil, to save life or to kill?" (Mark 3:4).

In deafening silence, pregnant with retreat, anxiety, and uncertainty, our Lord waited. He was deeply upset by their rigidity, callous indifference, and lack of compassion for a physically disabled man who was financially ruined. Our Lord's actions and words stood in stark contrast to the cold inaction and sterile, self-serving faith of the religious leaders. But it did not end there as Jesus commanded the man to stretch out his hand. The man obeyed and his hand was healed. What a change this was for the man and his family. As C. S. Lewis would say, he was "surprised by joy".

Jesus shamed the self-righteous religious elite by breaking their precious tradition. They were deeply shamed and felt abandoned, rejected, and humiliated. Moved by their shame to the point of hating Christ, they turned to destructive violence and determined among themselves that Jesus must die. They feared that his influence over the crowds would make him too powerful and would destroy all of their traditions and privileged status in society. As the culture of death and destruction appears as it does in each generation, the paschal mystery unfolds – Christ's passion begins in earnest.

Powerful and highly destructive, shame is the opposite of compassion. The deeper the shame core, the deeper the lack of compassion for ourselves and others. Compassion is not just a feeling. It is being pricked so deeply by the pain of another that we are propelled into action to meet their needs. In compassion there is no *other*. If you hurt, I hurt. If I hurt, you hurt. Our compassion can only be as deep as our love. Love without compassion is sentimentality and the acid test of love is compassion for one's neighbor, for community.

Ecce Homo: The Last Supper

The journey continues and we find our Lord at the Last Supper, that great feast of termination. In psychotherapy, termination is a very important part of the therapy because our mixed feelings of sadness, joy, and relief prepare us to hear messages of life-changing wisdom.

Guy Sottile, a well-known Italian evangelist told me an apocryphal story about Leonardo da Vinci that I will never forget. According to Sottile, da Vinci took about twenty years to paint the now famous painting of the Last Supper which was recently restored to its excellence and beauty in Milan. The painting took so long to complete because the artist Leonardo could not find a model for Judas. Walking along the streets of Milan after some twenty years and wanting to complete the painting, he came across a man who appeared hard, cruel, and evil. Maestro Leonardo felt the man would be an excellent model for Judas. Approaching the man he said, "Sir, would you consider being a model for Judas in my painting of the Last Supper?" The man replied, "Maestro, don't you remember me? Don't you know who I am? Twenty years and a lifetime ago you chose me as your model for Jesus."

The Last Supper is a powerful demonstration of compassion as our Lord says goodbye to his disciples before his crucifixion (John 13-17). The Last Supper illustrates eight qualities which help guide us in our spiritual journey toward authenticity: *love, communion, resistance, humility, simplicity, service, transcendence,* and *remembrance.*

A. Love

The Last Supper draws its intimacy from Jesus' expressions of love as he experienced them from the Father. Declaring his deep love for them, Jesus said to his disciples, "As the Father has loved me, so have I loved you" (John 15:9). Intimacy emanates from love and our Lord reminds us that his love reaches out to us at the most despairing and difficult points of life. This is especially meaningful because it challenges us to seek to live a life of love:

> Many waters cannot quench love;
> rivers cannot wash it away.
> If one were to give
> all the wealth of his house for love,
> it would be utterly scorned. —Song 8:7

Regardless of how much we may have failed, how far we have fallen or how much we feel like outcasts, Jesus reminds us that we are the *beloved of God*. Opening to the deep love of God melts away our false self and our shame and restores the true meaning of our identity in God. Our small *i* is swallowed up by the great *I Am*. As a result, we live in God and he lives in us.

The love of God begins, maintains, and completes the spiritual journey. According to Fr. Henri Nouwen, the journey involves three basic movements: *loneliness to solitude, hostility to hospitality*, and *illusion to prayer*. Each word represents a pole to which we are attracted. These three sets of poles are each a continuum along which we make our spiritual journey.[1]

1. Loneliness to Solitude

The journey from *loneliness to solitude* involves opening our hearts to the Love that never lets us go and the Face which never turns away. Loneliness is increasing in our culture. Studies show that all of us have fewer intimate relationships to share the deep feelings of our hearts than just ten years ago. Loneliness destroys community and leads us to the impersonal crowd.

In solitude we are alone with the *Alone*. Speaking of this, David says, "My soul waits in silence for you and you alone" (Ps. 62:1). Isaiah opens us to the victory of solitude, "Fear thou not, for I am with thee. Be not dismayed for I am thy God" (Isa. 41:10 KJV). Nurtured in solitude, we are prepared for community.

2. Hostility to Hospitality

Our underlying shame core periodically erupts into anger. We are often the object of our own anger. Anger is either internalized or projected onto others. It is in solitude that we are healed and lovingly moved from *hostility to hospitality*. Sadly, we often nurture our hostility leaving no space for the expression of the true self. Even where we are...*we* are what is missing! Emptying our hearts of hurt, fear, and anger is a grieving process that opens the door to intimacy. Jesus said, "Blessed are those who mourn, for they will be comforted" (Matt. 5:4).

Because of our losses, many of us live at the hostility pole which halts our spiritual journey. Anger or hostility may empower us temporarily, but it blocks us from opening the doors of our hearts to the love around us. On the other hand, if we could grieve our losses, we would open to a deeper love than we have ever known before. As a result, our hearts would overflow with love and hospitality instead of being incubators for anger and hostility.

3. Illusion to Prayer

The third movement of the spiritual life is from *illusion to prayer*. Stuck in the illusion of our false selves, we drown in selfishness or narcissism. We become attached to our possessions, bow to our idolatries, gratify our consumerism, and yield to our addictions. Hearts open to God's love melt away the illusions of the false self and shame allowing us to experience our true identity as the *beloved of God*. The true self exists only in God and it is there that we live in the awareness of the presence of God. God is love and he loves us to the uttermost. Love is the antidote of shame that makes us lovable and loving. "We love [God] because he first loved us" (I John 4:19).

God's love, our first love, is eternal, unconditional, and redemptive. It anchors us in the kingdom of God. All other loves are temporary, conditional, often disappointing. Secondary loves set us adrift in a temporal sea of illusory perspective. The true self cannot live outside the presence of God's love. Even so, we readily leave his presence and live out of the false self trapped in busy schedules and urgent time pressures without the awareness of his love. "Holy, holy, holy is the LORD Almighty; the whole earth is full of his glory [presence]" (Isa. 6:3).

B. Communion

The disciples were having a time of communion, intimacy, deep fellowship. The spiritual journey at its heart is really all about communion with God, others, the world around us, and with ourselves. The essence of the gospel is that God loves us and is always seeking communion with us. He is always reaching out to us. He comes to us through nature, a beautiful sunset or sunrise; he reaches out to us through animals, a dog that shows us unconditional love; he touches us through a child's face where you can sometimes see the face of an angel.

Sadly, because of the hurt in our hearts, we often miss him. We just do not trust love anymore because where we expected love in our home, family, or marriage, we received pain. So, we have closed the shutters of our lives to block out the pain of our woundedness. Unfortunately, whenever we close the shutters to block the view of the garbage, we also block out the gladioli, magnolias, and the beautiful bougainvillea. Unless we are vulnerable, we will miss the sweet communion with the love that seeks us saying: "Here I am! I stand at the door and knock. If anyone hears my voice and opens the door, I will come in and eat with him, and he with me" (Rev. 3:20).

Communion with God will always involve silence, "Be still and know that I am God" (Ps. 46:10). Opening ourselves to interior silence creates stillness and in stillness we sit and dine at the table set for two: "You prepare a table before me in the presence of my enemies" (Ps. 23:5).

Experiencing communion with God in silence is a discipline, a learning experience. David said, "I have stilled and quieted my soul.... Like a weaned child is my soul within me" (Ps. 131:2). In the silence of contemplation, we open ourselves to the naked love of God's presence which bathes our souls and creates the deepest form of intimacy and communion. That communion is enhanced by gratitude. When we are grateful, we give our deepest self. Gratitude is an appreciation that we are the *beloved of God.*

C. Resistance

All was not well in the beautiful Passover setting of the Last Supper. Judas was planning to betray the Son of God and sabotage his own life. There is always a Judas and often the Judas is us. Shame involves hurt and anger in our hearts. It makes us our own worst enemies as we are betrayed by self-sabotage.

Shame, **S**elf **H**atred **A**imed at **ME**, is self-destructive. Self-destruction is one of the most common ways that we create distance in our lives while at the same time destroying intimacy with God, others, and ourselves. Countering this, Jesus admonishes us to love our enemies (Luke 6:35). It is God's love that breaks down our resistance to intimacy. It allows us to face the hardened parts of our hearts and experience the deep healing of God's love.

Resistance is usually associated with, if not caused by, anger. Much anger comes from the effect repressed childhood trauma presenting itself in our adult lives. It may, of course, be provoked, but a person can only provoke the anger that is already in our hearts. As painful as it may seem, anger is a cry from the heart calling us to come home to ourselves. Working through the hurt and anger in our hearts opens us to the deep love of God.

D. Humility

Humility is the building block of spirituality and the enemy of shame. It always leads to intimacy. Humility is facing the truth about who we are, learning to accept ourselves as we are, not as we would like to be or should be. The road to humility is paved with multiple humiliations. Recognizing the magnificence and holiness of God is more sincerely humbling than focusing on the degradation we have suffered. Taking off his outer garment, our Lord put on the garment of a slave to serve his disciples by washing their feet. When we open to God's love, God exposes our prejudices, superior attitudes, competitive jealousies, and alienating tendencies. We have to be willing to let them go.

Derived from the Latin root *humus* meaning soil, humility implies a preparing of the soil of our hearts to grow the seeds of God's love in our lives. If we allow our hearts to harden, it is difficult for the seeds of love to grow. This unplowed ground must be tilled by working through the painful hurts and experiences of anger that so often characterize our deep inner selves. Opening our hearts to the presence of God creates fertile ground for the seeds of love to prosper.

E. Simplicity

Our Lord took a basin of water to wash his disciples' feet. At its heart, life is simple. A lady dying of cancer said to me, "Dying is so easy, no long sermons, not much food to eat, no bills to pay, just waiting for it to happen." But then, after being healed, she became vulnerable to the powerful consumerism surrounding our lives. She had increasing bills, bought a house, and said, "I wish I could live in health as I lived when I was dying." I will never forget her summary of life. Looking me straight in the face she said,

"David, at its heart, life is very simple, but we spend so much of our life making it complex."

Shame complicates life. In shame, we live beyond our means, work too hard, make poor choices, and do not exercise. As our lives become more and more complex, it becomes more difficult for us to be aware of the presence of God's love. The basin of water is a very powerful picture of simplicity. Parents must not forget that our children want us for ourselves, not for what we can give them. Similarly, people seek us for connection and being, not necessarily for what they can get from us.

Simplifying our lives in this very complex society is easier said than done. But if we are to make the journey without shame, we have to travel lighter. This requires making some very hard choices. The opportunities to simplify our lives seem to occur at specific times. If we do not take advantage of these opportunities, we may find ourselves experiencing an even greater sense of complexity.

Nothing is more painful than recognizing that we are caught up in the vortex of the hustle and bustle of life. We run around in circles to defend against our shame without the time or space to be present to ourselves or to God. Sadly, we all have experienced this reality pushing us further away from God, the figure and ground of our being.

F. Service

Dressed as a servant, our Lord bowed and washed his disciples' feet. What a paradox, the almighty and holy God washing the feet of ordinary, lowly human beings. This and this alone is God's love, providing a beautiful picture of intimacy. Though the Lord God is high and mighty, his love is always bent towards those who are humble and contrite. This foot washing demonstrates the love which never fails us. It is a love which reminds us that Christ still washes our feet by sending us friends to encourage us, children to admire us, and spouses to love us.

The story does not end there because when Jesus came to wash Peter's feet, Peter objected. Jesus, in a very simple but kind way, told Peter that if he refused to let him wash his feet, he could not belong to Christ. Many of us with our functional attachment disorders are very good at giving love, but have a very hard time receiving it. Deep spirituality is not just giving love. It is a deep appreciation of receiving love. It says sincerely from our hearts, "I appreciate you." What a revolution would occur if we learned to express gratitude and appreciation more freely to our children, spouses, and those who work with us. Thankfulness has a way of cleansing the air and creating a loving, open community.

Coming to Judas, we can imagine that Christ looked into his eyes and spoke inaudibly, "Judas, you don't need to do this. Even now we can work this out." But oh, the hardness of the human heart! When the false self forms onion-like layers around the heart, the shame triangle of abandonment, rejection, and humiliation becomes so deeply intractable that our hearts become like stone. Even though love may be very close, staring us in the face, shame makes it very difficult to open our hearts to receive it.

We do not have to live this self-destructive way. We can stop and change. I believe Jesus washed Judas' feet most carefully of all. This is a very powerful lesson that teaches us a love that is more than just getting along with those who appreciate us. In a very deep sense, it means moving toward those who abuse or reject us.

To love as he loves, we have to walk in hard places, our feet blistered and bleeding. We need to wash each other's feet. This may mean speaking a kind word, giving an encouraging hug, writing a letter, or making a phone call. As Jesus said, "Now that I, your Lord and Teacher, have washed your feet, you also should wash one another's feet" (John 13:14).

G. Transcendence and Immanence

Jesus told his disciples that he was going away, but that when they received each other they were receiving him. How important it is in our spiritual journey to recognize that Jesus often comes to us in other people. Shame prevents us from recognizing the visitation of Christ in others. Only when we transcend our shame can we see Christ in the people around us. Christ is in our midst in spite of all our hurt and pain. He is the immanent reality that blesses and renews us. What would happen today if we could see our own children as the Christ child? What if we could see our wives as Jesus? What would happen today if we could see our husbands or our best friends as Jesus coming to us and saying, "I want to love you"?

If this happens, something will change in our ability to be open to intimacy. Jesus is the lover who always seeks the beloved, he always comes for us. The tragedy is that because of the busyness in our lives, the fatigue in our hearts, and the resistance in our minds, we are often unaware of his presence. This is why we say, "Stop and smell the roses." A rose is a statement from God, blooming and booming in his loving voice that we are loved. As we open our hearts to the transcendent and imminent presence of God, we begin to see his presence in everything around us. He is in the roses, children, friends, lovers, and all of life. The ordinary becomes the bearer of the extraordinary.

H. Remembrance

Human beings are prone to forgetfulness. Not that we intend to forget, but with all of the stresses and strains of modern life, it is difficult to remain focused. Our internal shame core with the accumulated hurt from our ancestral heritage and personal experience covers or occludes much of the positive in life. We are then left to feast on only the negative. Negative thoughts produce a paralyzing internal addictive dialogue that distracts us from our true essence. As a result, we forget many a hard earned victory, beautiful experiences, and serendipitous moments of life.

Before going to his crucifixion, our Lord bids his disciples goodbye. He recognizes our human tendency to forget and so he institutes a special feast of remembrance. Frederick Buechner suggests Jesus saying by this act:

> When you remember me it means you have carried something of who I am with you, that I have left some mark of who I am on who you are. It means that you can summon me back to your mind even though countless years and miles may stand between us. It means that if we meet again, you will know me. It means that even after I die, you can still see my face and hear my voice and speak to me in your heart.[2]

Our Lord took the bread, blessed it and said, "This is my body which is broken for you" (1 Cor. 11:24 KJV). Then Jesus took the cup of wine and, to paraphrase his words, said, "This is my blood shed for the healing of the human heart." In this simple, but profoundly transcendent space-time moment, the mystery of the Eucharist was instituted. My professional experience of the deep shame of addicts in the culture of death and destruction in the world of crack cocaine has called me to a new simplicity. My only hope of living with the pain of the daily tragedy is the simple mystery of Christ coming to me, to us, to the world in the sacrament of the Eucharist.

A Sacrament is when something holy happens. It is transparent time, time which you can see through to something deep inside time...at such milestone moments as seeing a baby baptized or being baptized yourself, confessing your sins, getting married, dying, you are apt to catch a glimpse of the almost unbearable preciousness and mystery of life.

Needless to say, church is not the only place where the holy happens. Sacramental moments can occur at any moment, at any place and to anybody. Watching something get born. Making love. A walk on the beach. Somebody coming to see you when you're sick. A meal with people you love. Looking into a stranger's eyes and finding out he's not a stranger.

If we weren't blind as bats we might see life itself is sacramental.[3]

—Frederick Buechner

Thomas Merton maintained that Christ lives and acts in men by faith and by the sacrament of faith. For in his most holy sacrament, Jesus Christ himself is truly and substantially present. The blessed Eucharist is therefore the very heart of Christianity. It contains Christ himself in the mystery uniting with us in one body.

The Eucharist is our reminder of the perceptual shift God made on our behalf at Calvary. It was there that he delivered us from the shame of death and destruction. In its place we experience mystical union with our Lord and all his saints. In spite of ever-present death, the Eucharist teaches us that life is full of epiphanies of resurrection. The Eucharist is a prophetic witness to the bright hope of the future beyond this life. Our Lord said, "I tell you the truth, I will not drink again of the fruit of the vine until that day when I drink it anew in the kingdom of God" (Mark 14:25).

Ecce Homo: The Last Seven Words

The seven last words of Christ on the cross reflect the pathos, meaning, and hope of human life. As described earlier, shame, <u>S</u>elf <u>H</u>atred <u>A</u>imed at <u>ME</u>, is universal and strides like a colossus across the human heart. As the deep hurt and shame grows, our self-hatred invites the hatred of others. Shame produces a severe loneliness in which our pain is magnified and our perception of help is minimized as we walk into the darkness.

Eventually, the vertical pole of our self-hatred is intersected by the horizontal pole of our hatred and distrust of others producing the shame cross [Diagram 3]. Left to ourselves, we erect our own shame crosses and hanging ourselves on it. W.H. Auden says, "We prefer to be ruined, rather than changed!"

Our Lord had neither a shame core nor a hurt trail of abandonment, rejection, and humiliation. Yet when he bore our shame on the cross, he was abandoned by his followers, rejected as the Messiah, and publicly humiliated.

Shame as the *Master Emotion* underlying all sin is found in Isaiah's portrait of our Lord:

> He was wounded for our shame
> He was bruised for our inadequacy
> The punishment of our peace
> Was upon Him
> And by His suffering we are transformed.
> —Author's paraphrase Isa. 53:5

The cross is not a sentimental answer to human pain. It is mystery and in all our understanding we cannot fathom the depth of its meaning and healing. Love is the underside of shame, and the cross, in all its suffering, is that deep expression of love which is the antidote to shame.

The First Word - Luke 23:34

Father, forgive them for do not know what they are doing.

In the Lord's Prayer, Jesus taught his disciples that God's forgiveness of us is related to us forgiving others. In his pain and agony, Jesus asked his Father to forgive his persecutors. Forgiveness is the only process in life that can reach back into time and heal a wound from events which cannot be changed. As shame-prone persons, we need to forgive ourselves and those who hurt us. Forgiveness releases the prisoner from his cell. The prisoner is us!

Our Lord said, "Forgive them for they do not know what they are doing." Ignorance is not an excuse for cruelty, but many of our deepest wounds are inflicted by people who said or did things in ignorance. The release or elimination of our shame requires forgiveness.

"Forgiveness" is a poem written at a psychotherapy conference. Richard U. Rosenfeld describes forgiveness freeing us from the doubt that lies buried in the soul:

> And there I will languish
> Unless...unless...unless
> I seek forgiveness
> Not mere platitudes

> But soul-searching, gut wrenching acknowledgement
> That I am a prisoner in my own house
> You are not the enemy
> The enemy is the doubt I harbor about my worth
> Which lies buried in my bosom
> At the very core of my soul
> I have given you the most precious gift I have
> My own healing power
> And it is painful to realize
> That this gift belongs to no one else
> It is mine!

One of the defining characteristics of liberation from the pain of shame is the courage to forgive. Forgiveness is a process, not an isolated event. Forgiveness is not forgetting, it is disconnecting from our shame experiences. Through forgiveness our shame experiences come to consciousness, leaving what were shame-producing memories as mere empty shells devoid of painful feelings.

The Second Word – John 19:26, 27

Woman, here is your son; and...here is your mother.

There is no more piercing pain in a mother's heart than the tortured death of her child. Mary, the Blessed Virgin, chosen to give birth to the Son of God, was a person of deep thought and contemplation: "Mary treasured up all these things and pondered them in her heart" (Luke 2:19).

We can only imagine the wrenching pain and terrifying agony portrayed in Mary's face as her Son hung on the cross. Michelangelo helps us grasp the deep pathos and suffering of Mary as she holds her lifeless Son after the crucifixion in his famous sculpture *La Pieta*. Pain makes us self-absorbed and turns us in upon ourselves and away from others. In contrast, our Lord's love for his mother was deeply internalized and transcended his pain.

Jesus invited his mother into the reality and pathos of his suffering. He recognized the depth and pain of her suffering. He asked the disciple John to take his mother into his home and care for her. In the depth of his own suffering, Jesus reached out in compassion and empathy to his dear mother. In doing so he offered love to us all.

My lover is mine and I am His; He browses among the lilies, until the day breaks and the shadows flee, for love is as strong as death, many waters cannot quench love.
—Song 2:16, 17, 8:6, 7

The Third Word – Luke 23:43

I tell you the truth, today you will be with me in paradise.

Jesus was crucified between two thieves. Sneering at Jesus from the shame of pride and arrogance, one of the thieves challenged our Lord to do a miracle and save them all. The other thief, speaking from his brokenness, said, "Lord, remember me when you come into your kingdom." It was to the latter that our Lord said the profound and comforting words "Today you will be with me in paradise."

The word *paradise* is Persian and means *walled garden*.[5] When a Persian king honored his subjects, he chose them to walk in the garden with him as companions. Our Lord offered the penitent thief more than immortality; he promised him the honor of being his companion in the Garden of the Courts of Heaven.

As he was dying, our Lord revealed that there is an arena beyond this life. Life after death does not depend on what we have done, but on whether we humbly open our hearts in love with the words too deep for explanation, "Lord, remember me." Representing the two sides of our heart, the two thieves embodied shame and fear on one hand and love and humility on the other. Which side of our heart is victorious depends on which side we choose to feed.

We often die how we live. If we feed shame and fear, we become hardened in the self-limiting prison of arrogance and pride. Conversely, if we make the perceptual shift to surrender in humility and love, we experience the *eternal sunrise*. We can choose love as long as our hearts beat. A poet told of a man who was thrown from his horse and died:

> Betwixt the stirrup and the ground
> Mercy I asked, mercy I found.

Yeats describes humans as "dying animals attached to desire," but we can say with Paul: "Where O death, is your victory? Where, O death, is your sting?" (I Cor. 15:55).

The Fourth Word – Mt. 27:46

Eloi, Eloi, lama sabachthani.

"My God, my God, why have you forsaken me?" Piercing and gut wrenching, these words reverberate in the deepest part of the soul. We can all attest to times when heaven was silent and the words of even the most faithful person seemed irrelevant. But our hope and comfort is that our Lord identifies with our dark night of God's absence. He experienced the shame triangle of abandonment, rejection, and humiliation, he gives us courage to face our own shame when our faith runs dry and help eludes us. Walking our hurt trail and bearing our shame, our Lord gives us the courage to make the perceptual shift, to live in love.

Here we must be silent because we face a mystery too deep for words. His ultimate sacrifice for our sin and shame separated Jesus from God the Father with whom he had always been one. This is the cup our Lord asked to avoid in the agony of the garden. Then, in commitment to our broken hearts and shame-based lives, he said, "Not my will, but your will be done." Healing requires that we let go of our distractions, addictions, and compulsions. Only then can we turn our hearts, minds, and lives towards him.

The Fifth Word – John 19:28

I thirst.

The body is over seventy percent water and without water, life is impossible. Arid and dry are synonymous with thirst and emptiness. The Holy Spirit is the water of life and Jesus promised that if we trust him, our hearts will overflow with living water. But on the cross, rejected by the very Holy Spirit who united him with his Father, the eternal well is dry and Christ cries, "I thirst."

So often the Christ in us thirsts because of our rebellion and disobedience and we give him sour vinegar to drink. He has poured out himself for us; we in turn need to open our hearts in praise and thanksgiving, to let his living water flow through us. "As the deer pants for streams of water, so my soul pants for you, O God" (Ps. 42:1).

The Sixth Word – John 19:30

It is finished.

At this cry the temple veil was torn and the work of redemption was complete making the Holiest of Holies accessible to us. Earth is united with heaven and fear dethroned. Love wins and hope springs eternal in our breast as we open to the reality of God's will being done on earth as in heaven.

The Seventh Word – Luke 23:46

Father, into your hands I commit my spirit.

As he died, our Lord committed his Spirit to God. It is comforting to know that when we come to the end of our journey, God receives our spirit. But we must choose to commit. Jesus lived and died in commitment to God. O God, help us to live and die like our Lord. Through his cross and resurrection, you have freed us to both live and die.

Here is the ultimate act of surrender – letting go and letting God. Our Lord is teaching us about life and death. Since death is a part of life, we can only move beyond our shame if we surrender day by day hour to the Love that never lets us go and the Face that never turns away.

Brokenness and Passion in the Seven Last Words

The cross is the symbol of Christ's passion. It is filled with mystery and represents the shame and brokenness of the human condition. Our disjointed lives, wounded hearts, and overwhelmed spirits are awed as we contemplate in silence the passion and brokenness in these seven last words of our Lord. Yet the brokenness of the cross is a portal through which wholeness flows.

> There is a brokenness
> Out of which comes the unbroken.
> A shatteredness out
> Of which blooms the unshatterable,
> There is a sorrow
> Beyond all grief which leads to joy
> And a fragility
> Out of whose depths emerges strength.
>
> There is a hollow space
> Too vast for words
> Through which we pass with each loss,
> Out of whose darkness
> We are sanctioned into being
>
> There is a cry deeper than all sound
> Whose serrated edges cut the heart
> As we break open
> To the place inside which is unbreakable
> And whole,
> While learning to sing[4]
>   –Rashani, "The Unbroken"

Ecce Homo: The Resurrection

The resurrection of Christ completes the sacrificial journey of our Lord to overcome human sin and shame. The resurrection is not a peripheral phenomenon. It is the central point of our Lord's redemptive mission of love to heal the shame of the human condition. As Paul reminds the believers in Corinth:

> If Christ has not been raised, our preaching is useless and so is your faith.... And if Christ has not been raised...you are still in your sin [shame]. If only for this life we have hope in Christ, we are to be pitied more than all men.
> —I Cor. 15:14, 17, 19

Coming full circle, the resurrection fulfills God's promise to Adam and Eve. God foretold in Genesis 3:15 that the seed of the serpent (Satan) will bruise the heel of their seed, but their seed will crush the serpent's head bringing an end to shame, sin, and the culture of death and destruction. Paul explains this theologically: "For as in Adam all die, so in Christ all will be made alive.... The last enemy to be destroyed is death" (I Cor. 15:22, 26).

The victory of the resurrection is poignantly displayed in J.T. Pagliacci's opera *Cavalleria Rusticana*. On Easter Sunday morning the choir is heard singing the "Regina Coeli" in hushed voices. At the sound of the organ, Santuzza, deeply moved, begins to sing a passionate hymn and the people sing along with her.

> Let us sing His praise,
> The Lord is not dead,
> Resplendent, He has spread His wings
> Let us sing His praise,
> The Lord is risen
> And today ascended to the glory of Heaven

With triumphant blessing, Santuzza and the Easter worshipers' voices transport us to another realm reminding us over and over again of the victory of Easter:

> The Lord is not dead
> Let us sing His praise,
> The Lord is risen.

Mary Magdalene and the Resurrection

Nowhere are the significance, power, and witness of the resurrection more clear than through the eyes of Mary Magdalene recorded in John 20:1-18. Before meeting our Lord, Mary Magdalene was full of shame and at war with herself. The Scripture says that she had been delivered of seven demons, yet she was chosen by God to be the first person to see the risen Lord. This was no accident. What principles are found in the account of Mary Magdalene?

Mary was connected. As a follower of Jesus, Mary experienced a deep connection with our Lord who liberated her from the web of shame and destruction. In Christ her Ego Addictive False Self and shame melted away producing deep healing that allowed her to experience her true identity as the *beloved of God.* In *her* story, we see *our* story in the meaning of the resurrection. It is a movement from wounds to worship.

Mary was committed. True connection always leads to deep commitment. Remaining at the cross during the crucifixion, braving the jeers of the Roman soldiers, Mary demonstrated deep love and commitment. Unlike Pilate, Peter, Judas, and so many of us, Mary was no fair weather friend. True to her convictions, her love was real and no fear, danger, or opposition would deter her from that commitment to her Lord.

After the ghastly experience of witnessing the crucifixion, Mary went to the tomb looking for the body of

Jesus despite obvious danger. She went before dawn on the first day of the week. Mary Magdalene demonstrated that our ability to grasp the meaning of the resurrection depends on the depth of our personal commitment.

Mary had a sense of community. To Mary's surprise, the stone at the entrance of the tomb was moved. Excited and afraid, she ran to tell Peter and the other disciples. She was not a loner. She had a sense of community and shared her experience with them.

Community is important in the life of faith. We cannot go it alone. Community supports us and most of all enables us to find guidance in knowing the will of God. The resurrection enhances community, exposes our limitations, vulnerabilities, and woundedness, but it also showers us with grace, understanding, and forgiveness. How can different races get together? How can men and women have long-term relationships? Such unions can only succeed if there is a base for mutual forgiveness and love. We are admonished to forgive each other as God has forgiven us.

Mary was deeply contemplative. Contemplation is a transformation of consciousness with an awareness of God's healing love and a strong commitment to the mission of His love in the world.

> The experience of contemplation is the experience of God's life and presence within ourselves not as object but as the transcendent source of our own subjectivity. Contemplation is a mystery in which God reveals himself to us as the very center of our own most intimate self. When the realization of His presence bursts upon us, our own self disappears in Him and we pass mystically through the Red Sea of separation to lose ourselves [and thus find our true selves] in Him.[7]
>
> —Thomas Merton

She looked through the eyes of love. Mary anxiously told Peter and John what she had found at the tomb. Upon hearing the news, both Peter and John ran to the tomb. John arrived first at the tomb and looked in while Peter charged ahead and found the linen wrappings. John then went inside and found what Peter had seen. The Scriptures said that upon seeing this John believed.

Note that John and Mary Magdalene were the first disciples to believe in the resurrection. These two people were extremely close to Jesus and loved him dearly. Both of them remained at the cross during the crucifixion, risking their lives to be with the one they loved. They were rewarded with the first glimpse of the resurrection.

Love enables us to see with the eyes of the heart. The eyes of love are able to know others beyond physical appearance. St. Francis de Sales wrote long ago, *cor ad cor loquitur,* "heart speaks to heart." Relationship provides an empathic connection allowing us to know the mind and thought of others. Mary and John loved Jesus in a way that gave them that *heart to heart* insight on the interpretation of the meaning of his life, death, and resurrection.

Likewise, the life of faith flows from our relationship with God. Learning to be still quiets us and develops an inner silence that leads to knowing God. In stillness we love God and enjoy him in the midst of life's woundedness.

Mary learned the importance of Scripture. Although the other disciples saw the empty tomb, it was still not clear to them that Christ would rise again. The risen Christ met two disciples on the road to Emmaus and confronted them about their resistance to believing the Scripture.

How foolish you are, and how slow of heart to believe in all that the prophets have spoken! Did not the Christ have to suffer these things and then enter his glory?' And beginning with Moses and all the Prophets, he explained to them what was said in all the Scriptures concerning himself. —Luke 24:25-27

Clearly the Word of God is not optional to the spiritual life; it is an essential building block. For God who has revealed himself in his Son has also revealed himself in his Word. As Jesus said, "Heaven and earth will pass away, but my words will never pass away" (Mark 13:31).

Like we ourselves, the disciples were impeded in their ability to see the reality of the resurrection because they did not believe the Scripture. We live in ignorance and fear because we do not take seriously the discipline of studying and understanding and obeying his Word.

> The law of the LORD is perfect, reviving the soul. The statutes of the LORD are trustworthy, making wise the simple. The percepts of the LORD are right, giving joy to the heart. The commands of the LORD are right, giving light to the eyes. —Ps. 19:7-8

Mary showed persistence. After they had rushed to the tomb and found Jesus' body missing, the disciples returned home. Home is a place of rest, a place where we are sheltered. Home is familiar and sometimes we live in the prison of the familiar. It may seem strange that the disciples simply went home when they were faced with the most shattering event in history, but new happenings can have that effect.

Afraid, unsure, apprehensive, we drift toward the known. How many of us have lost great opportunities or have even turned away from potential greatness because we were unable to leave the prison of the familiar? Home sweet home it may well be, but it may also destroy ambition, reduce risk and encourage a triumphant mediocrity.

The disciples' motives for going home may have been mixed. Since the body of Jesus was missing, they might have feared being blamed and persecuted. Home may have been a meeting place; they may have gone back to let others know what was happening. We do not know.

What we do know is that Mary persisted, she stayed at the tomb. Persistence enhances faith and vice versa. In fact, many times faith just means "keeping on keeping on," "standing firm," or "holding on." As exemplified by Mary, faith means taking the risk of being persistent when others leave us, when our pseudo gods are gone, and we are left alone with the one true God.

Mary was blessed in her mourning. She not only persisted in staying by the tomb – she stood there weeping. As she wept, she kept looking into the tomb. She mourned for her Lord. She missed him. She wanted to be with him. Mourning means crying in our heart for those we love. We are promised that if we seek him, we shall find him. We are told that those who mourn will be comforted (Matt. 5:4) and, sure enough, as Mary mourned, she saw angels. They asked her why she was weeping. She replied, "They have taken away my Lord … and I do not know where they have put him" (John 20:13).

Persistence, faith, and an intense desire for God lead to sight. As someone has said, "Moses saw the burning bush. And the bush still burns, but only those who have eyes can see it." Mary focused on the tomb, unaware of the person standing behind her. The pain of death can be so powerful that the grave becomes our focus. Mary turned and saw a man who asked, "Why are you weeping? Whom are you seeking?" These are poignant questions. Christ confronts the motivation of the heart and questions us about our feelings. He challenges us about what we seek.

Seeking God sometimes means feeling his absence. How often do you cry because of the absence of God?

Yearning for him verifies our relationship with him. After all, how can we miss someone we have never known? She could not believe her eyes. Mary saw a man whom she supposed to be the gardener.

In cognitive development, according to Piaget, a little child develops schema for new experiences. When he sees a dog for the first time, he develops a schema in his brain for dog. It is an animal with a pointed head, four legs, and a tail. A little later the child sees a cow. The cow has a pointed head, four legs, and a tail. So the child says, "Ah, big dog!" He fits the cow into the existing dog schema. The child develops by creating a new schema for the cow.

We do the same as adults. Seeing a man in the garden graveyard, Mary supposed him to be the gardener, yet it was Jesus. How many times has he appeared to us and instead of developing a new schema we have compressed him into an existing schema? Thus we miss him. "That was only my neighbor, only a friend, only the pastor, only my wife, only my husband, only my child, only a coincidence." But the Christ always comes in the home, in the earthquake, in the illness, in the hurt, in the poverty. He always comes, but we do not always recognize him.

Mary heard him call her by name. Jesus called Mary by her name. What a touching moment. Faith has many common components, but above all it is personal. It is being called by one's own name. Each one of us is unique. We each have our own strengths, issues, and vocation. We have been called to be missionaries to our own hearts. When we lack a clear identity, we are reticent about our personal calling. We feel as if we are nothing but a face in the crowd. We look to someone else to validate our experience.

Some of us are so codependent that we do not even know our own name. Jesus loved Mary. She was His disciple. She sought him. She stuck by him. She was faithful and true to him. He knew her personally and he called her name. He revealed himself to her. Hearing her name and feeling the love of God, Mary recognized him and replied, "*Rabboni*," which means teacher or master. How amazing to think that the risen Christ was first revealed to an outcast, a woman of shame.

Her experience of celebration is intimately connected to her willingness to stay at the cross, to persist at the tomb, to mourn for him. We cannot expect the mountaintop experiences of faith without the valleys of commitment, persistence, and mourning. She was sent: "Go and tell!" Ecstatic, Mary clung to Jesus. She wanted to stay with him forever. But Jesus told her, "Go to my brothers and tell them, 'I am returning to my Father and your Father, to my God and your God'" (John 20:17).

The joy of knowing Christ is not to exhaust him with our emotion, but to allow him to guide us into his service. He sends us to go and create community. Go to the hungry, the hurting. Go to the imprisoned, the oppressed. Let them know Jesus lives. Tell them that because of the resurrection there is love and there is hope.

Mary Magdalene was an ordinary woman who had spent much of her life in disgrace. Deeply shamed and helplessly addicted to her pseudo gods, she miraculously found her way to the *Holy Other*, to the cross, and to the tomb in the darkness of that first Easter morning. She announced the resurrection, first, to her own life, then to her community. Finally, she brings the message of the resurrection to a broken world, i.e., to you and to me. Paul writes of the meaning of the resurrection and the healing of our deep shame: "I have been crucified with Christ and I no longer live, but Christ lives in me" (Gal. 2:20).

One of the keys to real religious experience is the shattering realization that no matter how hateful we are to ourselves, we are not hateful to God. This realization helps us to understand the difference between our love and His. Our love is a need, his a gift. We need to see good in ourselves in-order to love our selves. He does not. He loves us not because we are good but because He is. The root of Christian love is not the will to love but the faith that one is loved.[8] —Thomas Merton

Chapter 8

Stillness

Be still and know that I am God.
—Psalm 46:10

It is a quiet morning. The sea beats rhythmically upon the shore. A few birds glide across a cloudless sky. The trees stand at attention as the great ball of fire rises in the eastern sky. All is silent and still. Nature teaches stillness. Stillness born of silence is fast disappearing in our time. A cacophony of noise assaults us everywhere. There is noise in the home, noise in the restaurant, noise in the church, and, most sadly, noise in our hearts. Henri Nouwen once told a group of us that in our modern world the noise in our hearts is so loud it prevents us from hearing the singing of angels. With a twinkle in his eye, he said, "It's hard to live without hearing the angels sing."

Isaac of Nineveh, the Syrian monk, taught that prayer comes through stillness. He said, "If you love truth, be a lover of stillness."[1] Soren Kierkegaard, the nineteenth century Danish philosopher and theologian, said, "The present state of the world, the whole of life is diseased. Create silence! Bring men to silence. The words of God cannot be heard in the noisy world...."[2]

Creation occurs in the *silence of stillness*. The growth of a seed, the change of the seasons, the movement of the stars and planets, and the change of night to day happen in silence. The prophet Zechariah: "Be silent before the LORD" (Zech. 2:13). Habakkuk warns, "The LORD is in his holy temple; let all the earth be silent before him" (Hab. 2:20).

These words evoke a deep reverential stillness. John of the Cross calls silence the language of God, "And it is only in silence we hear it."

> Behold, my beloved, I have shown you the power of silence, how thoroughly it heals and how fully pleasing it is to God. Wherefore I have written to you to show yourselves strong in this work you have undertaken, so that you may know that it is by silence that the saints grew, that it was because of silence that the power of God dwelt in them, because of silence that the mysteries of God were known to them.[3]
> —Ammonas, disciple of St. Anthony

What is the Silence of Stillness?

> The endless cycle of idea and action,
> Endless invention, endless experiment,
> Brings knowledge of motion, but not of stillness,
> Knowledge of speech, but not of silence.[4]
> —T. S. Eliot

An empty room is silent, it has no choice. But a room where people choose not to speak or move is still. Silence is a given, the *silence of stillness* is a gift. As we journey further into interior silence, we open to stillness and a spaciousness of spirit. In the *silence of stillness* we are our true selves and sit at the interior table with God. "Thou preparest a table before me in the presence of mine enemies" (Ps. 23 KJV).

> Not only does silence give us a chance to understand ourselves better, to get a truer and more balanced perspective on our own life in relation to the lives of others: silence makes us whole if we let it. Silence helps to draw together the scattered and dissipated energies of a

fragmented existence. It helps us to concentrate on a purpose that really corresponds not only to the deeper needs of our own being but also to God's intentions for us.[5]
—Thomas Merton

God is love and, in his presence, our defensive Ego Addictive False Self and shame melt away revealing our true identity as the *beloved of God*. The stillness of silence is not the absence of noise, but the absence of our Ego Addictive False Self blocking us from our true essence in God and the interrelatedness of all things. When we lose touch with inner stillness, we lose touch with ourselves.[6] To lose touch with ourselves is to lose touch with "God in whom we live, breathe and have our being" (Acts 17:28).

A day of Silence
Can be a pilgrimage in itself.

A day of Silence
Can help you listen
To the Soul play
Its marvelous lute and drum.

Is not most talking
A crazed defense of a crumbling fort?

I thought we can hear
To surrender in Silence,

To yield to Light and Happiness,

To Dance within
In celebration of Love's Victory![7]
—Hafiz, "Silence"

Stillness is the awareness or the unified field of consciousness in which life is not a puzzle to be solved, but a mystery to be unfurled. We do not have a thought or see a flower. We are the awareness in which the thought is had and the flower is seen. There is an intimate connection between *being* and the *now*. The *now* is not only what is happening at the moment, but it is the unified field of knowledge in which life happens. Unfortunately, the constraints of humanity limit fully understanding *the now*:

> *Now* we see but a poor reflection as in a mirror; then we shall see face to face. I know in part; then I shall know fully, even as I am fully known.
> —I Cor. 13:12

Transcending intellectual, psychological, and cultural forms, stillness is formless. Jesus said, "The words I have spoken to you are spirit and they are life" (John 6:63). Stillness is related to the presence of the *Eternal Being*. "Be still and know that I am God" (Ps. 46:10). "In quietness [stillness] and confidence will be your strength" (Isa. 31:15). "He leadeth me beside still waters" (Ps. 23:2 KJV).

> Be still my soul
> The Lord is on thy side
> Bear patiently
> The cross of grief or pain.
> Leave to thy God
> To order and provide;
> In every change
> He faithful will remain.
> —Katharina Von Schlegel, "Be Still My Soul"

Stillness is the Gap Between Stimulus and Response

Labeling, naming, or interpreting before we really see, destroys the essence of what is seen. The sea becomes a body of salt water; the rose becomes a piece of vegetable matter; mountains become mounds of dirt and rock. Unable to adequately express the essence of reality, we label things as though to point at them. My mentor the late Dr. Gerald May used to say, "Pointing at a tree is not the tree!"

> The main thing is, knowing how to see.
> To see without starting to think,
> To see when you see,
> And not to think when you see.[8]
> —Thomas Merton

In our anxiety-laden culture with its time pressures, stillness evades us. Almost before seeing we start to label. As a result, we are "ever hearing, but never understanding; ever seeing, but never perceiving" (Isa. 6:9). How can we look at the Bahamian sea with all its myriad colors and not be grasped by its beauty? Between seeing and naming, between hearing and interpretation, is stillness. The longer we cultivate the gap between stimulus and response, the deeper the stillness, being, and presence.

Losing our true human connectedness, we end up creating a world of bland familiarity. Parents no longer see children. Husbands are not present to wives and vice versa. Friendship becomes shallow. No longer grasped by beauty and mystery, we create a world where strangers walk as friends and friends as strangers. Stillness means taking time to see before thinking, hearing, or interpreting.

Stillness is Knowing and Love

Stillness is *knowing* and *being known*. Turning doubt to faith and fear to love, stillness instills courage making our weak legs strong. When the priest Zachariah was told that his wife would have a baby in her old age and his name was to be John, he scoffed in unbelief. How did God get his attention? He shut Zachariah's mouth. He learned silence. When his wife had a child, in the transformation from unbelief to enlightenment, Zachariah wrote, "His name is to be called John" (Luke 1:13).

Akin to deep listening, stillness is acceptance and obedience. The word *stillness* is derived from the same Latin root *audiens* from which we get *audience*, and creates an intimate connection between listening and obedience. Stillness allows us to listen, obey, and follow the voice of love that speaks so loudly in all areas of life. "Holy, holy, holy, LORD God Almighty, heaven and earth are filled with his glory" (Isa. 6:6).

The word *absurd* is derived from the Latin root *absurdis* meaning *deafness*. Without stillness, life is absurd because we become deaf to the meaning and beauty of life. Without stillness the voice of love is faint and without the experience of the *Eternal Love*, it is difficult to be aware of God's presence.

Dr. Rob Norris is a respected theologian and pastor in Washington, D.C. He wrote on the deeper spiritual meaning of stillness in his church newsletter.

> There are times when, like the apostle Paul, [we] can see neither sun nor stars and life seems beset with tempests. Then there is only one thing [we] can do and only one way forward. Reason cannot help; past experiences offer no light. Even prayer brings only limited consolation; then [we] must put your [our] soul in one position and keep it there. [We] must stay [our] soul upon the Lord; and come what may – winds, waves, thunder and lightning – no matter what, [we] must lash [our self] to the helm, and hold fast [our] confidence in God's faithfulness, His covenant engagement, His everlasting love in Christ Jesus.

To rest in God calls for an inward stillness. Quiet tension is not trust; it is simply compressed anxiety. Why is it so difficult for us to be still and quiet and let God speak to us? Yet, in a still, quiet voice God continuously speaks to us saying,

> Come to me, you who labor and are overburdened and I will give you rest. Shoulder my yoke and learn from me, for I am gentle and humble in heart and you will find rest for your soul, my yoke is easy and my burden light.
>
> —Matt. 11:28-30

Meditation and Contemplation

These processes are often confused. Meditation is moving from the affairs of the secular world to the affairs of God. Jean Danielou says that meditation is a penetration into the meaning of things we already know – and what we think we know – even though our understanding is limited.[9]

Contemplation is turning from the things of God to the presence of God. Held by God's love, contemplation is a transformation of consciousness that motivates us to carry out the mission of love in the world. Although we may prepare for contemplation through any number of spiritual and psychological practices, contemplation, the awareness of the presence and communion with God, is a grace, a gift. We do not start at contemplation, we arrive there.

Chilean Nobel Laureate for Literature, Pablo Neruda expresses a similar thought, "and one day poetry arrived."

> And it was at that age … Poetry arrived
> in search of me. I don't know, I don't know where
> it came from, from winter or a river.
> I don't know how or when,
> no, they were not voices, they were not
> words, nor silence,
> but from a street I was summoned,
> from the branches of night,
> abruptly from the others,

among violent fires
or returning alone,
there I was without a face
and it touched me.[10]

Contemplation is surrender. Surrender is letting go, giving over control of our life from our Ego Addicted False Self. In surrender we move from the fear-based false self to our true, love-based self in God. It is a matter of simple awareness; contemplative prayer is opening to the stillness of silence. Stillness melts away our false self and shame which is based on our social status, our possessions, what we feel and what we do. In the stillness of contemplation, we experience our true identity as the *beloved of God*. Our most personal, true self is also universal in God. As the *beloved of God*, we open up in relationship to ourselves, to each other, and to God's garden, the world.

Contemplation makes us see the interconnectedness of all things. Jesus said, "Unless a grain of wheat falls into the ground and dies, it abides alone; but if it dies, it brings forth much fruit." The elimination of shame portends the death of our Ego Addictive False Self and a rebirth of the true self. Jesus said, "If anyone wishes to follow me, he must deny himself [surrender his false self] and take up his cross [his shame, pain body, and hurt trail] and become a disciple of my teaching and life" (Author's paraphrase, Mark 8:34, 35).

We cannot demand the gift of contemplation – union and communion with God. We can only be faithful because God is the giver of all good things including the gift of his presence. The presence of God is not something we choose depending on our will or wish. It is the condition of our very existence. When we become aware of the presence of God's love and willingly turn towards it, it becomes real and life changing. All things become new, he is near to all who seek him. As a result, the world becomes pregnant with God and life and the outpouring of his grace and love. Moses saw the burning bush and the bush still burns. But only those who have spiritual eyes – awareness – can see it.

> Earth's crammed with heaven,
> And every wild bush alive with God,
> And only he who sees takes off his shoes:
> The rest sit 'round and pluck blackberries.[11]
> —Elizabeth Barrett Browning

Unlike meditation, contemplation is not a method of prayer. It is an awareness of God in stillness leading us to surrender to God's presence, love, and action in the world. Awareness is not the same as thinking. Shannon says that thinking about God makes God an object and creates a subject-object dichotomy leading to dualism. Conversely, awareness of God transcends the subject-object dichotomy and our small *i* is swallowed up in God, the great *I Am*.[12]

Awareness of God's presence is the source and ground of the spiritual journey leading to contemplation. As we become more aware of his presence through the Holy Spirit, we become centered in him, and he in us, the hope of glory. Bourgeault calls this the magnetic center which acts as a G.P.S, God Positioning System, aligning our external life with the internal presence of God in us.[13]

Awareness of God's presence should accompany all our vocal prayer, whether personal or liturgical. Our private vocal prayers, our praying liturgy, our participation in Eucharist or Baptism or Reconciliation or Marriage take on a special depth, if we pray with this awareness of the Divine Presence. It will make us realize that when we pray we are never alone. Being aware that we are in the presence of God means being aware of our oneness with one another and with all of God's good creation. When we praise God and thank God, it is always with the awareness that we are totally dependent on God and that we are in God. When we pray for reconciliation, we are aware of our failure to live out all that intimacy which God requires of us. When we offer intercession, it is with the awareness of our radical need for God, since we are totally dependent on God for our existence and for our continued existence.[16]

–William Shannon

Merton says, "The experience of contemplation is the experience of God's life and presence within ourselves not as object but as the transcendent source of our own subjectivity."[14] Without true contemplation of God, life loses its gong; worship becomes empty and meditation turns into narcissistic gratification.

Contemplative Prayer

The goal of the inner spiritual life is to move toward contemplation, a deeper spirituality in the discovery of the soul's journey to God. According to Merton, contemplative prayer is the prayer of the heart.

The heart is the deepest psychological ground of one's personality, the inner sanctuary where self-awareness goes beyond analytical reflection and opens into metaphysical and theological confrontation with the abyss of the unknown yet present – one who is more intimate to us than we are to ourselves.[16]

Contemplation is the transformation of consciousness in which we discover our true identity as the *beloved of God* and live in the constant awareness of his love, mission, and healing presence in the world. Contemplation manifests itself through prayer, personal growth, relationships, work, appreciation of beauty, and compassionate service to others.

Contemplation is a commitment to the vision of God's love and to the mission of his love in the world.

Vision without the mission of his love is an empty illusion leading to a non-creative self-absorption. The mission without the vision of God's love leads to busyness, burnout, and non-redemptive activity. Contemplation must always be balanced by the vision and the mission of God's love. "Holy, holy, holy is the LORD Almighty [vision]; the whole earth [mission] is full of his glory" (Isa. 6:3).

Called to a mountain top fellowship with God, Moses had to return to the valley to serve the people. Always leading to compassion within and without, contemplation essentially means going to the mountain top only to return to kneel and wash the feet of our brothers and sisters.

> Contemplative prayer is addressed to the human situation just as it is. It is designed to heal the consequences of the human condition, which is basically the privation of the Divine Presence. Everyone suffers from this disease. If we accept the fact that we are suffering from a serious pathology, we possess a point of departure for the spiritual journey. The pathology is simply this: we have come to full reflective self-consciousness without the experience of intimacy with God. Because that crucial reassurance is missing, our fragile egos desperately seek other means of shoring up our weaknesses and defending ourselves from the [shame and] pain of alienation from God and other people. Contemplative prayer is the Divine remedy for this illness.[17]
>
> –Thomas Keating

St. John of the Cross says that when we are drawn to spend more time in the *silence of stillness*, the Lord is calling us to a new stage of prayer where we are required to *do* less and to be *present* more. Most of us are not good at being still and we cannot sustain contemplative prayer on our own ability, it is a gift from God.[18]

> The contemplative life is to retain with all one's mind the love of God and neighbor but to rest from exterior motion and cleave only to the desire of the Maker, that the mind may now take no pleasure in doing anything, but having spurned all cares may be aglow to see the face of its Creator: so that it already knows how to bear with sorrow the burden of the corruptible flesh, and with all its desires to seek to join the human-singing choirs of angels to mingle with the heavenly-citizens and to rejoice at its everlasting incorruption in the sight of God.[19]
>
> —St. Gregory

Lectio Divina

Lectio Divina, practiced for centuries in the ancient monasteries, is a process of spiritual transformation in daily life. The Lectio requires time to be aware of resting in God's presence. Lighting a candle during the Lectio is a helpful reminder of God's presence. Lectio Divina includes reading (Lectio), reflection (Reflectio), verbal prayer (Oratorio), and contemplation (Contemplatio).

Lectio – The Reading

Lectio is a short reading of Scripture. For maximum concentration, the passage can be read a number of times. After the reading, write down a significant word or phrase. Writing it down engraves it on our memory as the Holy Spirit uses it to teach us about God through the day.

Reflectio – The Reflection

After the reading, we are encouraged to reflect on the passage and the word or phrase God has given to us. It helps to ask ourselves how the passage relates to the vision and mission of God's love in the world. Particular emphasis should be placed on how the reading applies to our personal lives. Our goal is to rest in the awareness of the presence of God. This awareness helps to constantly remind us that contemplation is more about God than about us.

Oratorio – Verbal Prayer

Pray after listening to and reflecting on the reading. Verbally express to God your worship, praise, gratitude, confession, repentance, intercession, and petition. Prayer should be simple, sincere and succinct.

> Prayer with words is the type of prayer with which we are perhaps more at ease and which we generally have in mind when we think of "prayer." It is so named because it puts into words the various ways in which we are able to express our total dependence on God. Thus, we offer praise and thanks to God, first for our being and then for all the gifts that go with being. But in the context of our dependence on God there is a sense of gifts misused, and so prayer may take the form of repentance and a plea for forgiveness. Word prayer also looks to the present and the future, wherein we are just as dependent on God as in the past. So there is the prayer of intercession.[20]
>
> —William Shannon

Contemplatio – Entering Silence Too Deep for Words

Prepare for the silence by taking three deep breaths, holding to the count of four to allow the body to relax. Remain silent for twenty minutes. External silence leads to interior silence creating stillness and space to listen to God. In stillness and quietness, sit at the table of inwardness spread for two, God and you. The psalmist says, "Thou preparest a table for me in the presence of mine enemies"

(Ps. 23:5 KJV). Do not be discouraged if twenty minutes is too long. Take your time, grow into the silence. David claims he learned to calm and quiet his soul (Ps. 131). It takes time to learn to be quiet.

> Prayer without words is not so much expressing our dependence on God, but rather experiencing it and being so overwhelmed by that experience that words become so inadequate that they are useless. Nor are they really needed. Silence alone is appropriate. Wordless prayer is a kind of firm foundation for prayer with words. For without this deep awareness of God's dynamic presence in our lives, which comes with wordless prayer, we would probably become restless and uncertain in our prayer life (wondering whether we are doing it properly, worrying about our distractedness, etc.). With wordless prayer as the secure root of our spirituality, we shall never become overanxious (at least never for long), because we shall know that we are in God and so is all else that is. This is what really matters: all reality is charged with the glory of God's presence.[21] —William Shannon

In the silence, focus on a simple prayer, such as, "Lord God, come to me" or "Lord Jesus you are welcome." Let the thoughts, feelings, and reactions flow away like sail boats on a windy sea. When your mind wanders, quietly say "Lord" to refocus the mind. As the mind relaxes, the deep feelings of shame are evacuated unconsciously, leaving a sense of refreshment and peace.

In the silence we allow the Holy Spirit to pray in us: "The Spirit himself intercedes for us with groans that words cannot express" (Rom. 8:26). It is helpful to remember that we are resting in God and that contemplative prayer is a prayer of intention and not attention. Our Lord dwells in us through the Holy Spirit who prays in us even when we do not know how to pray. As we progress in interior prayer, the spirit within becomes more operational.

> If the Spirit of him who raised Jesus from the dead is living in you, he who raised Christ from the dead will also give life to your mortal bodies also through his Spirit, who lives in you.... Those who are led by the Spirit of God are sons [children] of God. For you did not receive a spirit that makes you a slave again to fear, but you have received the Spirit of sonship [childhood]. And by him we cry, "*Abba.* Father!" The Spirit himself testifies with our spirit that we are God's children .... In the same way, the Spirit helps us in our weakness. We do not know what we ought to pray for, but the Spirit himself intercedes for us with groans that words cannot express. And he who searches our hearts knows the mind of the Spirit, because the Spirit intercedes for the saints in accordance with God's will.
>
> —Rom. 8:11, 14-16, 26-27

Operatio – Opening to Our Life

We go into the throes of everyday life in the presence of God armed with the healing word or phrase. We are patiently aware of God's presence in people, nature, and situations. This openness is enhanced as we reflect on how we think about our thinking and how we feel about our feelings. It opens us to a deeper understanding of our inner motivations and intentions.

Review the word/phrase/sentence at midday and after supper followed by at least ten minutes of silence. Ask yourself how God's love has been shown to you throughout the day. End the day with twenty minutes of silence. This is best done shortly after dusk and completes the cycle and prepares us for the next day. Take time to prepare for sleep. It is helpful to avoid arguments or conflicts up to two hours before bed. If you dream, it is important to record them the following morning.

A Deeper Love

Our deepest desires express a hunger that only God can satisfy. Unfortunately, we often give our hearts to that which is not God, such as relationships, addictions, rituals, and possessions. The heart becomes free only by accepting an invitation to deeper love. But because of our narcissistic tendencies, we even use this love to seek ourselves. We need to learn to empty our hearts of all attachments and be filled by God. God's love gives life and slowly transforms us, healing our deepest wounds of shame.

Contemplative Prayer invites God into our life as a guest and then, as we surrender, we bow to make him the host of our life. God is inseparably linked to us in an eternal relationship, an *us-ness*, which is our home, life, joy. To surrender is to give up control, but the temptation to regain control is ever present with us when we become fed up or develop a feeling that we have arrived.

During our inward journey toward stillness, God transforms us into the image of Christ by breaking down the false self and eliminating shame to give birth to an awareness of the true self in God. The journey is filled with ups and downs because transformation occurs slowly and covertly. As we continue our journey in prayer, we open to the awareness of God's presence, not only at the time of prayer, but also in the hum drum experience of daily life.

In surrender, we are absorbed in the awareness of God and, as a result, our satisfaction is only found in his loving presence. "It is he who made us, and we are his" (Ps. 100:3). Experiencing the stillness of God's presence and love, we long for it and seek it with a passion. "For God alone my soul waits in silence" (Ps. 62:1).

It is easy to say we abandon ourselves to God. But living the abandonment out in practice is the real challenge. We come to realize that God is the dancer and the music in the cosmic dance of the music of love. Knowing God is not all joy, at times it is painful. It is like going to the dentist to prevent tooth decay or jogging for health. Job asked, "Shall we accept good from God, and not trouble?" (Job 2:10). The spiritual journey is not a sentimental trip of ecstasy. As God leads and directs our paths, we do not change the world as we know it, but we are changed and so is our vision of the world.

The Dark Night of the Soul

Transformation requires what St. John of the Cross describes as the *Dark Night of the Soul* where we walk by the light of faith in the love of God instead of human reason and understanding. Closing our eyes to the natural ways of human knowing, we experience darkness because our eyes have not adjusted to the bright light of divine faith. Frustrated and fatigued, we often seek to regain control of ourselves by withdrawing from prayer or giving up the spiritual journey. Like Elijah, sometimes the journey becomes too much for us and we even despair of living. *The Dark Night of the Soul* has many of stages which continue in and out of sequence.

Stage 1 - Attraction

We are pursued by the *Hound of Heaven* and enveloped in a cosmic love affair as we learn to navigate the light of God's glory, his presence. This may occur by an inspiring sermon, a work of art, or being overwhelmed by the mystery of nature.

Stage 2 – Fusion

As our relationship with God deepens and matures, we may experience epiphanies of ecstasy or insight. It is like heaven comes down and glory shines around. Our enthusiasm gives us an invincible attitude and, like Peter, we defy anyone to challenge our faith. Sadly, fusion is temporary and often our zeal is not tempered with knowledge or foresight.

Like Peter we succumb to circumstances and deny the Love that never lets us go and the Face that never turns away. We need to recall the words of Christ, "In this world you will have trouble. But take heart! I have overcome the world" (John 16:33).

Stage 3 – Crisis

The Dark Night of the Soul is lonely and it seems that God has abandoned us throwing us into crisis. As the crisis deepens, not only are we blocked from the natural light of human reason, we now experience a deep sense of isolation and confusion. Prayer becomes hard, dry, and painful and seems to boomerang back to us. At the height of the crisis, reaching the end of our rope, we recognize that God is holding us, we are not holding God. At this painful place in our faith journey, the fellowship, and support of the community of faith is extremely important.

Stage 4 – Commitment

Even without feeling the presence of God, and in spite of our pain, suffering, dryness, boredom, and frustration, we are left in love to commit ourselves to God. Like Job we say "Though he slay me, yet will I hope in him" (Job 13:15). Like Peter we say, "To whom shall we go? You have the words of eternal life" (John 6:68). At this point, we become strangely aware that commitment is a gift of God. "He

[God] who began a good work in you will carry it on to completion until the day of Jesus Christ" (Philip. 1:6).

Stage 5 – Intimacy

In faith, even the darkness beyond the light of natural reasoning becomes beautiful. Seeing the natural wonders of the sea, trees, stars, mountains, we experience a deep awareness of the oneness and interrelationship of all things. The most wonderful thing is that the warmth of God's embrace melts our defensive Ego Addictive False Self and shame and opens us to our true self in love.

According to Merton, our false self and shame are absorbed fully in God so that God becomes the transcendent source of our subjectivity. In so doing we experience the intimacy of being deeply loved by God. "He has taken me to his banquet hall, and his banner over me is love" (Song 2:4). It is no longer our way, but God's love living and working in and through us. Like David we learn to serve God's purpose for us in our generation.

The Journey of Elijah in Stillness

After a decisive victory over the prophets of Baal, the prophet Elijah retreats in fear when he learns that Queen Jezebel has put out a contract on his life. Queen Jezebel sent a message to Elijah saying, "May the gods deal with me, be it ever so severely, if by this time tomorrow I do not [destroy] your life" (1 Kings 19:2). Elijah then ran for his life feeling abandoned, rejected, and humiliated.

In spite of vast spiritual resources at his disposal, the mighty prophet of God is reduced to timidity by the power of his deep fear and shame. Is this not similar to us? How often has the glorious experience of victory brought to consciousness the pain of our deep fear and internal shame voices which magnify the threats and challenges of external circumstances? We can never absent ourselves from the presence of divine love, but overwhelmed by fear and shame, we often lose the awareness of that love.

As Shannon suggests, "If the Great Fact of our lives is that we are always in the presence of God, the Great Problem of our lives is that we are so often unaware of God's presence."[22] The great joy of contemplative prayer is that God never forgets us. But sadly, the contemplative must live with the realization that the experience of our intimacy with God is constantly slipping from our memory.

Having lost the awareness of divine love, Elijah leaves his help and companion behind. Absorbed in his Ego Addictive False Self he runs away to Beersheba. Elijah wanders alone in the desert and finally collapses under a solitary tree. Elijah feels hopeless and prays to die, "I have had enough, LORD…. Take my life. I am no better than my ancestors" (1 Kings 19:4). In this shameful state of failure, shattered dreams, and lost purpose, Elijah falls asleep.

The Lord Provides

In the midst of this darkness and hopelessness, God, the *Hound of Heaven*, reaches out in love to provide an angel to feed the terrified prophet. Awakened by the angel, Elijah arises, eats, and escapes once again to sleep. When we are overwhelmed, we should guard against retreating under the covers of our bed to find comfort in sleep. Shame seeks hiddeness and, as it intensifies, it will even negotiate our suicide or death to make us feel better.

Reaching out to Elijah again, the angel awaked him and told him to eat for he will need strength for the journey ahead. God acknowledges that the journey is too much for him. It is comforting to know that on our spiritual journey, we have an advocate, a compassionate God who identifies with our difficult times and painful feelings (Heb. 4:15).

God provides for us and always leads us to himself. For in the eternal perspective, our spiritual journey is more about God than about us. Given food for the forty days journey, Elijah is led by God himself to experience his presence at Mount Horeb, known as the mountain of God. Mount Horeb is surrounded by multiple deserts just as God, in times of great trial and testing, leads us through the deserts of our despair to himself.

> Our spiritual journey must lead through the desert or else our healing will be the product of our own will and wisdom. It is in the silence of the desert that we hear our dependence on noise. It is the poverty of the desert that we see clearly our attachments to the trinkets and baubles we cling to for security and pleasure. The desert shatters the soul's arrogance and leaves body and soul crying out in thirst and hunger. In the desert we trust God or die.[23] –Dan Allender

King David, whose life was punctuated by ripples of painful shame and fear, wrote:

> Send forth your light and your truth,
> Let them guide me;
> Let them bring me to your holy mountain,
> To the place where you dwell,
> Then will I go to the altar of God,
> To God, my joy and my delight. —Ps. 43:3-4

A Soul's Journey to God

Arriving at Mt. Horeb, Elijah enters into a cave to spend the night. We all have caves in which we seek shelter from the darkness of our despair. Some of the caves of our modern culture include money, addictions, possessions, and jobs. Sadly, we spend many years in our caves, hiding from the *Eternal Love* which is our true essence and purpose.

But the *Hound of Heaven* seeks us even in our caves. God probes us with the question he asked Elijah: What are you doing here? It pierces the heart. "The Word of God is living and active. Sharper than any double-edged sword, it penetrates even to dividing soul and spirit (Heb. 4:12).

Responding to God, Elijah says, "I have been very zealous for the LORD God Almighty. The Israelites have rejected your covenant, broken down your altars, and put your prophets to death." In anguish Elijah cries, "I am the only one left, and now they are trying to kill me too" (1 Kings 19:14). As we experience the pain, frustration, and despair of our own journey to stillness, these words cut to the core of the soul.

God tells the prophet to go out and stand on the mountain in the presence of the Lord as he passes by. In contemplation, regardless of our pain, we long for the healing presence of God. "My soul waits in silence for God only" (Ps. 62:1 NAS). Only the presence of God can satisfy the deepest longings of our heart. According to St. Augustine, "We shall ever restless be, until we find our rest in Thee."

Then God sent a great wind, but God was not in the wind. There was an earthquake, but God was not in the earthquake. Then there was a fire and God was not in the fire. After the fire there was a sound of silence – stillness, space, the still small voice of God.

The story of Elijah offers much insight in preparing us to experience the presence of God in the stillness of silence. When we go to silence, our minds are overwhelmed with a hurricane of powerful shame thoughts, which howl, blow, and distract us from stillness. We have to let go of the thoughts and let them float by like boats sailing on the sea. Blocking or resisting thoughts only empowers them to counteract and sabotage our journey to stillness.

Observing our thoughts as they pass through our mind is painful. Powerful and cataclysmic like an earthquake, these thoughts become voices that beat us down, break us up, and confront us with such painful questions as: How could this happen to me? Why did I do it? Am I that stupid? How could I fail so badly? As we move into silence, the powerful thoughts block and destroy our stillness. We have to focus our intention, persevere with patience and determination, and continue on our journey to stillness.

As we progress towards stillness, interior silence opens us to union and communion with God. The Ego Addictive False Self objects are consumed in the Holy of Holies by the fire of God's presence. As Elijah waits, God's presence is manifested by a sheer stillness. In the silent stillness we hear the still small voice telling us that we are deeply loved and highly esteemed. The *silence of stillness*, unlike any other silence, is unique. It is full of the presence of God manifested by a subtle but profound stirring of the soul, a gentle blowing, and a quiet whisper. It may even present a physical sensation, a vibration, a vision, or a voice.

> The climate in which the spiritual backbone of our inner life is discovered (or rather recovered) is the climate of prayer, especially that prayer without words, in which a Voice – deep within and inseparable from our truest self – speaks to us from the depths of our own silence, as that same Voice spoke to Moses from the burning bush. It was when Moses was in the wordless silence of the desert that God came to him; and Moses experienced a deep and abiding sense of the Divine Presence. The way God came to him changed Moses' life. For it set his silence on fire.[24]
> —William Shannon

Eternal Love purifies our soul. This is not an event but a process. God confronts Elijah again, "What are you doing here?" Like deep psychotherapy, repetitive deep questioning punctuated by silence in the loving presence of God, pierces the unbroken arid unfertilized soil of the heart. Pouring out his pain, Elijah repeats his litany of sadness about the rejection of God by his people, his own deep sense of loneliness, and the fear of being destroyed. In the stillness of silence, the mind empties or evacuates itself of its deep hurt and shame leading to the illumination and purification of the soul.

Serenity Prayer

God grant me the serenity
to accept the things I cannot change;
courage to change the things I can;
and wisdom to know the difference.
Living one day at a time;
enjoying one moment at a time;
accepting hardships as the pathway to peace;
taking, as He did, this sinful world as it is,
not as I would have it;
trusting that He will make all things right
if I surrender to His Will;
that I may be reasonably happy in this life
and supremely happy with Him Forever in the next. Amen.
—Reinhold Niebuhr

As Elijah goes through catharsis in the presence of the divine therapist, the discharge of the negative introjects of pain make space for the internalization of God's love. This becomes a healing self object transference relationship between God and Elijah providing affirmation, connection, and most of all, the comfort of God's presence. "Perfect love drives out fear" (I John 4:18).

After the evacuation of hurt and the healing of shame, Elijah is given his marching orders. In the stillness of silence, deep listening opens us to the vision of God's love; it clarifies our mission in the world. Elijah is told to go back to work, be focused, and stick with the program. Responding to Elijah's concerns, God promises to provide support in raising up the prophet Elisha as his help mate and successor. But most of all, God assures Elijah he is not alone because there is still a large remnant of people who faithfully seek and worship the true God.

Recognizing his inadequacy and utter dependence on God, Elijah's small *i* is swallowed up in the great *I Am*, the source and ground of all being and reality. Overwhelmed by shame and fear, the journey of Elijah to God in the *silence of stillness* illustrates how the experience of God's presence eliminates our fear and shame giving us courage and hope to continue the spiritual journey.

Our spirit is renewed when we come to the point of utter nothingness and rest in stillness. When we "walk in the light, as he is in the light" (1 John 1:7), he melts away the fear and paralysis of shame and we are empowered to continue on our spiritual journey. The psalmist recognized that God is the source of light and life, "For with you is the fountain of life; in your light we see light" (Ps. 36:9).

> I said to my soul, be still,
> > and wait without hope
> For hope would be hope for the wrong thing;
> > wait without love
> For love would be love of the wrong thing;
> > there is yet faith
> But the faith and the love and the hope are all
> > in the waiting.
> Wait without thought,
> > for you are not ready for thought;
> So the darkness shall be the light,
> > and the stillness the dancing.
> > > —T. S. Eliot, "East Coker"

In the *silence of stillness*, earth touches heaven and we experience the presence of the glory and majesty of the *Eternal Mystery*, God. In the *silence of stillness* we cry out:

> How lovely is your dwelling place
> O LORD Almighty!
> My soul yearns, even faints,
> For the courts of the LORD;
> My heart and my flesh cry out
> For the living God. —Ps. 84:1, 2

Conclusion

Mrs. Lilly Bethel tragically lost her husband and all of her six children one by one over the years. Words are inadequate to express the tragedy and brokenness of her life, but having a deep faith in God, she exuded a sense of peace and calm. Visiting her was such a pleasure because, in spite of her tragic life, peace and stillness pervaded her humble home. In the stillness of her home, I experienced the presence of the unseen reality of the Love that never lets us go and the Face that never turns away.

This island saint, a diamond purified by the refining fire of suffering, introduced me to God's love and presence, healing my shame, and giving me bread for the journey. Sister Lilly taught me and so many others that in spite of the tragedy of life, waiting patiently in the *silence of stillness* is the deepest form of healing prayer. Gone but not forgotten, absent but still present, she radiates the stillness that encourages us on our spiritual journey.

> It is only by breaking open entirely,
> by allowing our heart and whole being
> to break open again and again
> wider than we ever thought possible
> that the unbreakable jewel is revealed.
> —Rashani, "Again and Again"

Chapter 9

Love Wins

We love because God first loved us.

−1 John 4:14

We have explored the multidimensional aspects of shame including its formulation, dynamics, symptoms, and it manifestations in failure, arrogance, anger, addiction, and our tendencies toward idolatry.

Ignored for years, shame has become the Master Emotion rivaling Freud's emphasis on the sexual instinct. According to Michael Lewis, professor of Pediatrics and Psychiatry at the University of Medicine and Dentistry of New Jersey and, author of *Shame: The Exposed Self*,

> The species — specific feeling of shame is central in our lives. Shame, more that sex or aggression is responsible for controlling our psychic course.... Our internal struggles are not battles between instincts and reality, but conflicts that typically involve the understanding and negotiating of shame, its elicitors and its frequency.[1]

Similarly, popular books such as John Bradshaw's *Healing the Shame that Binds* and literature from the recovery movement emphasize the interrelationship of shame, addiction and dysfunctional family systems.[2]

Nowhere is the dynamic of shame more aptly described than in Buechner's novel about the Jewish patriarch Jacob in *The Son of Laughter*. According to Dr. Victoria Allen, "Buechner's Jacob is a man consumed by toxic shame which involves his identity and world view." Continuing, Allen claims that the cause and physical manifestation of Jacob's shame reflects the psychological understanding.

According to Michael Lewis:

> Shame is the product of a complex set of cognitive activities; the evaluation of an individual's action in regard to their standards, rules and goals and their global evaluation of the self. The phenomenological experience of the Pharaoh having shame is that of a wish to hide, disappear, or die. Shame is a highly negative and painful state that also result in the disruption of ongoing behavior, confusion in thought, and inability to speak.[4]

Even though coming to prominence as a central psychodynamic factor in the second half of the twentieth century, shame with its specific characteristics has been long acknowledged. For example, Charles Darwin in his *Expressions of Emotions in Man and Animals*,[5] described the overt physical manifestation of shame with an emphasis on the facial expressions: head averted or bent down with the eyes wandering or turned away (now referred to as gaze avert) and facial blushing. To illustrate, Darwin quoted the Old Testament prophet Ezra, "Oh my God, I am ashamed and I blush to lift my head to you, Oh God!" (Ezra 9:6).

The Friendship of David and Jonathan

Shame may be described as the underbelly of love. This is poignantly illustrated in the Old Testament by the soul friendship of David and Jonathan. After accomplishing the massive victory over Goliath the Philistine warrior, David was invited to dine at the court of King Saul. King Saul admired and respected David for his accomplishments until the people, including a band of women, berated him, shouting, "Saul has killed thousands, but David has killed tens of thousands" (1 Sam. 18:7). Angry and overwhelmed with shame and jealousy, King Saul plotted to kill David to prevent him from becoming king.

In spite of Saul's animosity toward David, Jonathan, King Saul's son, developed a deep friendship with David.

> Jonathan made a covenant with David because he loved him as himself. Jonathan took off the robe he was wearing and gave it to David, along with his tunic, and even his sword, his bow and his belt. —1 Sam 18:3-4

They became as one with a deep loyal commitment binding them. They promised to show each other unfailing kindness in life and their covenant of love extended to their families even after death. As Jonathan said, "[D]o not ever cut off your kindness from my family — not even when the LORD has cut off every one of David's enemies from the face of the earth" (1 Sam. 20:14, 15).

This covenant bound Jonathan and David together in life and death. Jonathan did all in his power to protect David his friend from the violence of King Saul, his father. With all the power of the army at his disposal, King Saul hunted David like a wounded animal. On one occasion, David, discouraged, frustrated, and tired, was trapped by King Saul at Horesh in the desert of Ziph. Reaching out to his friend, Jonathan traveled into the desert to be with David and "encouraged him in God" (1 Sam 23:16). In modern parlance, this phrase is not easily understood. It means that Jonathan identified with David's pain and surrendered him to God, the Eternal Love.

Encouraging people in God is powerful. But it is a lost art. One Wednesday afternoon, a young lady rushed into my family clinic crying that her brother was murdered. Angry and frustrated, she was determined to seek revenge by killing her brother's killer. According to the young lady, her brother was more than a brother. He was a surrogate father who provided for the family and paid for her education. Screaming loudly, she said that her brother's death catapulted her family back in to the pathos of poverty and destruction. Stunned by her sudden entrance into my office, I was shocked by her outburst. I found myself hoping that Ms. Burrows, a volunteer, whose son was murdered a year before, would come by to help me. She had worked through the shame of her own anger and revenge and had been very helpful to many persons facing tragic losses in the clinic.

On that particular day, Ms. Burrows was absent and I prayed that she would come. Suddenly, the door opened and in walked Ms. Burrows. Hearing the young lady's plight, Ms. Burrows hugged and comforted her by sharing her own experience and encouraged her to give up the desire for revenge. To my surprise, the young lady calmed down, but continued to mourn deeply the death of her brother. After a while, she left the clinic. A few days later, the young lady wrote that Ms. Burrows' support and encouragement opened her to a new perspective of God's love which melted her anger and desire for revenge. Ms. Burrows, a deeply spiritual lady, encouraged her in God.

The Death of King Saul and Jonathan

Tragically, King Saul and his son Jonathan were killed in battle on Mount Gilboa. When David heard the news, he was deeply saddened. David did not compensate for his shame by seeking revenge on King Saul for his cruel and brutal treatment of him. David mourned deeply for Saul and Jonathan. Grief is a deep revealer of the soul. We can only grieve as deeply as we love and vice versa, we can only love as deeply as we can grieve.

Hearing the news of King Saul and Jonathan's death, David cried out in deep lament:

> Thy glory, O Israel, is slain upon the high places
> How are the mighty fallen!
> Saul and Jonathan, beloved and lovely!
> In life and death they were not divided
> They were swifter than eagles,
> They were stronger than lions.
> —2 Sam. 1:19

Then, in a crescendo, David eulogized his friend Jonathan.

> How are the mighty fallen?
> In the midst of battle!
> Jonathan lies slain upon thy high places
> I am distanced from you, my brother Jonathan;
> Very pleasant have you been to me
> Your love to me was wonderful, passing the love of a woman.
> —2 Sam. 1:25, 26

These words are beautiful and portray the deep heartfelt feeling of a friend, brother, and soul partner. Warren Payne has said insightfully,

> The friendship between David and Jonathan has become a portrayal, the very meaning of what a friendship should be. It was long lasting and consistent even when they were parted; loyal and selfless yet it was realistic, and it was not allowed to override other relationships and responsibilities.[6]

King David and Mephibosheth

After becoming king, David remembered his covenant promise to treat Jonathan's family with kindness after

Jonathan's death (1 Sam. 20). When he assumed the throne, King David asked if there was anyone left of Jonathan's family to whom he might show kindness. After a national search, a son of Jonathan was found, named Mephibosheth, who was crippled in both legs and lived in a nondescript place called Lodebar, a city of dust at the end of the road to nowhere. Apparently, when Mephibosheth's nurse heard that King Saul and Prince Jonathan were killed in the battle on Mount Gilboa, she grabbed five-year old Mephibosheth and ran away to protect him. In her rush, she slipped and fell injuring Mephibosheth causing him to become crippled in both legs. In those days, physically and mentally challenged persons were disenfranchised, rejected from society, and, in some cases, were even killed. With his family displaced from power and discriminated against because of his physical handicap, Mephibosheth wallowed in shame in the poor dusty backwater town of Lodebar.

David summoned Mephibosheth to the palace where he welcomed him. King David told Mephibosheth about the covenant he made with his father, Jonathan, and that he would live at the palace and eat daily at the King's table. Overwhelmed by the Kings generosity, Mephibosheth asked King David how he could be so kind to such a dead dog as himself?

This is a beautiful example of how love conquers shame. The love and kindness of King David melted away the shame of abandonment, rejection, and humiliation of Mephibosheth. He made him a member of the royal household just as Christ makes us members of his royal household. Mephibosheth moved from the pathos of shame to the acceptance and honor of love.

"O Love that will not let me go
I give myself to Thee!"

The Shift from Shame to Love

As discussed earlier, our basic feelings can be reduced to shame (anger, fear) or love (compassion, hope). The challenge, however, is to move from the ethereal to the reality of daily life. We cannot help others move from shame to love unless we have faced and worked through our own shame. This is not easy. Life is wounded and our ancestral and personal hurts incline our hearts and psyche towards shame as anger, fear, or both.

Arising from the deep hurt in our hearts or psyche, shame produces negative thoughts and voices which control our perception. Making the perceptual shift from shame to love means choosing to see or value a person or a situation differently. Our internal shame thought patterns and feelings are projected onto others and situations forming perceptions which create our view of reality. It is not what another says or does that upsets us or makes us happy, but how we value and think about what they say or do. We do not see things as they are, but as we are!

Different people experiencing the same phenomenon have differing interpretive perceptions. Physics teaches us that an objective view of reality is influenced by our interactive participation. According to quantum physicist Neils Bohr, "What we experience is not external reality, but our interaction with it."[7] The minute we observe something or someone, that very act of observation influences our perception. This is also applies to relationships. Reality is influenced by what we think and feel about others. In essence, our inner reality determines the glasses through which we see other people.

So often, the qualities which upset us about other people are the projection of our own issues. It is difficult to change the world, but we can change our vision of the world by working through our inner hurt and shame. This is what is meant by making a "perceptual shift" and changing our perception of reality. Shifting from shame to love is an intentional choice to live in love instead of fear.

Shame based on fear produces anger which results in threatening or attacking behavior. But if we are courageous enough to look beneath the surface, we will see a person who is vulnerable, afraid, and making an appeal to be loved. For example, a jealous rage is essentially an appeal for love produced by our shame and fear. Attacking others or seeking revenge creates a vicious cycle of more fear which disturbs our wellbeing and exacerbates our problems. We are always choosing between shame or fear, illusion or reality, victimization or empowerment.

In our interaction with others, we either seek to extend love by loving behavior or, appeal for love through shame, anger, or fear. We move between these two options. When we love, we are being our true selves and are open to receiving love. If we are appealing for love through shame, fear, and anger, our false self uses threatening or attacking behavior as defenses. But if we are willing to shift from shame to love, we shed our false self-defenses and open up to the true self in compassion and understanding which enhances our happiness and wellbeing.

Choosing to live in love rather than shame spreads love in the world and liberates persons imprisoned by shame and fear. St. Paul wrote:

> If I speak in the tongues of men and of angels, but have not love, I am only a resounding gong or a clanging cymbal. If I have the gift of prophecy and can fathom all mysteries and all knowledge, and if I have a faith that can move mountains, but have not love, I am nothing. If I give all I possess to the poor and surrender my body to the flames, but have not love, I gain nothing. Love is patient, love is kind. It does not envy, it does not boast, it is not

proud. It is not rude, it is not self-seeking, it is not easily angered, it keeps no record of wrongs. Love does not delight in evil but rejoices with the truth. It always protects, always trust, always hopes, always perseveres.

—1 Cor. 13: 1-8

The Practice of making The Shift
From Shame (Fear) to Love (Compassion)

This simple, yet profound, process has blessed my own life and countless numbers of persons in my practice. It is a prayer, a relaxation technique, an anger management program, a shame elimination process and above all a form of self-transformation. Its effectiveness is based on practice, practice, and more practice.

I. Awareness that we can shift from shame to love.

Having been made in God's image, we come from love, to love, to be loved, and to return to love. "We love because God first loved us" (I John 4:19). We can never absent ourselves from the reach of divine love, but we can live without the awareness of that love. When we choose to remain in shame, we become victims because we have lost the awareness of the eternal "Love which will never let us go and the Face which never turns away."

Recognizing that we are loved creates the awareness of shifting from shame to love. According to Einstein, "A problem occurring at one level of consciousness cannot be solved at the same level." Awareness of being loved by the Eternal Love changes our conscious awareness, allowing us to surrender and make the shift form shame to love.

At any point in time we tend to be in either (a) the shame (fear, anger, hurt) or (b) the love (compassion, hope, humility) part of our heart or psyche. Once we become aware that shame is the predominant feeling in our heart and we can choose to make the shift from shame to love.

II. Stop – Take Time Out

If we are too busy to take time out, we are too busy. Excessive busyness is ignorance which produces emotional and physical fatigue. This blocks us from the unmanifested realities and mystery of life. Life involves chronological time (chronos) interspersed with eternal time (kairos). When we stop, we become open to appreciate the "still point" where chronological time intersects with kairos, the fullness of time. At the "still point" we are grasped by the eternal love which mediates the perceptual shift from shame to love. Love slows us down. On the other hand, shame, fear, and anger speed us up through physiological arousal. Our heart rate increases raising our blood pressure and because of the interconnection between the brain and the heart, our IQ drops. This explains why the internal phenomenon of shame is manifested by the external faces of violence, murder, abuse, intimacy dysfunction learned helplessness and so much more.

Time out breaks the vicious fatigue cycle resulting in clearer judgment and decision making. Better to stop and walk away than to wish we had!

More things are wrought by taking time out
than this world dreams of.

III. Face Shame Directly

When we feel afraid, angry, jealous, or hurt, regardless of the external circumstances, we are facing our deep seated shame core with its trail of shame scripts, thoughts, voices and perceptions. Try to recall the two or three of the most shameful or hurtful experiences in your life. For example, being fired from a job, failing an exam, the loss of a relationship, the shattering of a dream, a deep regret of something you did or did not do. Think of the shame scenes, scripts and persons doing or contributing to the shame experience and let yourself be present to them. Look for connections from those hurts to what you are feeling. What is the trigger for your present pain, anger, fear, hurt?

Ignore the pain and stay with the feeling, the fear, rage, sadness, etc. Although we can eventually learn to do this in our minds, it is initially helpful to write down your shame experiences and your feelings. This is our hurt trail which, metaphorically, is like a red hot pulsating wire extending through all aspects of our life relating us to past and present hurts and future fears.

Another way of doing this is to make a time line of our life, pinpointing the age and point at which the shame experience occurred. As we practice, we will find that our heart or psyche has a series of doors. When we open one door and work through the hurt or shame experiences, another door opens confronting us with other hurts.

At times, different shame schema from our unconscious emerges into consciousness depending on the triggers which discharge them. The gift of experiencing a shame schema is that it allows us to pinpoint the trigger giving us the opportunity to reduce its negative effect upon us. In other words, the willingness to empty our hearts of our shame schema opens us to love, the basic element and building block of life.

IV. Deep Breathing with Eyes Closed

Breathing is synonymous with life, "God breathed into man and he became a living soul." When we were young and carefree, we breathed deeply. But as we became older and burdened with the worries of life, we tend to breathe superficially leaving our lungs and brain less perfused by life-giving oxygen. The residual old air (carbon dioxide and its biochemical residues) increases anxiety and decreases impulse control making us insecure, irritable, and agitated. By closing our eyes while breathing deeply, the brain emits alpha waves which further relax us. Deeper relaxation is possible if we take time to focus on the relaxation of individual parts of the body.

V. Silence

Remaining silent for a few minutes settles our hearts. When a stirred pond is allowed to settle, we are able to see the bottom clearly. Likewise, allowing our hearts to settle makes us more aware of our deeper self. Merton speaks of the creative power and fruitfulness of silence:

> Not only does silence give us a chance to understand ourselves better, to get a truer and more balanced perspective on our own lives in relation to the lives of others: silence makes us whole if we let it. Silence helps to draw together the scattered and dissipated energies of a fragmented existence. It helps us to concentrate on a purpose that really corresponds not only to the deeper needs of our own being but also to God's intentions for us.[1]

As we turn to God in silence, our innermost self or soul is absorbed into the divine center and we experience solitude, the alone with the Alone. Our small *i* is swallowed up in the great *I Am*. We rest in contemplation and the experience of love in our true self in God. Shame is a defense against our aloneness. As we become aware of our true self based in the Eternal Love, our shame melts away.

Our aloneness is not eliminated but integrated into communion with God who is the real and all that is real. Love is reborn in solitude allowing us to reach out to others. One hour of solitude draws us closer to those we love more than many hours of communication. In solitude we are alone but not lonely, because the presence of God in Christ reaches out to us.

VI. Prayer

With our mind relaxed, we admit our problems and ask God, the source of all love, to open his love to us. We can never remove ourselves from the presence of his readily available love. Sadly, we can certainly lose the awareness of his love. God's love is unending, unchanging, unconditional. Human love is temporal, tentative, temperamental. We often lose awareness of eternal love and find ourselves condemned to live out of our second love which is temporal and limited. The shift from shame to love occurs as we become anchored in the Eternal Love which is always there for us.

Surrendering ourselves to his unchanging love enables us to shift from shame to love by a simple prayer such as, "Lord God, have mercy upon me and forgive my resistance to your love. I surrender my heart and shame to your healing and unfailing love. Amen."

VII. Opening to the Streams of Love

Becoming an adult is enhanced by our experience of unconditional love in childhood, which may come from a parent, relative, pastor, priest, rabbi, teacher, or a stranger. These acts of love create our love story and counteract our shame and hurt trail. These persons are streams of God's love to us, watering the dry and parched land of our shame prone heart. All love is God's love. Sometimes it is difficult to drink from the source, that is, pray or connect with God. But we can always drink from the love streams of others that flow through our lives. Who is a stream of love for you? Think of or write down those persons who have shown love to you. As you do this, you will relax and shift from shame to love.

In our beautiful, but often fragmented and confused world, our challenge is to become streams of God's love for each other. Many persons who have blessed us have passed away, but their love is stronger than death and is a powerful stream that comforts and encourages us. Are you a stream of love for some weary pilgrim passing through the marketplace of life? An unknown poet says it well:

In youth, because I could not be a singer,
I did not even try to write a song;
I set no little trees along the roadside,
Because I know their growth would take too long.

But now from wisdom that the years have brought me,
I know that it may be a blessed thing
To plant a tree for someone else to water,
Or make a song for someone else to sing.
—Unknown

VIII. Visit a Sacred place

God's love flows not only from the source and streams of love, but also from sacred spaces. Known as a thin space, a sacred place is where heaven and earth are very close. It is where we feel free, loved, and inspired. The beautiful Bahamian sea with its myriad colors is a thin space for me. It transports me to the eternal realm where I feel loved and experience the interconnectedness and oneness of all things. I have had the similar experiences in the Alps in Europe, the Rockies in the U.S., and the Serengeti plains in Africa.

Another special place for me is the Miller Park at the Chautauqua Institute where a small group of Sunday school teachers met many years ago for simple fellowship. This modest gathering has mushroomed into one of the world's leading think tanks providing spiritual, educational, and recreational refreshment for countless thousands of people. Visiting a sacred space, both physically or in our minds, relaxes us and allows us to shift from shame to love.

IX. Gratitude

Gratitude, as discussed previously, is a portal into love enabling us to move beyond shame to new vistas of self-transcendence and meaning. Life itself is a grace. Gratitude transports us into the united field of consciousness or awareness where we experience our deepest self in the good, the true, and the beautiful. Shame-busting gratitude extends even to what we so often take for granted such as health, family, job, friends, and the mystical beauty of nature. According to Tillich, thanksgiving is a consecration which transforms the secular world into a sacrament of grace changing shame to love.

Write down three things for which you are grateful. As you write, you will find yourself shifting from shame, fear, and anger to love.

To be grateful is to say yes,
To all that is good in life.
This in itself is love.

X. Practice Love

Having made the shift from shame to love, practice love, by reaching out to others. Make a commitment to see the world in love. Practice seeing without thinking, naming, or interpretation, just be present. As a result, you will experience the deepest form of love, that is, being and presence. The presence is always in the now. Now is not only what is happening in the present, but is the united field of consciousness in which the mystery of our lives unfurl. To so this, we have to slow down. According to Shannon, there is no way of being aware in a hurry. We can't see what is in front of us if we are always looking past it. We can't build relationships on the run. We can't see a flower unless we look at it. The philosopher Wittgenstein said admonished, "Don't think; look!"

Love wins. See every interaction in love. Whether the person is expressing love or appealing for love through anger, fear, or attacking, let us respond in love to create a more loving world.

A Love Story

While I was giving a lecture at a well-known church in Washington, D.C., a woman handed me an envelope. In it was what she said was a true story about Sally, a retired teacher who drove a school bus. Most of the kids were from upscale homes and were well groomed, intelligent, and well spoken. But Johnny was different. His mother was dead and his father who took care of him was an alcoholic. Johnny was poor, shame prone, and often unkempt. Shamed and victimized by the more fortunate kids. Johnny was isolated and rejected. But Sally, the bus driver, encouraged him by loving and speaking kindly to him.

One of the fortunate young girls named Joey showed her appreciation by giving Sally a silver heart inscribed with the words, "Sally loves me." Sally cherished the silver heart and kept it on the dashboard of the school bus. One day, Sally stopped the bus and told the kids that something very sad had happened. She said that the silver heart which Joey gave her was missing from the dashboard where she had placed it. All the kids blamed Johnny and said he stole it. Johnny was chastised by the other children and felt forlorn and ashamed.

The kids ridiculed him by calling him a thief and saying many other unkind things about him. Sally called Johnny to her and asked him if he took the silver heart. Apprehensive, nervous, and ashamed, Johnny shook with terror. Placing her hand in his left pocket, Sally felt the silver heart. Recognizing Johnny's shame and pain — Sally pulled her hand out of Johnny's pocket and remained silent. The kids continued to berate him, saying "Johnny took it; he is a thief and should be punished." They jeered and mocked him.

Years later, when Sally had retired from driving the school bus, she had a stroke and had to travel around in a wheel chair. One Saturday afternoon, while shopping at the mall, Sally was unable to get her wheelchair up the ramp. The manager was summoned. He was a middle aged man with a balding head. When the manager recognized Sally, he put his hand in his pocket and pulled out the silver heart with the words "Sally loves me" inscribed on it. Expressing his gratitude to Sally, Johnny said, "When everyone else shamed me and stopped loving me, you kept on loving in me. I only made it because you kept on loving me." Sally, against great odds, enabled Johnny to make the shift from shame to a meaningful life of love. Sally was a Christ figure whose love eliminated Johnny's shame and liberated him in love to reach his potential.

Is this not similar to the story where the religious elite (the privileged few) brought a woman caught in the act of adultery to Jesus to have her punished? Deeply ashamed and troubled, this woman felt abandoned, rejected, and humiliated. Guilty, she was condemned by her accusers and perhaps, more deeply, by her own conscience.

The religious aristocracy wanted her punished. According to the law, they were right. But they were so right, they were wrong. Acting in love, Jesus took time to reflect by writing on the ground. The irritated and frustrated accusers became increasingly outraged and challenged Jesus to punish the woman.

Jesus looked at them intently and said, "Let him who is without sin or failure cast the first stone" (John 8:7, author's paraphrase). One by one, the accusers left feeling convicted and ashamed. Turning to the woman, Jesus asked, "where are they? Has no one condemned you?" She answered, "No one, sir." Then Jesus spoke to her in love saying, "Neither do I condemn you...."

Released from her shame, the woman walked away in the freedom of love. In essence, the incarnation is God inciting the perceptual shift from shame to love.

> For He, the sun of righteousness was sent down from
> heaven to give light to us sitting in darkness (shame) and
> in the shadow of death, to guide our feet into way of peace
> (Love). —Luke 1:78, 79 (parentheses added)

Shakespeare's sonnet 116 reminds us of the victory of love:

> Love is not love
> Which alters when it alteration finds,
> Or bends with the remover to remove.
> Oh no! It is an ever-fixed mark
> That looks on tempests and is never shaken.[9]

LOVE WINS!

Epilogue

By Curt Ashburn

A Family Faces Shame

Get him, get him, get him, get him. Mark him.
—The Furies of Orestes

The Shame of a Mythological Family

The Greek drama *Orestia* by Aeschylus (BC 513-455) is a trilogy that chronicles the cycle of transgenerational shame that caused the destruction of a mythological family. It all began when Helen, the wife of King Agamemnon's brother, was kidnapped by the Trojans. The king prepared to sail to Troy to rescue her, but in order to have fair winds, he had to sacrifice his own daughter to Zeus. Predictably, this angered his wife, Clytemnestra. Even though Helen was her sister, she hated her husband for choosing her life over their daughter's. She punished him by being unfaithful while he was away rescuing Helen and fighting the Trojan War. Upon his triumphal return, she murdered him.

All this family shame now came to rest on their son, Orestes, who took revenge for his father's murder by killing his mother and her lover. After his shameful deed, he was pursued by the Furies, three goddesses who arose out of the flames of Clytemnestra to hunt, hinder, and haunt him. These foul demons of shame — abandonment, rejection, and humiliation — pursued Orestes relentlessly crying out, "Get him, get him, get him, get him, mark him."[1]

Orestes first fled to the temple of Apollo, the Greek god of prophecy and light. There he found forgiveness for his guilt. His shame, however, was not a matter so easy to assuage. Guilt says, "I made a mistake." Shame says, "I AM a mistake." The shame voices of our own Furies cry out *get them, get them, get them, get them, mark them!* This is why even those who believe in the forgiveness of a loving God, often remain nailed to the shame cross where they are hunted, hindered, and haunted by the Furies of shame.

Orestes eventually found freedom from the Furies in the temple of Athena, the Greek goddess of love. This is the story of how I found my freedom from shame. It is an old story, older than any Greek drama; it is the drama of the human condition. Shame is the *Master Emotion* and it did its best to master me and destroy me and everyone I love. This is the story of my shame and how my family, friends, the Church, and the teachings of Dr. David Allen lead me back to the temple of God's love, wounded and scarred, but unashamed.

The Shame of a Real Family

In spite of his many good qualities, my father was an angry, fearful, critical, overly sentimental, shame-based, and relentless bully. He picked on my brother and me mercilessly. For me, his disapproval came in spite my best attempts to please him. His disapproval of my brother was for the opposite reason. My brother defied him openly, refusing to try to please him in any way.

Neither my path of least resistance nor my brother's path of most resistance was able to break us free from the shame we carried. Our father's shame pursued us even when we left home for college. Shame never relents; it does not rest nor allow stillness of soul in its victims. It hinders, it hunts, and it haunts like the Furies of Orestes. Both of us carried our father's shame for over fifty years and both, in our own way, have now found release from the shame that was destroying us.

My brother found his escape from shame first. He had not spoken to me for more than a year. I had hurt him deeply. I had betrayed his trust and his generosity. I lied to him in order to hide my own shameful behavior. Since his early twenties, he had lived half a continent away where he tried unsuccessfully to run from his own Furies of shame. So, when the doorbell rang on that Tuesday morning, July 12, 2009, he was not on my mind.

When I opened the door, I saw my wife flanked by six Washington, D.C. police officers whose presence gripped me with fear. She had bad news. She elicited the support of the police because she was afraid I might have a heart attack or stroke in my despair. Was it one of our children? My legs went weak. "Your brother killed himself." When the police were sure that I was okay, they left.

My brother was dead by his own hand, but my hand was in it, too. Soon the police left, I looked at my wife and, with a cold calm, said, "There have not been many men since Cain who could say that they killed their brother."

An Inheritance of Shame

A video of our childhood would have recorded a typical 1950s and 60s family, but it would not reveal the invisible transfer of shame we were subjected to through my father's words, actions, and expectations. I was leading the All-American life and played the good son. My brother's shame was more obvious as he took the role of the bad son. We were both carrying our father's shame, but until I was in my late forties, no one could see the depth of destruction at work in me also.

The off-loading of shame is not always obvious, but it is real. As I recall my earliest emotional memories, it is as though my mother and two brothers did not even exist. In fact, my father was the emotional center of the family. I have no emotional memories attached to anyone else in my family except him. Each member of the family related to the others through him and knew each other primarily through him at the emotional level.

His existence was our existence, his being our being, his shame our shame. My words and actions were most often calculated to please him in order to keep him off my back. My brother's words and actions were calculated to hurt him with defiant behavior. Both of us made many self-destructive decisions in order to hide our shame and to protect ourselves from him. While our father bears responsibility for shaming us, we are responsible for the decisions we made in response to him. Accusations and assigning blame are unfruitful and misguided. What is important now is an awareness of the damaging effect that shame inflicts. A lack of that awareness in the past made it difficult to survive the burden of carrying my father's massive shame core.

The point of identifying the sources of our shame is to enable us to make the right choices [Diagram 5]. My brother ultimately made his choice in answer to Hamlet's dilemma, "To be or not to be, that is the question." The choice is ours. Are we going to choose to continue living out of the Ego Addictive False Self and worship the false gods of shame, or live out of the true self in Christ and worship him only? One way leads to life and the other to death. While we must acknowledge the shame voices in our lives, it is not so that we can accuse others or excuse ourselves. The purpose is to take responsibility for our shame-based behavior and attitudes from this moment forward.

My work with Dr. David Allen helped me became aware of the destructive power of carrying my father's shame. His shame distorted and destroyed my sense of self, not just as a son, but as a brother, husband, father, and pastor. When the present continually reminds us of our shameful past, we cease to exist in the now. The *Real Presence* of Christ in us, the hope of glory, is exchanged for the cross of shame, a cross that we were never intended to bear. We are each choosing every day to "die by our own hand" or to truly *be* in spite of "the slings and arrows of outrageous fortune."

Shaming the Good Son

From an early age, my strategy for dealing with my father's expectations was over achievement. First, I used my size and athletic ability to meet his requirement that his sons play football. Fortunately, I loved football, but I was also living his life and carrying his unfulfilled dreams in the form of shame. He bragged about me in public as though my success belonged to him, but in private, nothing I did on the field was good enough for him.

My second strategy was to excel in school, but I soon found that my intelligence and academic success were no defense against his need to shame and degrade me. His nickname for me was a shortened version of *stupid*. He called me *Stupe*. Any time I did the least thing wrong or in a way that he did not like, he would sneer the epithet, *Stupe*. Day after day for as long as I can remember from age six until I was married, he called me *Stupe*. And when he said the word, it dripped from his tongue with disgust.

The only time I ever challenged him in any way was over politics and religion at the dinner table. I always knew that I was smarter than he was, but that did not keep him from "winning" every argument. When he could not defeat the reasoning of my arguments, he used sarcasm or his rage to shame me into silence. My brother once told me that those frequent dinner table battles were some of his best and most frightening memories. Best because no one ever challenged him like that, but frightening because they always ended with my father's vitriol and my humiliation. He never laid a hand on me, but that would have been better than the contemptuous jack hammering of my soul day after day.

Stupe was his name to degrade me intellectually, but calling me a *sissy* was the most common way for him to transfer his shame. Being tough was so valued that he even named our little rat-like dog Tuffy. There was no crying in our home even though he himself was overly sentimental. Crying was an unauthorized feeling for everyone except for him. If we did cry or show any other kind of *sissy* behavior or emotion, he would point an index finger at us and rub off the top of it with his other index finger and say, "Shame on you sissy."

I have a theory as to where *Stupe* came from. My father had a lisp until after his service in the navy during WWII. He told me that he was very self-conscious about it. It was not until after the war that he got speech therapy to correct it. As to *sissy*, I that likely came from him being small in stature. He never tired of repeating the story of how he was cut from his junior high football team simply for his lack of size. It seems reasonable that even though he eventually got rid of the lisp and went on to play college football, he never stopped trying to make up for sounding dumb and being small. I have to wonder if these experiences were the seeds of *Stupe* and *sissy*.

Overall, my dual strategies worked, my athletic and academic achievements pleased my father and they were an escape from his bitter and unrelenting verbal assaults. But it was my inner thought life and imagination that were my true refuge. My father chided me for always reading, but his shaming words had no power in that world. It was there that I secretly nurtured my own dreams of being a husband, a father, writer, coach, and preacher. I created my own dreams in a world where he could not make me ashamed.

Shaming the Bad Son

The compensations developed by the Ego Addictive False Self are different in different people, but the purpose is always the same, a place to hide from the Furies of our shame. My brother's response to being shamed was not over achievement, but a war of rebellion leading to his own self-destruction. To the outside world, his shame appeared more obvious than mine. Four years younger than I, he took the opposite approach to my golden-boy strategy. His way was to fight my father's expectations, to contradict and to act counter to everything that his shame demanded of us. My brother seemed to live and breathe just to find new and creative ways to tell our father to "go to hell."

I was the clean-living straight arrow, he used drugs, drank heavily, and eventually moved on to drug dealing. I was built to play football, starred in high school, and played four years in college. In contrast, even my brother's late growth spurt seemed to be an intentional jab in the eye to my father. He forced my brother to play anyway because playing football was necessary in his mind for manhood.

I remember a passage from the 1970's best seller *The Boys of Summer* in which the author, Roger Kahn, observed that the highest compliment his father could give was, "He's an intelligent man." My father's greatest compliment was, "He's a big man." The fact that I was big for my age and my brother was small for his was symbolic of the dynamics between my father and each of his sons. My brother was physically intimidated and eventually quit football just adding to his shame. I was his big son and he never tired of saying to anyone who would listen, "Big boy isn't he?"

We also differed in our responses to his shame-based religious sentimentality. I preached my first sermon at age sixteen and my brother hated church, hated or did not believe in God and said so until the day he died. It tortured my father and that, of course, was the point. He was always openly defiant. Like all children, he went through different phases, but all were rebellious. He had a pyromaniac phase and one of just plain meanness destroying old, irreplaceable photos of my father and his college friends by poking their eyes out with a pencil. He underachieved and was truant over fifty percent of his senior year of high school spending his days on the Jersey shore drinking and using drugs.

My brother did not want to go to college, but it was expected. He went to Shippensburg University just as our father had and, predictably, he dropped out his sophomore year. My father is still not over him dropping out of college. Imagine, the son is in his grave and the father's shame lives on. He moved to Florida and then Colorado sometimes not returning home for years at a time. He became a successful real estate agent, but suffered from both drug and alcohol addiction and the severest and most debilitating depression which plagued to the day he died.

A Brother's Shame

Being the *ideal* son was not enough for me. I wanted to be the *ideal* brother. Because my brother was picked on at school as well as at home, I tried to become his protector. Unfortunately, no one could protect him once his fear and anger drove him to find acceptance in bad company. That was just the ticket to thumb our father in the eye. It was also when he began to avoid me, his *ideal* older brother. When we were both in our forties, he told me that I had seemed too perfect for him. To him I was everything that our father wanted in his sons and all that my brother hated. Apparently I fooled him, too.

His self-imposed exile in Florida and Colorado lasted thirty years. I had resented both my father and my brother for those lost years. I resented my father for driving my brother away and resented my brother for running away. We regained some contact in the mid-nineties because of his love for my children who adored their uncle.

In 2005, we began to talk for the first time about what it was like for each of us growing up. I had always denied ever having negative feelings toward our father. I wanted to retain the *ideal* childhood that was fixed in my mind. I wanted the edited version of my childhood video, not the raw footage. But my brother's bitterness, the pain I heard in his voice, and his tears opened my eyes to the reality of my own hurt and shame. Soon I hated our father as much as he did. My darkness began as I marinated in newly found bitter memories. I wished my father would die and free us from our shame, but the reality was that I was never the *ideal* anything. I was too wrapped up in pleasing my father and trying to be *his ideal* and failing at that, too.

A Star Athlete's Shame

As with everything else, my football career looked like a fairy tale. As a high school senior, I was recruited by the University of Texas Longhorns which had just won the national championship, but my father wanted me to play for the U.S. Naval Academy in Annapolis, MD. I loved the idea of playing for Navy, but I was seventeen and choosing to play for the best team in the country was easy.

Unknown to me, my father had been writing letters and doing all he could to get me accepted to the academy. He himself had applied unsuccessfully after WWII. Now he would be able to rectify that injustice through me. So, with a mixture of both pride and disappointment, I went to the Naval Academy.

When a football injury ended my future in the navy, I was given the option of being the first academy graduate to be commissioned as a chaplain. I declined and finished my education and football career at Shippensburg. I am proud to have attended both schools, but the irony is just too rich and the shame too deep to ignore the fact that I ended up graduating from the same college as my father.

A Husband's Shame

At Shippensburg University, I found the *fusion* of my life. That is what Dr. Allen calls that stage of a relationship when the sun rises and sets on the girl or guy of your dreams. We were married just before I graduated from college and set off for seminary. That is where fusion turned to confusion and the sweet voice of the girl I fell in love with and married became the shaming voice of my father. It was not what she said, but what I heard that shamed me. In her innocent comments, I heard my father's criticism rather than really listening to her.

I wanted to be the *ideal* husband, but any comment by her that was even mildly critical of me destroyed my self-worth. She felt my shame deeply, but that unfortunately led to her losing her voice as a person. I should have been the voice that called her to self-acceptance, but my shame silenced her. Nevertheless, more than anyone else, she preserved my life while waiting for me to come out of the darkness where I wandered about aimlessly for years.

One of the most touching and important ways she preserved my life was how she supported me when I got back into coaching football. In those darkest years, when everything was going wrong, she encouraged me to keep coaching high school football. Coaching ate up twenty hours a week August through November and brought in virtually no money. She asked me one day if I knew why she kept coming to my games even after our son was no longer playing. I did not know and she said tenderly, "Because the football field is the only place where I can see the man I love happy and just being himself."

That opened my eyes to the damage that worshiping at the altar of the *ideal* had done to me. No one is the *ideal* coach, but it was only as a coach that I was being my true self. I saw that it was the real me that she loved and not the *ideal* me. The *ideal* is only an illusion which fools us into thinking we are something that we are not.

A Pastor's Shame

At eight years old I wept at the realization that Jesus Christ gave his life for mine. From that point on, I willed to be the *ideal* disciple. I discovered at sixteen that I had a gift for preaching and again I was determined to achieve the ideal. After seminary, I became the associate pastor in a high profile church on Capitol Hill in Washington, D.C.

However, becoming the *ideal* pastor did not work out any better than being the *ideal* son or husband. Even though I received tremendous affirmation from ninety-five percent of the congregation, it only took one wealthy deacon and his small power group to disapprove and bring out my shame. The shame voice of my father through that group drowned out hundreds of voices of affirmation.

It is not hard for a pastor to find shame voices in the church. Pastors, young and old, are being destroyed by shame every day. Someone has called it clergicide and it did ultimately end my life as a pastor. When I disagreed with the wealthy deacon on the nature of outreach to the community, no one else in leadership stood with me. My refusal to give in eventually led him to offer me thirty thousand dollars in cash to leave the church. In 1985, that was a large lump sum of money for a pastor with young children. I heard in that deacon's words my father's voice criticizing me. I refused the money and resigned as pastor.

A Savior's Shame

The Jews of Jesus' time were looking for the *ideal* Messiah. He would be a great king and military leader. He would deliver Israel from under the heel of the Roman Empire. That search for the ideal is precisely why they did not recognize him when he came in a humble manger. He was not the *ideal*. He was the Word made flesh, he was God made man, incarnational reality, the *Real Presence*.

His band of men abandoned him at his greatest time of need. His most faithful followers were a handful of women which brought him the scorn of the religious elite. After conquering sin and death, he identified himself to his disciples by showing them the marks of his suffering. He was not the idealized, sanitized Hollywood Messiah. He was a wounded and betrayed "man of sorrows, acquainted with grief," shamefully nailed to a Roman cross, rejected, abandoned, and humiliated. Since he had no shame of his own, was it not for your shame and mine that he died?

A Hero's Shame

The most painful aspect of my journey was the shame I felt looking into the eyes of my children. I especially recall once having coffee with my daughter. She was visibly sad and hurt and said to me the words no father ever wants to hear, "Dad, you were my hero." I was a past-tense, classic hero, tragically flawed.

Those words were heartbreaking because I knew they were true. I also knew that she had forgiven me for my behavior and that God had forgiven my sins. It was not the guilt of my actions, but the shame of what I had done to a little girl's heart, to sons who looked up to me as a man, to a wife who had to watch as shame destroyed the man she loved. It was not the guilt, but the shame that I could not live with. I had wanted more than anything in my life to be the *ideal* father and husband. My shame was so deep at that moment that I wanted to die.

It took me a long time to realize that there is no such thing as an *ideal* father or anything else. Those who love us are not looking for the *ideal*. The *ideal* is an illusion that makes for empty hugs and lonely beds. Ideals are just thoughts; it is incarnational reality — *Real Presence* — that our loved ones are looking for in us. Like our Lord, we are most truly identified by our scars, not our ideals. Rejecting the idolatry of the *ideal* is critical in eliminating the shame gap between what we aspire to be and who we really are.

Intervention

Shame is interior darkness; it hides, deceives, and isolates its victims. Darkness had done all those things in me and everyone was beginning to see it. An intervention by my wife, best friend, and both brothers in September 2006 was the beginning of my long journey out of darkness. After a week in a psychiatric ward, four months living with my youngest brother's family, two weeks living in my car, and four months in the attic of a community center in north Philadelphia, the darkness began to lift. I spent a year working for the Fellowship of Christian Athletes and it was then that my wife invited me to come home.

It was the month before my brother's suicide that I started teaching Dr. Allen's book *In Search of the Heart* at Gospel Rescue Ministries. It was during that month of teaching his "Recovery to Discovery" approach to relapse prevention, the hurt trail, the identity card, and the love story that I felt the light dawning in my darkened heart. The depression began to lift from my mind and healing was coming to my damaged spirit. Then came the news that I had killed my brother. My father may have dug his grave over a lifetime, but I had finished him off.

It was not an enemy spear that killed Uriah; it was King David. In the eyes of God, David committed murder to cover the shame of his adulterous relationship with Bathsheba. The prophet Nathan, speaking for God said, "You are the man." Cain killed his brother, Abel, to cover the humiliation of his rejected offering. God asked Cain, "Where is your brother?" Now he was asking me the same question and my brother's blood cried out from his grave and every voice in my head whispered, "You are the man."

The Perceptual Shift

During Dr. Allen's first trip to D.C. after my brother's suicide, he asked me how I was doing. I answered, "Not so good, Doc, I killed my brother, you know. Tell me how many men I have to help at the mission to make up for killing my brother?" My words stunned him for a moment and then he leaned forward, eyes blazing, pointing his finger at me. It was during that summer that he had been outlining his understanding of shame as the *Master Emotion* for this book. He reminded me of the garment of shame that I had begun to remove during that first month of teaching. He said with a gentle intensity, "Your brother is responsible for his decision to die. The shame must die with him. You must not take his shame on yourself."

Doc helped me remember that the guilt for my actions had been confessed by me and forgiven by Christ. The shame my brother carried needed to be buried with him and mine must be nailed to the shame cross of Christ. Still pointing at me he declared, "Neither you nor your father killed your brother. He killed himself. Grieve and grieve deeply, but do not be ashamed anymore."

That was the beginning of my perceptual shift [Diagram 8], the death throes of my shame. It was then that I began to live and love out of my true self. I exchanged my guilt-ridden Ego Addictive False Self, my shame core, for the light of his glory and grace. It is a daily dying. Shame does "not go gentle into that good night."[1] Shame is a false god arising out of the ashes each day and looking for my permission to shame me anew, to convince me to live out of my Old Man, Adam, not Christ.

Why do we give destructive shame permission to ruin us? Why do we exchange the clean robes of the glory of God for the nakedness of shame? Because we, like Orestes, are fleeing our shame voices who taught us to hide our shame. With our eyes downcast, our shoulders slumped; we cover our nakedness with fig leaves from the very tree that was the source of our shame. Only by being clothed in the glory of the slain Lamb of God can we again walk unashamed.

At the mission, I often challenged each man to wake up in the morning, look himself in the mirror and ask, "What can I do today to be a better man?" The better man is the new man or woman in we are called to be in Jesus Christ. But with any honest assessment of ourselves we see that we are broken and worthless in our rags of shame.

To all of them and to all of you who are broken, I commend the lyrics of Leonard Cohen's "Anthem":

> Ring the bells that still can ring
> Forget your perfect offering
> There is a crack in everything
> That's how the light gets in.

Shame is a relentless foe and there are days when we will fail miserably. It is then that we must go to our knees and confess our failure in the realization that "there is a crack in everything" including us. Then we can sleep "the sleep of the righteous". In the morning, when God's mercy rises like the sun, we must dare to look at the broken image in the mirror, "forget the perfect offering" and, without shame, have the courage to once again ask, "What can I do today to be a better man?" For some it is the man or woman we used to be, for others it is who we never were, but for all of us, it is the person we were meant to be. Either way, "ring the bells that still can ring."

Conclusion

Countless men and women are dying of the shame they carry and the shame of being ashamed. Understanding the nature of shame as Dr. Allen presents it in this book will help anyone who was shamed as a child and is still re-living a shamed-based past. What we learn from Dr. Allen is not how to change or blame those who have shamed us. It was I who was changed as I edited this book, as I read and re-read the message of hope and peered with Mary Magdalene into the empty tomb of the risen Christ. This book is about developing an awareness of our shame and how to exchange it for the lost glory of God. It is about finding our identity in Jesus Christ in whom there is no condemnation or shame.

For over fifty years, I let shame make my choices for me and that was the story of my life. I carried my father's shame as a constant fear of failure, of being a *sissy*, of living up to my nickname, *Stupe*. The shame that is in us from childhood, if left unresolved, will pursue us through the voices of other people. They become the echo of our primary shame voice which was, in my case, my father's voice. It was his voice that I heard no matter who was talking.

I no longer seek to be the *ideal* anything, just a broken and wounded incarnational reality in Jesus Christ. Now my wife, sons, and daughter all know me by my scars, not my successes or even failures. In this humble and inadequate confession, I identify myself with the *Wounded Healer*, the one whose Love will never let us go and whose Face will never turn away. Now, with all my faults, failings, and fears, I am a *real* husband to my wife, a *real* father to my children. I also have another brother to whom I can now be a *real* brother and I can even be a *real* son to the father I once hated. Now I am as much myself every day as I used to be only as a coach on the football field.

Months after my brother's death, my father took me to visit his grave. I stood beside him as he remembered his son. As we left, he began to cry. I put my arm around his shoulders. When we got to the car, referring to his tears, he said to me, "I guess I'm the sissy in the family now." I did not know how to tell him even then that he is not a sissy; he is just a man, *memento mori*. A man with two sons, one freed from his shame by the empty tomb of Christ, the other by his own grave, hunted down, and chased there by the Furies of shame. It is true to the ending of a Greek tragedy that the father of those two liberated sons is still pursued by his own shame.

Recently, my daughter, now twenty-two, was spending a few days with us. She was reading her old journals that go back to when she was in ninth grade. She brought me a paragraph torn from the pages of her 11/21/2003 entry. It was a prayer written when she was fifteen and when I was engulfed in darkness. I wept as I read these words —

Dear God,

Help my dad to receive the motivation to get out and do something about his shameful feelings he's been carrying for so long. Help him know he is truly an amazing person and he should share his gifts with others.

She has a *real* dad now, a new kind of hero, wounded, but unashamed. I was indeed Orestes, hunted, haunted, and hindered by the Furies of transgenerational shame. Once guilt ridden, shamed based, and banished from the paradise of God's presence, I now declare that the Ashburn family shame ends with me. The last lines from Leonard Cohen's "Hallelujah" are a fitting conclusion, not simply to my story, but to every story of victory over shame:

> I did my best, it wasn't much
> I couldn't feel, so I learned to touch
> I told the truth, I didn't come here just to fool you
> And even though it all went wrong
> I'll stand before the Lord of Song
> With nothing on my tongue, but hallelujah!

SHAME DIAGRAMS

Diagram 1 | 277

Basic Life Needs and Woundedness

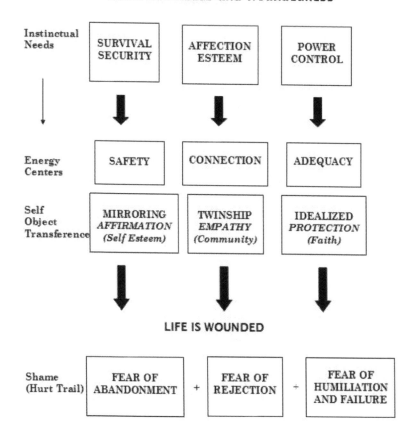

Instinctual Needs	SURVIVAL SECURITY	AFFECTION ESTEEM	POWER CONTROL
Energy Centers	SAFETY	CONNECTION	ADEQUACY
Self Object Transference	MIRRORING *AFFIRMATION (Self Esteem)*	TWINSHIP *EMPATHY (Community)*	IDEALIZED *PROTECTION (Faith)*

LIFE IS WOUNDED

Shame (Hurt Trail)	FEAR OF ABANDONMENT	+	FEAR OF REJECTION	+	FEAR OF HUMILIATION AND FAILURE

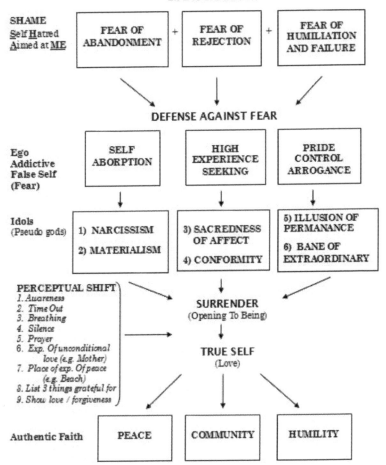

Fear Defenses, Surrender and the True Self

Diagram 3 | 279

Shame Addiction Cycle
With The Shame Cross

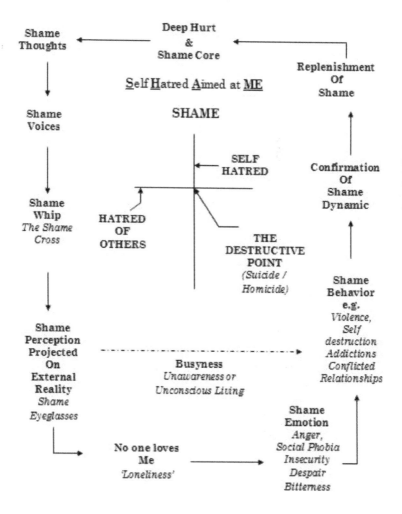

Shame Addiction Cycle
With The Shame Shield

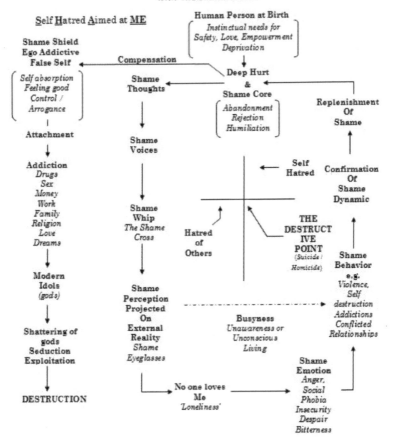

Diagram 5 | 281

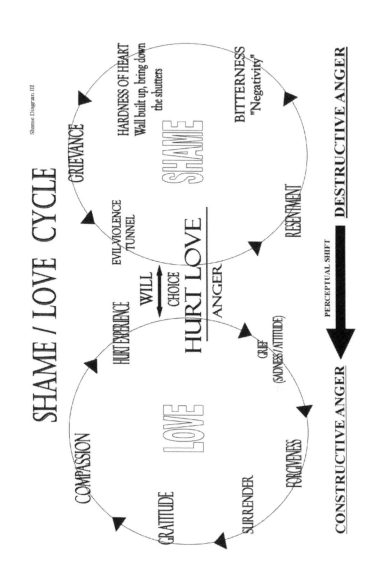

SHAME / LOVE CYCLE

Shame Diagram III

DESTRUCTIVE ANGER

GRIEVANCE

HARDNESS OF HEART
Wall built up, bring down
the shutters

SHAME

BITTERNESS
"Negativity"

RESENTMENT

EVIL/VIOLENCE
TUNNEL

HURT EXPERIENCE

WILL

CHOICE

HURT LOVE

ANGER

PERCEPTUAL SHIFT

COMPASSION

LOVE

GRATITUDE

SURRENDER

FORGIVENESS

GRIEF
(SADNESS/ATTITUDE)

CONSTRUCTIVE ANGER

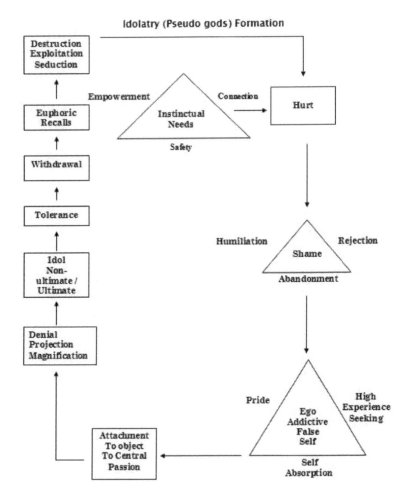

Diagram 7 | 283

SURRENDER

SUR = OVER   RENDE = GIVE BACK

Life Situations
(Defended by Shame Based
Ego Addictive False Self)

True Self
(Being)

Eternal Being
(God)

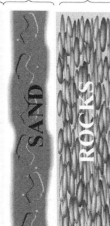

SEA

SAND

ROCKS

Shame Diagram VI

The Perceptual Shift

'We don't see things as they are, but as we are!'

Focus on Present
Humility
Connection
Solitude
Courage
Honesty
Beauty
Nature
Surrender
Forgiveness
Acceptance
Peace
Tolerance
Understanding
Gratitude
Hope
Power
Discipline

(Portals - Silence, Suffering, Nature, Music, Dance, Poetry)

Perceptual Shift

Will Choice

Practise

LOVE
(COMPASSION)

SHAME
(FEAR)

Anger
Worry
Complaining
Stress
Distracted
Gossip
Resentful
Blaming
Dwell on Past (regret)
Lying
Isolation
Loneliness
Cowardness
Defensive
Criticism
Contempt
Stonewalling

HURT

Perceptual Shift

1) Time Out / Silence-Stillness
2) Deep Breathing (Relaxation)
3) Prayer
4) Think of someone who loved you
5) Think of some place where you felt relaxed
   or at peace, e.g. beach, lake, etc.
6) Express Gratitude

Shame Diagram V

End Notes

Introduction - Shame: The Human Nemesis

1. Gershen Kaufman and Lev Raphael, *Coming Out of Shame : Transforming Gay and Lesbian Lives* (San Francisco: Main Street Books, 1996), 11.

2. Heinz Kohut, *The Analysis of the Self: A Systematic Approach to the Psychoanalytic Treatment of Narcissistic Personality Disorders* 11th ed ed (New York: International Universities Press, 1971).

3. Leon Wurmser, *The Mask of Shame* (The Master Work Series) (Northvale, New Jersey: Jason Aronson, 1994), 108.

4. Ibid. 16.

5. Ibid. 33.

6. Anonymous. *The Cloud of Unknowing and The Book of Privy Counsel* (Image Book Original), Ed. William Johnston (New York: Image, 1996), 43.

Chapter 1 - Shame: The Human Condition

1. Andrew P. Morrison, *Culture of Shame*, 1 ed. (Chicago: Ballantine Books, 1996), IX.

2. Ralph Ellison, *Invisible Man (Penguin Modern Classics)*. New Ed ed. (London: Penguin Classics, 2001).

3. Morrison, Andrew P.. *Culture of Shame*. 1 ed. Chicago: Ballantine Books, 1996. 175.

4. S. S Tomkins, *Affect Imagery Consciousness: Volume II: The Negative Affects*. 1 ed. (New York: Springer Publishing Company, LLC, 1963), 118.

5. Thomas Keating, *Open Mind Open Heart: The Contemplative Dimension of the Gospel*. 20 Anv ed. (New York: Continuum International Publishing Group, 2006).

6. Ibid.

7. Margaret S. Mahler, Anni Bergman, and Fred Pine, *The Psychological Birth of the Human Infant: Symbiosis and Individuation* (unknown: Karnac Books, 2002).

8. Heinz Kohut, *How Does Analysis Cure?* 1 ed. (Chicago: University Of Chicago Press, 1984).

9. Ronald Rolheiser, *The Restless Heart: Finding Our Spiritual Home in Times of Loneliness* (New York: Image, 2006).

10. Thomas Keating, *Open Mind Open Heart*, 2006.

11. Frederick Buechner, *Whistling in the Dark: An ABC Theologized* (New York: HarperOne, 1993), 83.

Chapter 2 – The Shame of Arrogance: The March of Folly

1. Leon Wurmser, *The Mask of Shame*, 1994. 308.

2. Frederick Buechner, *Telling Secrets* (New York: HarperOne, 1992).

3. Jean-Paul Sartre, *Being And Nothingness* (New York: Washington Square Press, 1993), 221.

Chapter 3 – The Shame of Failure: The Silent Killer

Chapter 4 – The Shame of Anger: The Evil Violence Tunnel

1. Sigmund Freud, *Civilization and Its Discontents* (Complete Psychological Works of Sigmund Freud) (New York: W.W. Norton & Co., 2010).

2. Anne Morrow Lindbergh, *Gift from the Sea: 50th Anniversary Edition*, Reissue ed. (New York: Pantheon, 1991).

Chapter 5 – Shame and the Dance of Idols & Pseudo gods

1. Diarmuid O'Murchu, *Quantum Theology, Revised Edition: Spiritual Implications of the New Physics*, Rev Upd ed (New York: Crossroad General Interest, 2004), 25.

2. Fyodor Dostoyevsky, *The Idiot* (New York: Signet Classics, 2010).

3. Timothy Keller, *Counterfeit Gods: The Empty Promises of Money, Sex, and Power, and the Only Hope that Matters* (New York: Dutton Adult, 2009), X-XI.

4. Peter Kreeft, *Back to Virtue: Traditional Moral Wisdom for Modern Moral Confusion* (San Francisco: Ignatius Press, 1992), 73.

5. Gerald G. May, *Addiction and Grace: Love and Spirituality in the Healing of Addictions* (Plus) (New York: HarperOne, 2007), 1.

6. M. Scott Peck, *Further Along the Road Less Traveled: The Unending Journey Towards Spiritual Growth,* 2 ed. (New York: Touchstone, 1998).

7. Erich Fromm, *You Shall Be As Gods: A Radical Interpretation of the Old Testament and Its Tradition.* null. Reprint, New York: Henry Holt & Company, 1991. 43.

8. Ronald Rolheiser, *The Restless Heart,* (2006).

9. Bruno Bettelheim, *Freud and Man's Soul: An Important Re-Interpretation of Freudian Theory,* 1st Vintage Books ed ed (New York: Vintage, 1983), 15.

10. Rollo May, *Psychology and the Human Dilemma* (New York: W. W. Norton & Company), 1996.

11. Bryan Appleyard, *Understanding the Present: Science and the Soul of Modern Man* (New York: Anchor, 1994), 7.

12. Diarmuid O'Murchu, *Quantum Theology* (2004).

13. Scott Peck, *Further Along the Road* (1998).

14. Diarmuid O'Murchu, *Quantum Theology* (2004).

Chapter 6 – Surrender: Making the Perceptual Shift

1. Viktor E. Frankl, *Man's Search for Meaning* (Boston: Beacon Press, 2006).

2. Henri J. Nouwen, *Here and Now: Living in the Spirit* (New York: Crossroad General Interest, 2002), 20.

Chapter 7 – Ecce Homo: Behold the Man

1. Henri Nouwen, *Reaching Out,* Special ed (Grand Rapids, Michigan: Zondervan, 1998).

2. Frederick Buechner, *Whistling in the Dark: An ABC Theologized* (New York: HarperOne, 1993), 110.

3. Frederick Buechner, *Wishful Thinking: A Seeker's ABC.* Rev Exp ed (SanFrancisco: HarperSanFrancisco, 1993), 101.

4. Estelle Frankel, *Sacred Therapy: Jewish Spiritual Teachings on Emotional Healing and Inner Wholeness* (Boston & London: Shambhala, 2005), 34.

5. William Barclay, *The Gospel of* Luke (The Daily Study Bible Series), Rev ed (Louisville: Westminster John Knox Press, 1975), 287.

6. Elizabeth Barrett Browning, *Aurora Leigh* (Oxford World's Classics) (London: Oxford University Press, 2008), Book VII.

7. Thomas Merton, *The New Man* (New York: Farrar, Straus and Giroux, 1999), 19.

8. Thomas Merton, *The New Man* (New York: Farrar Stairs, 1999), 90.

Chapter 8 - Stillness: The Silence of Shame

1. Donald Spoto, *In Silence: Why We Pray* (Non-Classics) (Boston: Penguin 2005), 193.

2. Donald Spoto, *In Silence: Why We Pray* (Non-Classics) (Boston: Penguin 2005), 190.

3. Thomas Merton, *Contemplative Prayer* (New York: Image, 1971), 42.

4. T. S. Eliot, "Two Chorus from the Rock", *The Wasteland and Other Poems* (Mass Paperback Edition) (Toronto: Harcourt Brace Jovanovich, 1962), 81.

5. William Henry Shannon, *Seeds of Peace: contemplation and Non-violence* (New York: Crossroad Classic, 1996), 70.

6. Eckhart Tolle, *Stillness Speaks* (Novato, CA: New World Library, 2003), 3.

7. Hafiz, *I Heard God Laughing: Poems of Hope and Joy* (Non-Classics) (Boston: Penguin 2006), 67.

8. William Henry Shannon, *Seeds of Peace: contemplation and Non-violence* (New York: Crossroad Classic, 1996).

9. Donald Spoto, *In Silence: Why We Pray* (Non-Classics) (Boston: Penguin 2005), 192.

10. Pablo Neruda, "Poetry by Pablo Neruda." PoemHunter.Com - Thousands of poems and poets. Poetry Search Engine. http://www.poemhunter.com/poem/poetry-2/ (accessed August 14, 2010).

11. Elizabeth Barrett Browning, *Aurora* Leigh (Oxford World's Classics) (London: Oxford University Press, 2008), Book VII.

12. William Henry Shannon, *Seeds of Peace: contemplation and Non-violence* (New York: Crossroad Classic, 1996).

13. Cynthia Bourgeault, *Centering Prayer and Inner Awakening* (Boston: Cowley Publications, 2004), 163.

14. Thomas Merton, *Contemplative Prayer* (New York: Image, 1971), 19.

15. William Henry Shannon, *Seeds of Peace: contemplation and Non-violence*. New York: Crossroad Classic, 1996. 54.

16. Thomas Merton, *Contemplative Prayer* (New York: Image, 1971), 13.

17. Thomas Keating, *Invitation to Love: The Way of Christian Contemplation,* New ed (New York: Continuum International Publishing Group, 1994).

18. Murhadh O'Madagain, *Centering Prayer and the Healing of the Unconscious* (New York: Lantern Books, 2007), 80.

19. Thomas Merton, *Contemplative Prayer* (New York: Image, 1971), 51.

20. William H. Shannon, *Silence on Fire: Prayer of Awareness*, Revised ed (New York, New York: The Crossroad Publishing Company, 2000), 11.

21. William H. Shannon, *Silence on Fire: Prayer of Awareness*, Revised ed (New York, New York: The Crossroad Publishing Company, 2000),11.

22. William H. Shannon, *Silence on Fire: Prayer of Awareness*, Revised ed (New York, New York: The Crossroad Publishing Company, 2000), 14.

23. Allender, Dan B. *The Healing Path: How the Hurts in Your Past Can Lead You to a More Abundant Life*. Colorado Springs: WaterBrook Press, 2000.

24. William H. Shannon, *Silence on Fire: Prayer of Awareness*, Revised ed (New York, New York: The Crossroad Publishing Company, 2000).

Chapter 9 – Love Wins

1. Michael Lewis MD, PhD.
2. John Bradshaw, *Healing the Shame that Binds.*
3. Frederick Buechner – Son laughter.
4. Michael Lewis MD, PhD.
5. Charles Darwin 'Expressions of emotions in man and animals'.
6. Warren Payne *Commentary on 1 & 2 Samuel* P.161 Westminster press publication, 1982.
7. Neils Bohr, in *Mindful Loving* by Henry Grayson Ph.D. (Gotham books published by Penguin Group USA Inc., New York, New York 10014, USA), 46.
8. Thomas Merton, in *Seeds of Peace* by William Shannon, (Crossword Publishing Co., New York, NY 10017, 1996), 76, 70.
9. William Shakespeare, "Sonnet 116".

Prologue – A Pastor Confronts Shame

1. Richard Lattimore, trans, *Aeschylus 1 - Oresteia Agamemnon; Libation Bearers; Eumenides* (Chicago: University Of Chicago Press, 1979) 139.

Bibliography

Bibliography

Allender, Dan B. *The Healing Path: How the Hurts in Your Past Can Lead You to a More Abundant Life*. Colorado Springs: WaterBrook Press, 2000.

Anonymous. *The Cloud of Unknowing and The Book of Privy Counsel* (Image Book Original). Ed. William Johnston. New York: Image, 1996.

Appleyard, Bryan. Understanding the Present: Science and the Soul of Modern Man. New York: Anchor, 1994.

Barclay, William. *The Gospel of Luke (The Daily Study Bible Series. -- Rev. ed)*. Louisville: Westminster John Knox Press, 1975.

Barton, R. Ruth, and Ruth Haley Barton. *Invitation to Solitude and Silence: Experiencing God's Transforming Presence*. Downers Grove, IL: InterVarsity Press, 2004.

Bettelheim, Bruno. Freud and Man's Soul: An Important Re-Interpretation of Freudian Theory. 1st Vintage Books ed ed. New York: Vintage, 1983.

Bourgeault, Cynthia. *Centering Prayer and Inner Awakening*. Boston: Cowley Publications, 2004.

Browning, Elizabeth Barrett. *Aurora Leigh (Oxford World's Classics)*. London: Oxford University Press, 2008.

Buechner, Frederick. *Telling Secrets*. New York: Harperone, 1992.

Buechner, Frederick. *Whistling in the Dark: An ABC Theologized*. New York: HarperOne, 1993.

Buechner, Frederick. *Wishful Thinking: A Seeker's ABC*. Rev Exp ed. SanFrancisco: HarperSanFrancisco, 1993.

Dostoyevsky, Fyodor. *The Idiot*. New York: Signet Classics, 2010.

Eliot, T. S. "Two Chorus from the Rock". *The Wasteland and Other Poems*. Mass Paperback Edition ed. Toronto: Harcourt Brace Jovanovich, 1962.

Ellison, Ralph. *Invisible Man (Penguin Modern Classics)*. New Ed ed. London: Penguin Classics, 2001.

Frankel, Estelle. *Sacred Therapy: Jewish Spiritual Teachings on Emotional Healing and Inner Wholeness*. Boston & London: Shambhala, 2005.

Frankl, Viktor E. *Man's Search for Meaning*. Boston: Beacon Press, 2006.

Freud, Sigmund. *Civilization and Its Discontents* (Complete Psychological Works of Sigmund Freud). New York: W.W. Norton & Co., 2010.

Fromm, Erich. *You Shall Be As Gods: A Radical Interpretation of the Old Testament and Its Tradition*. null. Reprint, New York: Henry Holt & Company, 1991.

Hafiz. *I Heard God Laughing: Poems of Hope and Joy*. Boston: Penguin (Non-Classics), 2006.

Keating, Thomas. *Invitation to Love: The Way of Christian Contemplation*. New Ed ed. New York: Continuum International Publishing Group, 1994.

Keating, Thomas. *Open Mind Open Heart: The Contemplative Dimension of the Gospel*. 20 Anv ed. New York: Continuum International Publishing Group, 2006.

Keller, Timothy. *Counterfeit Gods: The Empty Promises of Money, Sex, and Power, and the Only Hope that Matters*. New York: Dutton Adult, 2009.

Kohut, Heinz. *The Analysis of the Self: A Systematic Approach to the Psychoanalytic Treatment of Narcissistic Personality Disorders*. 11th ed. New York: International Universities Press, 1971.

Kohut, Heinz. *How Does Analysis Cure?* 1 ed. Chicago: University Of Chicago Press, 1984.

Kreeft, Peter. *Back to Virtue: Traditional Moral Wisdom for Modern Moral Confusion*. San Francisco: Ignatius Press, 1992.

Lattimore, Richard, trans. *Aeschylus 1 - Oresteia Agamemnon; Libation Bearers; Eumenides*. Chicago: University Of Chicago Press, 1979.

Lindbergh, Anne Morrow. *Gift from the Sea: 50th Anniversary Edition*. Reissue ed. New York: Pantheon, 1991.

Mahler, Margaret S, Anni Bergman and Fred Pine. *The Psychological Birth of the Human Infant: Symbiosis and Individuation*. unknown: Karnac Books, 2002.

May, Gerald G. *Addiction and Grace: Love and Spirituality in the Healing of Addictions* (Plus). New York: HarperOne, 2007.

May, Rollo. *Psychology and the Human Dilemma*. New York: W. W. Norton & Company, 1996.

Merton, Thomas. *Contemplative Prayer*. New York: Image, 1971.

Merton, Thomas. *The New Man*. New York: Farrar, Straus and Giroux, 1999.

Morrison, Andrew P. *Culture of Shame*. 1 ed. Chicago: Ballantine Books, 1996.

Neruda, Pablo. "Poetry by Pablo Neruda." PoemHunter.Com - Thousands of poems and poets.. Poetry Search Engine. http://www.poemhunter.com/poem/poetry-2/ (accessed August 14, 2010).

Nietzsche, Friedrich. *The Gay Science: With a Prelude in Rhymes and an Appendix of Songs*. 1st ed. New York: Vintage, 1974.

Nouwen, Henri J. *Here and Now: Living in the Spirit*. New York: Crossroad General Interest, 2002.

Nouwen, Henri. *Reaching Out*. Special ed. Grand Rapids, Michigan: Zondervan, 1998.

O'Madagain, Murhadh. *Centering Prayer and The Healing Of The Unconscious*. New York: Lantern Books, 2007.

O'Murchu, Diarmuid. *Quantum Theology, Revised Edition: Spiritual Implications of the New Physics*. Rev Upd ed. New York: Crossroad General Interest, 2004.

Peck, M. Scott. *Further Along the Road Less Traveled: The Unending Journey Towards Spiritual Growth*. 2 ed. New York: Touchstone, 1998.

Rolheiser, Ronald. *The Restless Heart: Finding Our Spiritual Home in Times of Loneliness*. New York: Image, 2006.

Sartre, Jean-Paul. *Being And Nothingness*. New York: Washington Square Press, 1993.

Shannon, William Henry. *Seeds of Peace: contemplation and Non-violence*. New York: Crossroad Classic, 1996.

Shannon, William H. *Silence on Fire: Prayer of Awareness*. Revised ed. New York, New York: The Crossroad Publishing Company, 2000.

Spoto, Donald. *In Silence: Why We Pray*. Boston: Penguin (Non-Classics), 2005.

Tolle, Eckhart. *Stillness Speaks*. Novato, CA: New World Library, 2003.

Tomkins, S. S. *Affect Imagery Consciousness: Volume II: The Negative Affects*. 1 ed. New York: Springer Publishing Company, Llc., 1963.

Wurmser, Leon. *The Mask of Shame (The Master Work Series)*. Northvale, New Jersey: Jason Aronson, 1994.

Made in the USA
Lexington, KY
27 March 2019